BETTER TO RELY ON OURSELVES

NORDIC INSTITUTE OF ASIAN STUDIES

Recent Monographs

67. Asta Olesen: *Islam and Politics in Afghanistan*
68. Hans Antlöv: *Exemplary Centre, Administrative Periphery*
69. Arne Kalland: *Fishing Villages in Tokugawa Japan*
70. Weng Eang Cheong: *The Hong Merchants of Canton*
71. Christine Dobbin: *Asian Entrepreneurial Minorities*
72. Eldrid Mageli: *Organising Women's Protest*
73. Vibeke Børdahl: *The Oral Tradition of Yangzhou Storytelling*
74. Cecilia Nathansen Milwertz: *Accepting Population Control*
75. Sharifah Zaleha Syed Hassan and Sven Cederroth: Managing *Marital Disputes in Malaysia*
76. Antoon Geels: *Subud and the Javanese Mystical Tradition*
77. Kristina Lindell, Jan-Öjvind Swahn and Damrong Tayanin: *Folk Tales from Kammu – VI: A Story-Teller's Last Tales*
78. Alain Lefebvre: *Kinship, Honour and Money in Rural Pakistan*
79. Christopher E. Goscha: *Thailand and the Southeast Asian Networks of the Vietnamese Revolution, 1885–1954*
80. Helle Bundgaard: *Indian Art Worlds in Contention*
81. Niels Brimnes: *Constructing the Colonial Encounter*
82. Ian Reader: *Religious Violence in Contemporary Japan*
83. Bat-Ochir Bold: *Mongolian Nomadic Society*
84. Shaheen Sardar Ali and Javaid Rehman: *Indigenous Peoples and Ethnic Minorities of Pakistan*
85. Michael D. Barr: *Lee Kuan Yew: The Beliefs Behind the Man*
86. Tessa Carroll: *Language Planning and Language Change in Japan*
87. Minna Säävälä: *Fertility and Familial Power*
88. Mario Rutten: *Rural Capitalists in Asia*
89. Jörgen Hellman: *Performing the Nation*
90. Olof G. Lidin: *Tanegashima – The Arrival of Europe in Japan*
91. Lian H. Sakhong: *In Search of Chin Identity*
92. Margaret Mehl: *Private Academies of Chinese Learning in Meiji Japan*
93. Andrew Hardy: *Red Hills*
94. Susan M. Martin: *The UP Saga*
95. Anna Lindberg: *Modernization and Effeminization in India*
96. Heidi Fjeld: *Commoners and Nobles*
97. Hatla Thelle: *Better to Rely on Ourselves*
98. Alexandra Kent: *Divinity and Diversity*
99. Somchai Phatharathananunth: *Civil Society and Democratization*
100. Nordin Hussin: *Trade and Society in the Straits of Melaka*

Better to Rely on Ourselves

Changing Social Rights in Urban China since 1979

Hatla Thelle

NIAS
Press

First published in 2004 by NIAS Press
Nordic Institute of Asian Studies (NIAS)
Leifsgade 33, 2300 Copenhagen S, Denmark
Tel: +45 3532 9501• Fax: +45 3532 9549
E-mail: books@nias.ku.dk
Online: www.niaspress.dk

Typesetting by Donald B. Wagner
Printed and bound in Great Britain
Production by Bookchase

British Library Cataloguing in Publication Data

Thelle, Hatla

Better to rely on ourselves : changing social rights in urban China since 1979. – (NIAS monograph ; 97)
1.Social rights - China 2.China - Social conditions - 1976-2000 3.China - Social policy 4.China - Economic conditions - 1976-2000 5.China - Economic policy - 1976-2000
I.Title II.Nordic Institute of Asian Studies
361.6'1'0951

ISBN 87-91114-26-8
ISSN 0069 1712

Table of Contents

Charts

只能靠自己

Preface

This book is the combined result of two different projects generously funded by the Carlsberg Foundation, The Research Council for Social Sciences and the Research Council for Development Research, all in Copenhagen, Denmark. On the Chinese side the People's University in Beijing, Zhongshan University in Guangzhou and the State Council Development Research Centre in Beijing were the academic cooperation partners. In Denmark the work has been based at the Danish Institute for Human Rights in Copenhagen during the period 1997 to 2002. Without financial help and scholarly support from all these institutions the study could not have been completed, and I express my sincere thanks and acknowledgments to all colleagues and staff that participated in the process.

Special thoughts go to the people who have been willing to use their time and intellect to discuss my doubts with me and correct my errors and misunderstandings so far. Without doubt many remain as my own responsibility. Thank you to scholars at the research department of DCHR and other academic institutions in Scandinavia, China and the rest of the world. Especially helpful were Chen Min, Gong Sen, Vibeke Hemmel, Ida Elisabeth Koch, Li Hua, Cecilia Milwertz, Shi Guang and last but not least, my partners in China Li Lulu, Zhou Daming and Ge Yanfeng.

Hatla Thelle

只能靠自己

Abbreviations

BLS: *Basic Living Subsidy*

BR: *Beijing Review*. Before 1979 *Peking Review* (*PR*)

CCP: Chinese Communist Party

CEDAW: Convention on the Elimination of All Forms of Discrimination against Women

CEL: Compulsory Education Law, see Bibliography

CESCR: Committee of Economic, Social and Cultural Rights

CTN: Chengshi tongji nianjian [Urban statistical yearbook]

CRC: Convention on the Rights of the Child

CSISY: *China Social Insurance Statistical Yearbook*

ECOSOC: UN Economic and Social Council

EL: Education Law, see Bibliography

FEER: *Far Eastern Economic Review*

GWYGB: Guowuyuan gongbao [Bulletin of the State Council]

GTN: Guangzhou tongji nianjian [Guangzhou statistical yearbook]

HJN: Hebei jingji nianjian [Hebei statistical yearbook]

HRC: Human Rights Committee

ICESCR: International Covenant of Economic, Social and Cultural Rights

ICCPR: International Covenant of Civil and Political Rights

MOCA: Ministry of Civil Affairs

MOFA: Ministry of Foreign Affairs

MOLSS: Ministry of Labour and Social Security

NPC: National People's Congress: China's Parliament

PR: *Peking Review*. After 1979 *Beijing Review* (*BR*)

PRC: People's Republic of China

RMB: *Renminbi*, literally translated as 'People's Money'. The official name for the Chinese currency, *yuan*.

SC: State Council; China's Government

SCMP: *South China Morning Post*, Hong Kong.

SOE: State owned enterprise

SSA: Social security agency

UDHR: Universal Declaration of Human Rights

UNDP: United Nations Development Programme

UNRISD: United Nations Research Institute for Social Development, Geneva

ZJJTN: Zhongguo jiaoyu jingfei tongji nianjian [China educational finance statistical yearbook]

ZLTN: *Zhongguo laodong tongji nianjian* [China labour statistical yearbook]

ZMTN: Zhongguo minzheng tongji nianjian [China civil affairs' statistical yearbook]

ZRGLSBFQ: Zhonghua Renmin Gongheguo laodong he shehui baozhang fagui quanshu [Laws and regulations on labour and social security of the PRC]

ZTN: Zhongguo tongji nianjian [Statistical yearbook of China]

ZZZG: Zhongguo zhufang zhidu gaige [Reform of the housing system in China]

只能靠自己

Glossary and Definitions

Administrative urban structure
- City (*shi*)
- City district (*qu*)
- Street office (*jiedao banshichu*)
- Neighbourhood committee (*jumin weiyuanhui*)
- Prefectural level city (*diji shi*)
- Town (*zhen*)
- County (*xian*)
- County city (*xianji shi*)
- Township (*xiang*)

Combination system (*tongzhang jiehe*)
: Short for 'Combination of social pooling funds and individual accounts (*Shehui tongchou yu geren zhanghu xiangjiehe*)', first mentioned in 1994. See Chapter 6 for details.

Household registration system (*hukou zhidu*)
: An administrative device demanding that every citizen is registered by the public security organs in his or her place of residence. The registration status defines a whole range of civil and social entitlements. For further discussion see Chapter 4.

Inheriting job (*dingti*)
: A policy whereby one child in a family could get one parent's position in the work unit after retirement of the parent. *Dingti* is also referred to as *neizhao*: internal recruitment, or *jieban*: to take over a job. The system was formally abolished in 1986.

Internally retired (*neitui*)
: Another form of being laid-off with a slightly better subsidy, usually at the initiative of the work unit.

Iron rice bowl (*tie fan wan*)
A widely used name for the work unit system, meaning that it gave every worker a rice bowl that could not break.

Laid off (*xiagang*)
A formal category for persons who do not work in their work place; they receive Basic Living Subsidy but keep relation with the work unit that is responsible for social welfare.

Minimum living standard (*zuidi shenghuo xian*)
The lowest limit of income under which citizens with no other means of support are entitled to a subsidy from the local government. Regulations entered into force 1 October 1999. The Neighbourhood Committee registers the families whose income per person is under the limit fixed by the local government.

PAYG (*xianshou xianfu*)
Pay as you go, an institutional setup whereby present needs are paid with present money: no savings involved. The principle covers tax-based universal social security systems like those of Northern Europe.

Personal file (*dang'an*)
Each employee has an individual file recording his or her past. Information on political, professional and family history is kept in this document by the work unit and the material has in the past been widely used to identify victims of political campaigns. The person is not informed about the content of the file.

Poverty card (*tekun zheng*)
A poverty card can be obtained by recommendation of the work unit when being laid off. It entitles the holder to a reduction in prices of essential goods, including school fees, as well as tax reductions.

Schooling
In this work the following English terms are used:
Xiaoxue: Primary school, five or six years duration
Chuzhong: Junior middle school, three years
Gaozhong: Senior middle school, three years

Send-down-to-the-countryside (*xiafang*)
During the 1950s and 1960s cadres and students in different political campaigns were sent from the cities to live in the countryside for long periods.

Seniority (*gongling*)
The number of years an employee has worked in the same work unit. The figure is important in deciding a whole range of social benefits, like pension, health care benefit, access to subsidized housing, etc.

Serious illness scheme (*dabing tongchou*)
Insurance scheme covering high health care costs. Serious illness is defined according to kinds of illness and/or level of expenses.

Three no's people
No income, no support from children, no work ability (*wu shouru, wu shanyang, wu laodongli*). These people get social assistance (*jiuji*) from MOCA.

Two guarantees (*liangge quebao*)
Campaign begun in May 1998 based on promises of the 15th Party Congress with the aim of speeding up reform of state-owned enterprises. The two guarantees are basic livelihood of laid-off people and that retirees should get the full amount of their pension in time.

Two 'not caring' (*liangge bu zhao*)
An agreement between the work unit and the worker that neither part pays anything to each other but the employer-employee relationship still exists.

Work unit (*danwei*)
The name for the workplace in cities and towns involving a comprehensive package of social support and social control.

Waiting-for-job (*dai ye*)
Designation from the pre-reform labour allocation system covering the period from leaving school until receiving a job allocation.

只能靠自己

Introduction

BACKGROUND

The title of this book (*zhi neng kao ziji* in Chinese) summarises the sentiments and attitudes shared by the people who provided the information it is based on. A number of families in two urban communities were interviewed about their daily lives in relation to basic social security in order to paint a picture of the protection of social rights in urban China during the reform period 1979 to 2002. The ambition was to study how protection of social and economic rights is affected by the transition from plan to market in a former centrally planned economy like the Chinese.

The concept of human rights – forming the constitutive element of the United Nations – has gained more and more strength on a global scale in recent decades, some 190 states being members of the UN and having signed many or some of the international conventions and declarations. Human rights involve global standards for living conditions of human beings across the globe, meting out the ultimate responsibility for these standards to national governments. The standards involve both protection against interference from governments and state obligations to secure basic means of livelihood. The countries under economic restructuring like China encompass some 25 states with a combined population of 1.7 billion people. The economic transition from plan to market thus involves a radical restructuring of economic and social conditions for almost one-third of the world's population. It is a long and complicated process, far from being accomplished at the moment of writing.

China is somewhat of a newcomer in the international community in general and in the human rights arena in particular. Becoming a member of the UN in 1971 and of the Human Rights Commission in 1982, the country has had two to three decades to adapt to international cooperation and the supervision mechanisms this cooperation contains. During this time China has signed or ratified all of the most important international conventions, has been accepted as a member of the World Trade Organization and has embarked on a long road of building a legal and administrative system to safeguard economic development and to underpin its participation in the international community.

The pre-reform social system in China was characterized by a clear division between different segments of the population and by a strong link between social benefits and employment status. The most important distinction was the one between urban and rural citizens. Protection of social rights for these two groups was governed by different policies and based in different institutional settings. Within each category benefits, furthermore, differed according to the place of birth for the farmer and the political status of the workplace for the urbanite. Income and resource distribution was done through administrative rather than monetary means. The state apparatus administered the wealth created by collective productive activities, and people obtained necessary goods and services through the decision of bureaucrats with access to these assets that could not be bought for money. Their power was built on position in a political hierarchy. Those outside the elite came to depend on office decisions to act economically or even to get the most basic means of livelihood.

The availability and abundance of social goods differed from place to place and from time to time during the Maoist period, 1949–1979, but the system possessed a universal quality in the fact that everyone was assigned a work place where some kind of collective assistance was formally guaranteed in case of failure of individual capability or family support. The guarantee co-existed with dependence on bureaucratic decisions and lack of institutional channels for formulation of needs and wants. Social security was bought at the expense of personal freedom of thought and action.

With the economic and/or political reforms in the socialist bloc, a new contract between state and citizen is coming into being; administrative distribution is gradually replaced by market mechanisms and the opportunities of and demands on citizens have changed drastically in the process. The balance between freedom and security has tipped; basically and simplistically spoken civil rights like freedom of movement and choice have been strengthened while social rights like certainty of at least some source of income have been weakened. But how does this new social contract protect people in need and how is it perceived by citizens not accustomed to the new balance of opportunities?

AIMS AND ARGUMENTS

The broader aim of the present study is on the one hand to investigate the diversity of ways rights can be protected under different political and economic systems in order to deepen the debate on human rights and reconcile seemingly opposing views on the 'right' way to organize societies. A study of the former and present special Chinese variety of socio-economic protection will reveal some measures different from the ones usually discussed in academic literature, but maybe in some respects as valuable.

On the other hand the empirical parts of the study are meant to introduce light and shade into the picture of human rights protection in China as it is presented in the Western public space. In parts of the international discourse the Chinese government scores high on the list of perpetrators of human rights violations, with a steady focus on the treatment of political dissidents, on administrative punishments, excessive use of the death penalty, abusive implementation of a one-child policy, etc. The aim here is neither to defend nor discuss these practices but to add to the picture by presenting general political measures in the field of social protection and discussing the substantial problems encountered in a transformation process as huge as the one we see in the Middle Kingdom.

Social rights are in all societies protected by social policies while social policies in turn are influenced by economic performance and level as well as cultural and political traditions. To make a nuanced assessment of the protection of social rights in China during the last part of the 20th century it is therefore necessary to combine an empirical investigation of how people in their homes, workplaces and daily lives are protected against social risks with knowledge of the proposed or implemented political measures and to view these in relation to the international obligations of the government.

The approach is to compare the international standard with national legal norms and administrative institutions designed to protect economic and social welfare, and to focus on how these institutions protect the individual in relation to the international standard. The analysis contains a discussion of the emerging division of responsibility between state, market, civil society and family/individual. In the present study there will be no distinction between the family and the individual because most research shows that important decisions in Chinese lives still are taken as family, not individual, decisions.

Thus, the study deals with the relationship between rights protection as defined at the international scene and a specific (rapidly changing) economic and social system. The present situation in China is seen as a phase in an ongoing process and the intention is to illustrate the change from one kind of system to another yet unknown and poorly defined one, and to discuss how the traditional structure influences the designing and implementation of new policies. Transformation is not a uni-linear movement from one point to another. It consists of a multitude of changes going in many directions, but certain common new principles guide them, notably the commercialization or 'monetization' of social transactions and the resulting individualization of social rights that has profoundly influenced everyday life in the People's Republic. The course of transformation is, however, not only steered by new principles but also adjusted in relation to existing structures and practices.

A transformation of this scope can fruitfully be viewed as a layered process, where the new system is coexisting with or attached to the old for an unknown period of time. As no system – be it driven by market forces or by administrative decisions – exists in a pure form, this attachment eventually shapes the resulting social structure and creates a new form, combining traits from the two different systems. To bridge the old and the new, the actors – government, associations, people, academics – invent and use what could be called *transformative mechanisms*, used as tools to fill gaps and settle accounts before a new system is viable. These mechanisms are shaped by the existing social and political structure. At stake here is to grasp and define this process of creating new tools and to identify if and how traits of the transformative mechanisms shape the 'final', or at least a more stable, outcome. Knowledge about the specific traits of the new system is necessary to make an assessment of the social protection at the bottom level of society.

The central argument of this investigation is that the protection of social rights in reform China is dominated by social structures surviving from pre-reform days and these structures inhibit the attainment of the expressed goals of reform. The two most important surviving elements are the continued position of the workplace as central administrator of welfare allocation, and the persistence of social segmentation between rural and urban citizens and between the employed and the unemployed part of the economically active population. The aim of reform is to broaden the coverage of social security benefits, but the practice has resulted in a failure to elevate social responsibility to an appropriate state level possessing sufficient funding to fulfill the welfare obligations.

STRUCTURE OF THE BOOK

Four areas have been chosen for their character as necessary means to guarantee the basic right to life and dignity in modern society. These are employment, housing, social security and education. For reasons explained later the special Chinese characteristics make it interesting to focus on how to get a job; how to pay and own housing; how to obtain basic social security, primarily health care and old-age pension; and finally how the right to free basic schooling is protected in the new order. The sources are from different societal layers: at the 'bottom' interviews from two urban communities, 'in between' documents and discussions of national reform policies, and at the 'top' the international conventions and interpretations thereof.

The book discusses social protection for the middle-income level of the urban population, that is, the group in Chinese society that prior to the reform period was protected – or even pampered – by the special labour allocation system of the PRC. So especially vulnerable groups like peasants and migrants or especially privileged groups like the new private entrepreneurs are excluded from the study; they are covered by other mechanisms and institutions than the majority of urban citizens.

Basic data are interviews with families in two urban communities in North and South China conducted from the end of 1997 to the beginning of 1998. The interviewed people are not selected as being representative of urban people in general or even necessarily of the neighbourhood they live in. Their stories must be viewed as unique but *possible* results of reform at the local level. Nevertheless, general impressions from visits to the country and talks with both scholars and people on the streets suggest that the life situations described here are reality for an identifiable, up to a 100-million-strong group of people 'caught' in a certain stage of the transition. On the national level the Constitution, laws and important policy documents concerning the area in question will be used to discuss the changes in the character of social rights protection. On the international level the sources used will be the specific articles in the International Convention on Economic, Social and Cultural Rights, as well as the general comments on them by the UN Committee on Economic, Social and Cultural Rights and the core literature of the concepts, in order to identify the international obligations of States Parties.

Chapter 1 sets the scene by describing the geographical, social and historical context. The two communities are introduced and the reform process in general is outlined to place the reform of the specific areas in a relevant context. Furthermore the methodology in the use of sources is discussed.

Chapters 2 and 3 introduce the two theoretical discourses used as reference points. The area includes legal as well as social science, and an attempt will be made to bridge the two. The assumption is that no single theory will cover the problem area under scrutiny, so several tools have to be used in interpreting the empirical material. The human rights discourse is self-evidently in focus as the main basis of reference, but, for reasons that will be elaborated on in the beginning of each chapter, it is not very useful either in discussing policy choices or in distinguishing the inner mechanisms of the social and economic institutions. But the two fields – human rights and social policy – share certain features and mutual references are seen in the literature:

- Both are focussed on the role of the state and the relationship between state intervention and individual conditions of life.
- Both harbour a strong ethical and normative element. The concept of human rights presupposes the idea of the equality of human beings, while the social policy field to a certain extent is built on the idea of a state obligation to oversee the well-being of citizens.

The theoretical structure of this study interlinks the different approaches as both preconditions for and instrumental to each other. The human rights discourse is about certain *standards to be met*, but does not address in detail the question of how to obtain a certain result, while social policy theories *propose how to establish institutions and systems* that are capable of protecting certain rights in a sustainable way, and the empirical data *provide information* feeding into the process of designing new institutions and systems. The aim – protection of human rights – cannot be reached without effective political interventions and without basic knowledge of existing conditions. Consequently, social policy and social science analysis are seen as preconditions for protection of social and economic rights, and have to be included in a discussion of this field in a special historical setting. Furthermore, the book is meant for a heterogeneous audience, primarily legal experts, social policy scholars and researchers in Chinese studies as well as students in these disciplines and any other interested parties. So the two chapters are also meant as introductions to non-specialists in the respective fields; a human rights expert only has to skim through Chapter 2, while a social policy scholar can read Chapter 3 lightly, and the development of the Chinese reforms generally will be known to many China scholars.

Chapters 4 to 7 contain discussions of each of the areas treated, introduced by quotations from the interviews that specifically address the topic. The chapters all treat the local implementation of reform policies, the historical development in the area concerned and a short introduction to the relevant international standard. Efforts have been made in each field to include the legal environment in the form of the new laws and regulations, the economic status in the form of statistics as well as the social consequences in the form of scholarly debates and local information. Due to different types of problems and failure in identifying sources, the weighting within each subject might not be totally consistent.

Chapter 8 traces the reactions and perceptions of the people interviewed. While the foregoing chapters have tried to describe changes objectively taking place, this part searches for information on how people perceive and react to their new life situations. Of course we can only know what people say, not what they really think and feel, but what they say about their feelings can be supplemented by stories of what they do or what their neighbours do and a more coherent picture will emerge.

Chapter 9 analyses the results by repeating the principles behind the reform process and discussing the implications for the following: at the 'top' the social policies adopted by the government and at the 'bottom' the protection of social rights of urban citizens. Finally a short summary sums up an overview in time and concentrates the results in a short simplified list of progress and lingering problems in social rights protection. In two appendices examples from the interviews are given to convey the type of information given and to show the way the interviews were conducted.

1 只能靠自己

Setting the Scene

> *In the whole period of transformation of the economic system, we must handle correctly the balance between development, reform and social stability. Development is the goal, reform is the motive force, stability is the precondition. This is the general rule for all the work, and it goes for social insurance as well.* (Hu Xiaoyi 1998: 35)

The background to the story told here consists of reform processes at the national and local levels in China. The goal of the study has been to grasp the process of change over a period of time at different levels of society. This is done with a basic reference point to the winter of 1997–1998 in two localities, from where lines are drawn in time from the past to the future, and in space from the family level to the level of national reform and further on to the level of international law. This last jump seems huge, and some might doubt the meaningfulness of applying human rights standards to the Yao family in Sheepmarket Street. Nevertheless, the effort is not as complicated as it sounds because the link between international standards and everyday life in cities and villages all over the world is ready at hand in the form of national governments and their local counterparts. There are few direct connections between the 'man in the street' and the international conventions, but the latter impose a duty on the state apparatus to take or not take specific actions regarding the former. The thinking behind the present study is to test whether this duty can be done only by asking how policies and administrative practices affect individual life situations. So individual conditions and reactions will be presented together with new policies and implementation problems on protection of social rights in the four selected areas: employment, housing, social security and education. Individual experiences are thus the sources used to evaluate state compliance with implementation of human rights.

Before introducing the local and national background a few words on social policy terminology are needed. A premise is that social rights are protected by social policies. The content of the rights regime and social policy theory will be discussed separately in the next two chapters as the basic theoretical framework for the analysis of the empirical data. The interface between them consists exactly of the state responsibility referred to above. Seen from a human rights perspective, states are obliged to protect individuals against the state itself and against other risks coming from third parties or from natural conditions, while social policy is characterized by 'public management of social risks' (Esping-Andersen 1999: 36), meaning the role of the state is pivotal in this arena as well. Social policy terminology in academic literature is complex and not always consistent. The words social welfare, social security, social insurance and social assistance are all used with more or less common and explicit definitions. In China scholars tend to use social security (*shehui baozhang*) as consisting of four components: social insurance (*shehui baoxian*), social relief (*shehui yuanzhu* or *jiuzhu*), welfare (*fuli*) and personal savings (*chuxu jijin*) (Hu Xiaoyi 1998: 9; Li Jingwen 2000: 9), terms supplemented since 1994 by two items, preferential treatment for military veterans (*youdai liejun*) and mutual aid (*huzhu*) (Wong and Flynn 2001: 42). In the West, welfare is often the broadest term covering more items than social security (Tang Kwong-leung 2000: 175; Goodman and White 1998: 9).[1]

Based on Western and Chinese sources, an attempt has been made to order the different terms in relation to the degree of protection. The differentiation concerns how many areas are covered, how many beneficiaries are involved and how sufficient the benefits are in fulfilling 'an adequate standard of living', the somewhat

1. The language varies, e.g. Tang and Parish use the word social security for pension and unemployment, while health care is separated as a special item (Tang and Parish 2000: 36). Another confusing example: in an American context the Social Security Act of 1935 is an insurance scheme while the word welfare is used for the far less generous social assistance offered by the Federal Government.

vague term used in international conventions. There is no statistical backing for the listing in chart 1.1, only a general understanding that more items covered and independence from the labour market give a more all-round and effective protection.

A useful dichotomy to be introduced right away is 'the balance between equity (*gongping*) and efficiency (*xiaolü*)', which occurs in both Western and Chinese literature to address the problem that the quest for social justice and redistribution of resources will often impede economic development, so a choice has to be made or a balance has to be found between the moral humanistic concern of collective responsibility for members of society and the need for economic growth. The balance reflects in some ways a core dilemma in social policy and, as will be discussed later, the two objectives are sometimes treated as competing forces fighting for the same resources, while other analyses stress the fact that they can be mutually reinforcing when social security funds like pension funds,

Chart 1.1 Social policy terminology used in this study

Social policies addressing joint needs in society	higher (universal) protection	1. **State subsidies**, direct or hidden.[a] Cover all citizens.
		2. **Social Welfare** including housing and education. Covers all citizens.
		3. **Social security**, 9 branches.[b] Most often only covers workers.
		4. **Social insurance**, method used to secure health care, pension, unemployment or other items.
	lower (selective) protection	5. **Social assistance**, all items at minimum level. Covers groups and individuals in need.

a. Meaning state policies affecting social conditions in a broad sense, like tax exemption rules, preferential treatment of employers hiring people from vulnerable groups, subsidized housing, etc. (Leung and Nann 1995: xxi).

b. According to the principal ILO document on social security, the term covers medical care, sickness benefit, unemployment benefit, old age benefit, employment injury benefit, family benefit, maternity benefit, invalidity benefit and survivors benefit. See Chapter 6.

created with the aim of redistribution, spur economic development (Hort and Kuhnle 1999: 4).

The following chapters address what in the chart is called social welfare, i.e. covering social security items or (in ILO language) branches as well as housing and education, as protection of these areas in Chinese cities before reform was inextricably woven together in one institutional arrangement. The reforms aimed at untangling them and spreading them out to new actors, thereby lifting some of the burden from the shoulders of the government. The scenes to be set in this chapter proceed in space and time, from the level of local implementation to the arrangements that historically have shaped the experiences and reaction patterns of the local people, and then progress in time to a short overview of the new national policies.

LOCAL SETTING AND RESEARCH METHODOLOGY

The two researched sites belong to North and South China, Hebei and Guangdong provinces, respectively. Both are coastal provinces and as such part of the area mostly affected by economic reform and bureaucratic decentralization. The differences between them are, however, significant. Hebei is, in spite of its proximity to the two metropolises of Beijing and Tianjin, the least economically developed of all the coastal provinces (Hong 1998: 18), while Guangdong is the province with the highest growth rate in the whole country for the last two decades. The average official salary in Guangdong is about double that of Hebei (*CTN* 1997: 441 and 453) and four times as many people in Guangdong compared to Hebei are employed in units other than state or collectively owned enterprises.[2] From a political viewpoint Hebei is close to the site of national government but in Guangdong 'the emperor is far away' as the Chinese saying goes. In relation to the reform process, without further investigation one would expect to find the most radical de-

2. The regional statistics give 17 per cent in Guangdong employed by 'other than state or collective owned units', a category mainly consisting of private companies, compared with 4 per cent in Hebei (*ZLTN* 1996: 17).

partures from the socialist pre-reform system in Guangdong, both because of its high level of economic development and its location far away from the political centre. Guangdong is usually depicted as being difficult to control from Beijing, prompting discussions about the possibilities of China splitting up into at least two parts: a rich Southeastern and a poor Northwestern area.[3] However, the results of the present study do not support this proposition.

Xingtai city, Hebei province

Hebei province has traditionally served as supplier of raw materials to the two economic centres of Beijing and Tianjin, because the area possesses precious minerals as well as coal and iron ore, but its own technological development has been slow.[4] Inside this relatively poor province Xingtai, the city studied, is among the least developed of the bigger cities in terms of industrial and agricultural output, coming after the much bigger heavy industrial urban centres like Shijiazhuang, Tangshan, Handan and Baoding. Xingtai is a middle-sized town in the southern part of the province, situated on the Beijing–Shanghai railway line. It has a population of half a million people. The town looks 'oldfashioned', with earthen roads off the main streets and dilapidated old residential buildings in the centre. Only three high structures – ten stories – tower over the main street. One is the new department store, another is a joint venture hotel and the third is a new office building. The latter is quite empty, though it looks like it has been finished for some time. At the outskirts of the city one can see factories with smoky chimneys all around the horizon. All in all it seems to be a place only slightly touched by the new times, despite its location on an important transportation line and only four-hours' drive from Beijing.

The neighbourhood studied is situated in the very old part of the centre in the Sheepmarket Street (*Yangshi jie*), crossed by the

3. For an overview of this discussion, see Goodman 1997: 4–6.
4. Hong Yang argues that the economic development has been slow *because* of the province's proximity to Beijing and Tianjin. The two metropolises have reduced Hebei's possibilities of getting foreign investment and technological development (Hong 1998: 18).

Ox-, Horse- and Flowermarket streets. Sheepmarket Street was baptized Great Leap Forward Street during the Cultural Revolution. In 1974 the 'right wing'[5] protested against the name as a vestige of leftist thinking and the name was changed again. It was an area for trading hides before. Foreigners came there to buy leather and the market streets were bustling with leather shops. So the street got its old name back and the market atmosphere has also been revived. The street is full of vendors selling fish, vegetables and other daily necessities. Some are from the countryside, rural people coming here to trade their goods and returning to their villages in the evening. Others are residents who try to supplement their meagre income by selling all sorts of things. The area has a spacious and comfortable touch due to the willows planted on both sides of the relatively wide street. The houses are ostensibly from the 1930s, three stories high, though some are really old and only one story.

Xingtai City in 1996 consisted of 2 districts (*qu*), 15 counties (*xian*) and 2 county towns (*xianji shi*). The Sheepmarket Street Neighbourhood Committee (*jumin weiyuanhui*[6]) is one of 38 committees belonging to the Sheepmarket Street Office (*jiedao banshichu*). The committee has jurisdiction over 300 families, almost 1,000 persons in all. It employs three people full time and these and the committee members are chosen at a residents' meeting where all families are invited. The election subsequently has to be approved by the Street Office but this is normally just a formality. The District Civil Affairs Bureau pays a small salary of 40 yuan each month to the staff and additional income is generated from renting small shops to individuals. The primary functions of the committee are household registration, population control, mediation of disputes and economic activities, like offering service to elderly people and at the same time creating income possibilities for the young people 'waiting for job', i.e. the unemployed.

In Xingtai 41 families were interviewed and the age of the family members is equally divided between younger people (25–35),

---

5. Expression used in one interview.
6. *Jumin weiyuanhui* is often in English translated as Residents' Committee.

middle-aged people (35–50) and retirees. Their educational level is relatively low, most stopped schooling at junior middle school level or below. Of the adults over 25 years of age only about one-fourth graduated from junior middle school and none from a university. The rest completed primary school or dropped out somewhere in the process. A few per cent are designated as illiterates. Of the school-age youngsters the 7 to 12 year olds all attend school and of the teenagers only a few do not attend junior middle school. The parents' present or previous jobs are mostly factory work or some kind of trading business inside a traditional work unit, in state or collectively run enterprises. Few are cadres,[7] and two have served in the military. Eight per cent of members of the interviewed families belong to the party. Average household size is 4.9

Chart 1.2 City administration in China

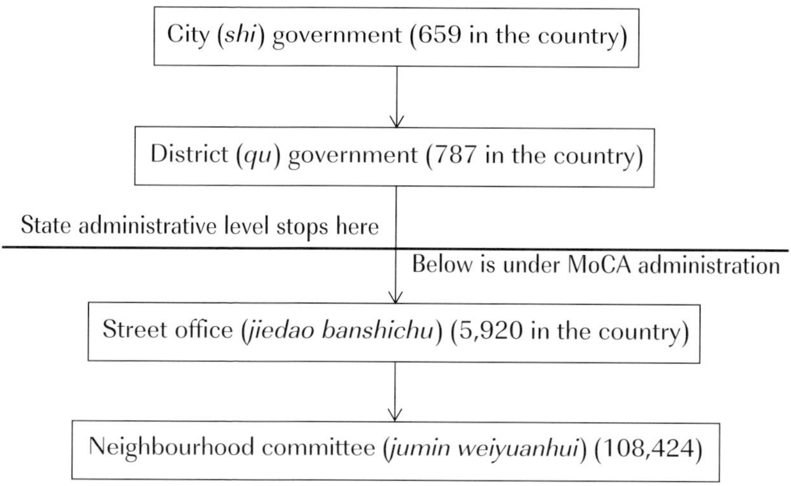

The cities referred to here are both prefectural level cities (*diji shi*) and county level cities (*xianji shi*). In 2000 there were 659 cities in the whole country with the jurisdiction of 787 districts. There were 2.074 counties ruling over 400 county level cities (*ZTN* 2001: 3). The organs below state level is under MOCA and figure in the statistics of this ministry (*ZMTN* 2001: 94).

7. The normal English word used for the Chinese word *ganbu*, meaning leading personnel at all levels.

persons and 13 of 41 households include three generations or parents living with married children.[8]

Most grown-up family members are what could be called 'economically active', as they have an affiliation to a work place. Only four elderly women are reported as having been housewives all their lives. Despite this ostensibly almost full employment, the incomes of the families are unstable and unpredictable. More than 80 per cent of the 53 work units mentioned as employing or having employed the people from Sheepmarket Street are not paying salary or paying only irregularly on the grounds of bad economic performance. One factory is dominant in the area, the Dyeworks (*zhiran chang*). It has some kind of affiliation with 70 per cent of the families. It is situated just to the south of the residential area and this factory is luckily not doing too badly economically. The average nominal salary per person is reported to be 300–400 yuan a month, being around 75 per cent of the 5,692 as average annual pay for urban workers in 1997, which is the official figure for the province as a whole (*HJN* 1998: 373).

Guangzhou city, Guangdong province

Guangzhou is the capital of Guangdong province and the city in China most affected by the new open policy. The province has generated the highest economic growth in the country for the last two decades. The city looks like one big construction site, crisscrossed by roaring highways. The studied Neighbourhood Committee in Haizhu district is situated south of the Pearl River, near Zhongshan University. The neighbourhood is, like the rest of the city, characterized by buildings under construction, muddy roads full of motor bikes and local market stalls in provisional shelters. The Haizhu district is one of the biggest districts in the city of Guangzhou, with a population of 750,000 people divided in 20 Street Offices, almost 400 Neighbourhood Committees and one

8. This is a smaller percentage (33 per cent) of three-generation families than Martin Whyte's findings in Baoding – a place very similar to Xingtai – in 1994, where 44 per cent of surveyed parents lived with a married child (Whyte 1997: 19).

town (*zhen*) (*GTN* 1997: 9 and 39). The district has only recently been administratively converted from agricultural area to city district and it is still the most rural of Guangzhou's four core urban districts, having a relatively large population registered as rural citizens.

The researched Neighbourhood Committee of Xinjiao rules over 1,437 persons in 547 families with an urban registration and about 1,000 peasants with an agricultural household registration. On top of that, 20,000 migrants are reported as living in the area, which gives the amazing figure of almost ten migrants for each permanent resident! The situation of this migrant population is not discussed in this book as all those interviewed were permanent residents. The migrants are administratively dealt with by the Neighbourhood Committee via a so-called 'small group for outsiders' (*wailai xiaozu*) that among other things is in charge of residence permits, in which cases it refers to the public security system. The Neighbourhood Committee has nine members and two full-time employees appointed by the district leadership. Their salary is paid by the District Civil Affairs Bureau. The committee members are chosen at residents' meetings every third year, where each family has one vote. If no one from the family can participate themselves they can send someone else to represent them. Furthermore, annual meetings are held where people can voice their opinions and complaints. The committee deals mostly with the permanent residents but it is also responsible for implementing the one-child policy among migrants.

The role of the committee is similar to that in Xingtai, except for the fact that it is not allowed to undertake economic activities. According to the committee member interviewed, the administration of births, deaths, marriages and divorces is especially troublesome and mediation in marriage cases takes a lot of time. A typical pattern is that the husband goes away on business and finds another woman with whom he establishes a new relationship or even a new family. Another time-consuming task is related to drug addiction and prostitution which involves preventive social work among young people. Population control is a new duty since 1995 and very difficult to implement. The many outsiders do not comply with the policy. When they get a child they send it back to their village and then they get another child. The police can be contacted and asked to send them back if they do not obey the rules, but it is impossible to prevent them from returning to the city.

In Xinjiao Neighbourhood 42 families were interviewed, mostly middle-age couples, and the great majority of them are regular state employees inside the socialist work unit system. The average household size is 3.8 persons, with only 6 out of 42 including 3 generations or collateral nuclear families coresiding.[9] Interestingly 10 out of 43 families have only one breadwinner and 53 per cent of the people employed had been assigned a job through the state allocation system.[10] Eleven characterize themselves or their spouses as housewives. The average monthly income of the families is reported as 1,300 yuan in Xinjiao Neighbourhood, less than the official Guangzhou average of 1,021 yuan per person per month (*GTN* 1997: 371). The educational level is a bit higher than in the northern community of Xingtai, about 35 per cent having left school at the junior middle school level and several young people attending a university or higher vocational training institution.

Methodology

From each of the two Neighbourhood Committees around 40 families were selected to be interviewed about changes in their living conditions since 1980. Due to different procedures the results from the two places are of a different character, the Xingtai material being much more detailed than the Guangzhou interviews, which are therefore supplemented by secondary sources. The time of interviewing was autumn 1997 and spring 1998. For 'bureaucratic' reasons[11] the family interviews were done by the Chinese counterparts

9. Only 14 per cent compared to the 33 and 44 per cent from Hebei just mentioned.
10. After leaving school everyone would be offered a job through a local government organ – the Labour Bureau (Wang Feiling 1998: 100). Ikels likewise observes that the system of unified job allocation was still basically in force, while experiments were conducted in 1998 forcing graduating students from seven selected schools to find jobs on their own (Ikels 1996: 190 and 191).
11. Foreigners are subject to restrictions in doing social science research in China so it is difficult to conduct systematic interviews and visits in people's homes.

and their students, while the author participated in and conducted interviews with authorities and scholars. The family interviews from Xingtai were taped and subsequently written out in Chinese and are on file with the author, while the Guangzhou interviews exist in written form as filled-out questionnaires.

The family interviews were semi-structured and questions were arranged around the four themes: employment, housing, social security and education. Within each area the history of the family since 1980 was recorded, focussing on any changes and the reasons for these changes. A typical question on employment would be how many job changes had occurred for each member of the family. For each change the reasons behind losing the job and channels used to find a new job would be discussed. Furthermore, the interviewee would be asked of his or her evaluation of changes during the reform period. The interviewee would be asked if life was better now than before and questions were raised concerning individual knowledge of social policies and personal opinions on the obligation of the state. Only one person in each household was questioned about the situation of all members.

Many interviews involve biassed answers and untrue information. The biases in this investigation involved a tendency to overstate problems and difficulties, as the informants could very well get the impression that the interviewers, coming from central and important local research institutions, would be able to influence policymaking to the benefit of complainants. The same impression could cause them to blame their problems on local bosses rather than state policies. But some of the stated problems could actually be *seen* also by this author, like the many sellers without customers being idle people in their best age, e.g. a young man selling sunglasses on a bitterly cold November afternoon, or beggars showing their handicapped child to the public. The bad economic performance of enterprises could also be verified by identical descriptions from people at many different levels. The sincerity of the respondents' targets of blame and criticism is of course difficult to ascertain, all that is known for sure is that no physical opposition to government organs were reported, while tales were told of sporadic gatherings protesting against employing work units. Demonstrations against local and even central government have been reported from other places, so protests over living conditions are far from unknown in China. The inner 'true' feeling of the interviewed persons will of course always be beyond the reach of the researcher. A well-known inclination to understate income for fear of involvement of taxing authorities can furthermore be discerned in some answers. Therefore, information on income should not be taken too seriously and exact figures are not decisive for the analysis, either.

The two localities are seen to represent a part of the Chinese population that is influenced by the economic reforms to a fairly high degree, but at different stages of economic development. Common for the situation of the two sets of families is that they are neither very well-off nor extremely poor. Their economic situation is generally slightly below the average for their part of the country and it was part of the objective of the study to describe the situation for 'ordinary' people, neither the newly-rich in the glittering streets of Shanghai, nor the destitute peasant migrant in the backstreets of Lanzhou.

These 'ordinary' people represent a large group of the Chinese urban population. 96 million workers were in 2000 employed in either state owned or collective enterprises (*ZTN* 2001: 107) and as a third or maybe even half of these were not earning a profit, their employees in some ways have lost out in the reform process. Many of them worked half a lifetime at low pay as exchange for a promise that the state would take care of their social needs. Those over 30 years of age have lived through turbulent times, giving their lives what Tang and Parish have called a 'geologically layered quality' (Tang and Parish 2000: 17). The term refers to the very different times most presently living Chinese have gone through. The oldest have experienced a devastated China from the beginning of the 20th century, the 'Liberation' of 1949, the 1950s' optimism and hope, the 1960s' violence, the 1970s' political struggle and subsequently two decades of drastic social change.[12] Their common

12. The idea of the very different generations in modern Chinese history is developed in a popular Chinese sociology book called 'The Fourth Generation' (*Di sidai ren*), which describes the experiences and personal characters of four generations of modern Chinese (Whyte 1997: 3).

place of residence gives them a common social status and a common frame of mind. Within each community their reactions and perceptions are remarkably alike, as will be shown in Chapter 8 describing their personal reactions to a turbulent and multi-layered history. In the past they occupied a special position as 'the vanguard of socialist society', which maybe made some of them less able to cope with the new freedoms. No matter what, the social protection they enjoyed since the 1950s possessed unique qualities in a complex patchwork of social security and social control.

SOCIALIST WELFARE WITH CHINESE CHARACTERISTICS, 1949–1979

The economic and political system of socialist China is amply described in existing literature and the information will not be repeated here. Important in the present context, however, is the establishment of institutions for providing urban people with employment, housing, education and social security after the Communist take-over in 1949, where a fairly generous protection of social rights for urbanites was developed in the period between the birth of the People's Republic and the shift in economic policy in 1979. The young Chinese government rapidly committed itself to a strategy of forced industrialization, supported by the Soviet Union, and urban workers became the core force of the state to realize its goals for the nation. To protect the industrial work force, so important to survival and development of the communist state, the regime rather quickly after 1949 established mechanisms for protecting white- and blue-collar workers against loss of working ability on different grounds. As early as 1951 'Regulations for Labour Insurance of the PRC' were published by the State Council, in 1952 followed by regulations guaranteeing health care to employees in party and government organs (*ZRGLSBFQ* 1999: 304–314). As a result, workers and managerial staff were protected in five vulnerable situations: work injury/disability, illness, death of breadwinner, old age and maternity.

Social protection of urban residents continued along two tracks: one for employees in productive enterprises (*laodong baoxian*) and one for staff in administrative institutions like government organs or other public institutions like schools and hospitals (*gongfei yiliao* was the name for health care insurance in public institutions). Workers and cadres each had their own system. The enterprise system was originally designed only for workers in state owned enterprises, but big collective enterprises followed suit and established similar kinds of protection.[13] The level and kind of benefits, financial sources and administrative responsibility differed, however, according to the size and position of the work unit. The participating units had to pay 3 per cent of their total salary to a welfare fund, which in turn paid pensions and other allowances, while the work unit paid medical costs (Dixon 1981: 42–43). The enterprise system was financed by the units and managed by the trade union, while the system for public institutions was financed by the local or central state budget and managed by the Ministry of Health for health care and the Ministry of Personnel for the other items.

During the Cultural Revolution from 1966 to 1969 the general chaos disturbed institutional arrangements, and welfare funds were seized by the Red Guards and distributed to workers. After the turmoil a reconstructed system meant that each work unit received an allocation from the state budget, amounting to around 15 per cent af total wage bill, to cover welfare expenditures. The sum was to be negotiated between the workplace and the relevant local government bureau (Dixon 1981: 131). The system had become 'work unit insurance', constituting a pure form of a pay-as-you-go system (Gu 2001: 132; Hu Xiaoyi 1998: 9; Wu Jinglian 1998: 230).[14] Pensions and other subsidies were paid directly from the enterprise budget before tax. The usual method for health expenses – if treatment was not done in institutions owned by the work unit – was

13. Chinese industry under the planned economy was under two kinds of ownership, state and collective. The state enterprises (SOEs) involved big national industries of strategic importance, like heavy industry and transportation. The collective industries ranged from big province level factories to small rural industries.

14. Abbreviated as PAYG is the expression for systems where present contributors pay for obligations accumulated in the past. It is, thus, opposed to savings systems, where individuals or institutions collect funds to cover future expenses, see Chapter 3.

that the individual paid and got the money refunded on request. Only relatively high ranking work units paid health expenses for their employees directly to the hospital or clinic providing the service.

In this way, beginning with the early 1950s, the work unit system (*danwei zhidu*) was born. The unit gradually became the focal point of urban family life in China and, on behalf of the state, it became the only provider of social protection for the majority of urban employees. In principle everyone received a job allocation – and only one – upon graduation from school. A person's attachment to the work unit was normally for life and involved the fulfilment of material needs like food, health care and housing; future security in the form of pensions, as well as education and job opportunities for children; immaterial support like mediation and consultation in matters of marriage and family life; and social control in relation to behaviour, movement and criminal activity. Social safety and restrictions on personal freedom were interwoven in a tight net around the family and personified in the leadership of the work unit. In practice and in people's minds work and social security were *given* by the state to cadres and workers, and rights thinking, consequently, became somewhat irrelevant, as welfare was inbuilt in the top-down hierarchy and not separated from other life areas.

Protection of social rights in China before reform thereby came to constitute a pure form of occupational welfare known from other socialist systems (Lee Ming-kwan 2000: 2). The relatively generous protection was made possible by the 'high employment, high subsidy and low salary' principle behind the package. It can be said to be just and in principle fairly equitable in relation to a certain group of people, i.e. those who were entitled to a job and thus also to the social benefits of employment.

During the 1950s this social security system developed to cover more than 90 per cent of urban workers and staff in state and collective enterprises, in 1979 amounting to 89 million people: 75 million workers, including dependants who were covered with 50 per cent, and 14 million administrative personnel. For the others – employees in small collective enterprises or people without job and their dependents – ruled the motto of the civil affairs departments of MOCA, quoted by Linda Wong: '. . . self-reliance by the masses, mutual aid, dependence on the collective, and state help as the last resort' (Wong 1998: 61). People without a work unit were managed by the Ministry of Civil Affairs with a quite different budget and level of social protection. And because China was still a predominantly agricultural country, less than 15 per cent of the total population was covered by this relatively generous protection for urban citizens. Farmers were for most of the time to rely on family or rural collective resources, providing a much lower level of services. In other words a disproportionately large share of the government budget was spent on a small number of people, which in fact was only one of many manifestations of the huge gap between the urban and the rural population in socialist China. The inequalities were linked not to individual performance or preference, but firstly to urban citizenship and secondly to the status of the work unit, the choice of which in turn depended on family background, political connections or sheer chance. Because the work units were far from equal in wealth and power they provided far from equal opportunities for their employees.

The system was – or gradually became – problematic in other ways. Firstly, the obligation to employ an administratively fixed number of people and to provide social services for them resulted in productive enterprises having to bear the economic burden of overstaffing and management expenses. Secondly, big enterprises would often choose to have their own welfare institutions, like clinics, hospitals and schools, which were typically less cost effective than comparable independent institutions. And thirdly, the universal guarantee created a dependency mentality among employees who got used to, or resigned to, the fact that the work unit took care of every aspect of daily life (Tang and Parish 2000: 5).

A problem of such a structure is that entitlements and obligations are disjointed (Zhu Ling 2000: 80). No limits to spending existed and the individual had no duty to contribute, once the employment relation was in place. With no duty follows no responsibility and no interest in rationalizing the use of resources. The intermediate levels of work units and local governments, likewise, were not held accountable for excessive spending, so the distance between beneficiary and provider was too great, diminishing the profitability of service provision. In the long run the system was not sustainable, as expenses grew more than the economy as a whole developed. The same phenomenon was seen in other socialist systems, e.g. in Eastern Europe (Kornai 1997).

But worst of all, especially in relation to the later aim of developing market mechanisms, the system immobilized the labour force. A job change presupposed endless bureaucratic negotiations and the social benefits earned in the old place of work could not automatically be transferred to the new. When a market economy was put on the agenda, the work unit system had to be reformed because the old system in important ways was in direct opposition to the new. And social security, like health care, education, housing, pensions, etc., had to be taken care of by other actors to enable enterprises to bear the responsibility for their own profits and losses.

To sum up, on the eve of reform social protection in important areas like health care, housing, old age, maternity, injury, etc. was covered from the same source and under unified management for urban employees. There were no provisions for unemployment, claimed to be non-existent, and no family allowance was established, two branches that traditionally in international documents are included among the lowest standards of social security. In the reform process the different items were separated, as we shall see, but the transformative mechanisms possessed basic common traits.

Work unit research

Social sciences within Chinese academia were revived by the reform policy after having been confined to the straitjacket of Marxist political economy, and the opening-up policy meant new opportunities for Western scholarship on the Chinese social structure. Sociology, anthropology, law and economics were reestablished at Chinese universities and American and European scholars were allowed to do research on-the-spot in the form of anthropological fieldwork or social surveys. In this new field the work unit was discovered as a unique cultural and social construction important for understanding the urban social structure, and extensive research has since then been conducted on the institution (Lee Ming-kwan 2000; Li Hanlin, Li Lulu and Wang Fenyu 1996; Liu Jianjun 2000; Lü and Perry 1997; Lu Feng 1993; Meng Xin 2000; Walder 1986; Whyte and Parish 1984).

The Chinese work unit includes all possible kinds of employers, divided into two main groups, corresponding to the two types of social security mentioned above: one consists of *enterprise work units* (*qiye danwei*) like factories, mines, trade corporations, etc. and the other includes *public service units* (*shiye danwei*) like educational or health service institutions and *state institutions* (*xingzheng danwei*) like professional organizations or administrative units under party or government. Work units can be owned by the state (*guoying qiye*) or by a collective of workers (*jiti qiye*) or by a residential committee, and they are carefully graded in a hierarchy, determining the decision-making power of the leadership and the amount of fringe benefits employees are entitled to.[15] The ranking also determines which kind of information from government and party the leaders are permitted to receive and thus affects their possibilities of acting successfully in the economic sphere (Lü and Perry 1997: 6). During the reform years in some places a non-productive unit was considered safer to be employed in than a factory because it had a 'financial guarantee' (*chi caizheng baoxian*), i.e. it was paid by the government and did not depend on the market forces to the same degree as enterprise units.[16]

The work unit has been analysed from a range of different angles and with different conclusions as to its viability in a reformed social structure. Some scholars see it as a natural successor to the traditional Chinese clan system that also had the responsibility of both protecting and controlling its members (Li Hanlin and Wang Qi 1996: 104; Dutton 1998: 55), while others stress the difference between the clan and the work unit, notably that the clan is eco-

15. As an example it was explained in an interview that different levels could build apartment buildings of different height. Grade 1 – the highest – was allowed to build as many storeys as they wanted, while collective units could only build to six storeys or below. Interview, 5 November 1997.

16. Interview information.

nomically self-sufficient, while the unit depends on the state for its resources. Political scientists stress the political role of the work unit as supporter of the ruling establishment; sociologists stress the function as basic social entity, criminologists focus on its contribution to crime control and prevention, etc. (Liu Jianjun 2000: 21–33).

A general idea is that the system remained essentially unchanged up through two decades of reform though with competition from other employers like private companies. Some look favourably on the survival of the work unit system even under a market economy (Liu Jianjun 2000), while others regard the system as an obstacle to reform (Lu Feng 1993: 88; Lo and Cheng 1996: 51). Tang and Parish assume that the importance of the work unit began to fade in the 1990s and the continued growth of the private sector with its alternative employment structure will accelerate the decline in its importance (Tang and Parish 2000: 29). The wide spectrum of approaches and theories confirm the picture of the Chinese work unit as a comprehensive system of social production, reproduction and regulation, and its caretaker functions makes it essential for an understanding of social security as well.[17]

SOCIAL WELFARE AND REFORMS

Overview of economic reform development

At this stage it is important to note that the transition to a market economy in China is caused by a need to solve a range of concrete problems, most prominently declining productivity,[18] stagnating living standards and international isolation. The change of leadership and of the thinking of the political establishment in China took

17. What Lü and Perry elegantly term the 'maternalistic' function. 'The functions of the *danwei* can be divided into two main areas: political and social. As in a traditional family, the *danwei* acts as a patriarch who disciplines and sanctions his children, while at the same time serving as a maternal provider of care and daily necessities.' (Lü and Perry 1997: 8)
18. See calculation by Tong that 100 yuan of investment produced 34.8 yuan in 1957, but only 22.7 yuan in 1975, and labour productivity only increased 0.3 per cent in this period when the national product grew at an annual rate of 8 per cent (Tong 1987: 5).

place within the existing formal political structure and the reforms did not signal a basic change in ideas about relations between state and individual or a commitment to a new political ideology, as did the fall of communist regimes in Eastern Europe and Central Asia a decade later.

The Chinese system by the end of the 1970s constituted a strong amalgamation of political and economic power. Productive enterprises were managed by a dual leadership of a professional and a political cadre, with the latter as the final decision maker, and state or collective ownership were the only possible ownership forms in both agriculture and industry. No market worthy of the name existed and resources were distributed by administrative means. All profits from production were transferred to the national coffers and business expenses of enterprises and institutions were allocated each year on the basis of negotiations between central and local levels of government. Power depended on position and connections in the political hierarchy, not on wealth. The reform process became one great exercise in dividing up sectors and areas, marking new boundaries, re-structuring old frames, and especially dividing the political and the economic spheres. Politicians should restrict themselves to macro-economic decisions like regulations on taxation, capital and finance institutions, etc. and professionals should be responsible for profit-generating activities. The aim was economic development, rising living standards and international recognition, and the means were to graft market mechanisms onto the planned economy and to open up for foreign business relations.

The Chinese reforms have attracted widespread attention both in and outside of China (Howe 2001; Shirk 1993; Wang Shaoguang and Hu Angang 2001; White 1993), and only the basic principles and turning points will be summed up here. The radical break emerged from the 'Communique of the Third Plenary Session of the 11th Central Committee of the CCP' (*PR*, no. 52, 1978: 6–16). The session endorsed a shift of emphasis to a new principle called *socialist modernization* that had to be speeded up to improve people's living standards, and concerning economic management the serious shortcoming pointed out was over-concentration of authority.

Important new policies were introduced in 1979, 1984, 1989, 1992 and 1997. The first sectors to be affected were agriculture and foreign relations. A contract system was at once introduced in the countryside, allowing families to contract land from the agricultural collective – at that time the basic unit was called the production team. The team and the individual/family signed a contract, obliging the farmer to produce a certain amount of something, usually grain. Any excess amount could be kept and used by the discretion of the families themselves. Production soared almost immediately and within less than one year all regions had introduced the new so-called contract responsibility system. Side productions were allowed and the former ban on private marketing was lifted. The increase in production lasted five years to level off in the last half of the 1980s (Ash and Kueh 1996: 58).

Economic relations with the outside world were also reformed immediately by establishing four special export zones with preferential treatment for foreign investors in the southeastern part of China and by passing a law allowing foreign companies to invest in Chinese production. The economic decision making in foreign trade that formerly belonged to around ten powerful import and export corporations were decentralized to lower levels of government. These were allowed to keep a certain percentage of earned foreign currency for further investment or trade. Foreign trade likewise rose rapidly, by more then 10 per cent anually in the following decade (Ash and Kueh 1996: 221).

In 1984 economic reforms entered the cities by way of a 'Decision of the Central Committee of the Communist Party on Reform of the Economic Structure' (*BR*, vol. 27, no. 44, 1984: I–XVI). Socialist modernization was still the basic aim, now to be achieved by building *socialism with Chinese characteristics.*[19] Urban enterprises were targeted as directly responsible for growth in production and commodity circulation, and they would from now on have to be responsible for their own profit and loss (*zifu yingkui*). The principle of distribution according to work performance was stressed, in-

19. The phrase was defined as 'integrating the basic tenets of Marxism with actual conditions in China' (*BR*, vol. 27, no. 44, 1984: III).

volving widened income difference and a denunciation of egalitarianism as 'utterly incompatible with scientific, Marxist view on socialism' (*BR*, vol. 27, no. 44: XII). Contract responsibility was to be introduced in industry, as in agriculture, with the manager at the top assuming ultimate responsibility. Thus the power of the professional manager was strengthened at the expense of the party secretary. Experiments had been conducted in Sichuan province from 1978 to 1980 with profit retention and management autonomy (Tong 1987: 10) and these measures were extended to other parts of the country. A new labour allocation system broke radically with the tradition of life-long employment by replacing 'the iron rice bowl' (*tiefan wan*) with contract employment. Employers got the right to hire and fire workers in 1986[20] and a bankruptcy law was passed the same year. Productivity was enhanced by introducing new principles of remuneration, like bonus systems and piecework, exactly the two forms that were most violently attacked during the Cultural Revolution as means of capitalist exploitation.

The establishment of special zones continued by opening 14 cities for foreign investment in 1984 and by the end of the 1980s the coastal area had manifested itself as the dynamo in economic development. A splitting up of the country in an advanced and a backward part became a reality, with economic growth in the east surpassing development in the western regions (Yao and Zhang 2001: 169). The basic economic changes mentioned above had been introduced, but in fact they were far from being effectively implemented. Work units in the cities still kept a cradle-to-grave obligation towards their employees.

1989 became a turning point in many ways. Economic growth had slowed down, leading to uncontrolled inflation. Large parts of the population were dissatisfied with their share of the economic boom, and voices demanding political changes grew louder and louder.

> The economic difficulties may be summarised as follows: accelerating inflation leading to a deterioration in the real income of the urban population in the face of rising expectations; fiscal

20. The four important State Council documents can be found in *GWYGB*, no. 25, 1986: 739–750.

> problems due to a decline in state revenues; mounting foreign debt and accumulating trade deficits; inadequate investment; worsening problems in agriculture, ecological balance, education, transport, and so on. (Wing and Cheng 1996: 17)

The brutal crackdown on students and workers in June[21] tarnished the reputation of the Communist Party, toppled party secretary Zhao Ziyang and brought Chinese human rights violations to the top of the international agenda.

The following three years were marked by retrenchment policies and ideological regimentation, until Deng Xiaoping in January 1992 set out on a so called 'Southern Tour' (*nanxun*) widely covered by the media (*FEER*, 13 February 1992: 10). In Guangdong province he expressed his full support to an ongoing reform process and this symbolic gesture signalled renewed strength for reformists within the party though without reinstating the dethroned party head, Zhao Ziyang. In October of the same year, at the 14th Party Congress, the new party head, Jiang Zemin, delivered a report on 'Building Socialism with Chinese Characteristics' (*BR*, vol. 34, no. 43, 1992: 9–32)[22] as another new stage in socialist modernization. In an accompanying interview a party spokesman stated that market economy as a mechanism does not belong to capitalism, but is '. . . a common achievement brought about by the economic development of the modern world . . .' (*BR*, vol. 34, no. 43, 1992: 33). The formulation of the new policy took a further step in November 1993 with a party decision to create the term 'socialist market economy'.[23] In the new stage the market would play 'the fundamental role in resource allocations under macroeconomic control by the state' (*BR*, vol. 36, no. 47, 1993: 12). The pressure for a genuine transition to market conditions intensified, but many problems still existed in implementation, which were revealed in

21. On the night between 3 and 4 June 1989, army tanks cleared a demonstration in Tiananmen Square in Beijing of demonstrators who had been active for more than a month. An unknown number were killed and the events are still the object of political conflict within China and between the Chinese government and the international community (Oksenberg et al. 1990).
22. The full title is 'Accelerating the Reform, the Opening to the Outside World and the Drive for Modernization, so as to Achieve Greater Succes in Building Socialism With Chinese Characteristics'.
23. Full title 'Decision of the CPC Central Committee on Some Issues Concerning the Establishment of a Socialist Market Economic Structure'.

September 1997 when the 15th Party Congress once again called for an effective marketization of state-owned industry. In the government report party general secretary Jiang Zemin repeated the ambition to promote a fundamental shift of the economic system, and promised that the government would not directly intervene in the operation of enterprises (*BR*, vol. 40, no. 40, 1997: 20).[24] Finally, at the CCP Central Plenum in September 1999, it was declared that 'The transformation of the SOEs' system and their structural readjustments have reached *a crucial stage*, with some deep-rooted contradictions and all the problems having emerged' (emphasis added) (*BR*, vol. 42, no. 41, 1999: 18).

The picture above clearly reveals the gradual character of the urban reform policies. There is no big bang over the process, but rather a two-steps-forward-one-step-back approach.[25] The ambition to reform state-owned enterprises and raise living standards is expressed all the way from 1984 and in stronger and stronger terms, reflecting how complicated the process turned out to be. It emerges from words and deeds that the attitude of the leadership was cautious. New measures were tried out in selected areas before they became national policy, concessions granted to lower levels were withdrawn when problems cropped up or resistance turned out to be serious. The trials in the different areas were conducted by so called 'small leadership groups' (*lingdao xiaozu*) set up by the SC and chaired by the politburo member responsible for the field (Tanner 1999: 55, n. 12). The groups would consist of not only professionals from the given ministry but also representatives from other stakeholders, like the Ministry of Finance, banks or line commissions depending on the issue in question. The mandate of the group would be to decide on the content of a new policy, select places for experimentation on the basis of economic level and political orientation of the leadership in different localities, receive reports on results and finally formulate proposals to the State Council or the National Peoples Congress. Local authorities were

---

24. Full title 'Hold High the Great Banner of Deng Xiaoping Theory for an All-round Advancement of the Cause of Building Socialism With Chinese Characteristics'.
25. By Deng Xiaoping called to 'cross the river by groping for the stones' (*mo shitou guohe*).

eager to be selected as an experimental site because this would often attract extra funding and provide political status to their areas, and good connections to central leadership were necessary to be permitted to conduct trial reforms. There was no open procedure on how to be selected or which kind of benefits would follow from a selection, it was all a matter of negotiations between the involved parties.

The pivotal point in urban reform was the work unit system in state owned and collective industry, and the really difficult decisions were how to make industry self-supporting without sending millions of unemployed people home or out in the streets to demonstrate. The lack of social security became the obstacle to establishing an effective and profitable industrial sector, because the social burden of the work units made them more and more unable to compete on equal terms with the newly established private sector and rural industry, which did not have a large and old work force to feed and care for (Saunders and Shang 2001: 278). According to contemporary estimates one fifth of state enterprises were losing money in 1986, one third in 1991 and almost one half in 1994 (Lo and Cheng 1996: 15 and 21). A clearly unsustainable situation prompted a speeding up of efforts to establish new mechanisms for social security.

Legal reform

Following the economic re-structuring, a gradual 'legalization' has taken place as the new order of things had to be backed by law to gain confidence both from the population and from the international community. A comprehensive legal system has been created almost from scratch during the two reform decades; some laws relevant in this context are a Law on Civil Procedure (1991), an Inheritance Law (1985), a Lawyers Law (1996), a Women's Law (1992), a Marriage Law (1981) and a Labour Law (1994), but no law on social security as such has been passed. Apart from these national laws adopted by the NPC, provinces have corresponding laws and regulations that are subordinate to the national one. And the SC and departmental ministries issue decisions, circulars, regulations, etc. both broad on policy lines and detailed as explanations and specifications in law implementation (Tanner 1999).

But laws and regulations are violated as everybody knows and systems to provide remedies have been integrated in the legal reform process. They run along two lines: one to seek redress for administrative mismanagement generally and one within the ambit of the Ministry of Labour and Social Security. With the aim of controlling the bureaucracy and preventing abuse of power an Administrative Litigation Law was enacted in March 1989,[26] according to which administrative cases can be heard by specialized units within the People's Courts system (Potter 2001: 21). The drafting of the law is said to have been both one of the more controversial processes of legislation but also an extremely public one involving strong expressions of interests from executive bodies worrying about court interference in administrative procedures (Buhmann 2001: 353).

With a less legal character, a bridge between the citizens and the administrative power holders exists in the form of a system for 'filing of grievances' (*xinfang zhidu*) operated by local governments, which at each level has to assign staff members or an organizational unit to receive and answer approaches – by mail, telephone and in person – from citizens with problems.[27] At the central level a unit within the SC General Office treats questions to the NPC or the Party Central. A lot of the enquiries can be solved on the spot, some times by contacting the work unit or other involved parties and negotiating a solution, but the possibility of proceeding to the court system exists.

Especially relevant to social security is the system for settling of labour disputes (*laodong zhengyi*) codified in the Labour Law of 1994, chapter 10. In case of a dispute between a work unit and an employee three stages of conflict resolution are set up. At the unit level a mediation committee (*zhongcai weiyuanhui*) has to be established with representatives from the staff and

26. *Zhonghua Renmin Gongheguo Xingzheng Susong Fa.* (*GWYGB*, no. 7, 1989: 297–307).
27. *Zhonghua Renmin Gongheguo Xinfang Tiaoli*, promulgated by the SC 10 October 1995 to go into effect 1 January 1996 (*GWYGB*, 9 November, no. 26, 1995: 1046–1051).

workers, the unit leadership and the trade union. If mediation fails the dispute can be brought before an arbitration committee at the level of the local Labour Bureau, with participation of unit leadership and the trade union – no staff representatives are included at this level. If the arbitration award is not acceptable or is not implemented in due time a lawsuit might be brought to a basic-level People's Court. Disputes over social insurance benefits are specifically mentioned in an interpretation from the Supreme People's Court as falling within the scope of the articles in the Labour Law.[28] The number of cases accepted under the system grew from 94,000 in 1995 (*ZLTN* 1996: 551) to 135,000 in 2000; of these latter, 31,350 were cases of 'social insurance and welfare' (*ZLTN* 2001: 429). The outcome of the social insurance cases are not recorded separately, but of the total number of accepted cases in 2000, 30 per cent were settled by mediation, 40 per cent by arbitration and the remaining 30 per cent by 'other' means.[29]

Chart 1.3 Complaints and remedies

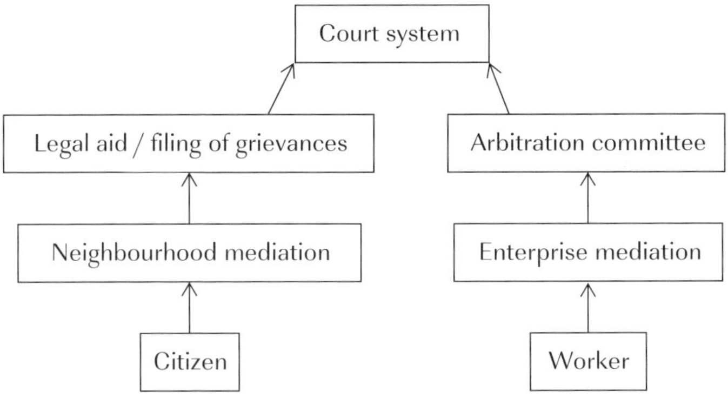

28. 'The Interpretation provides that the people's court will accept the following disputes: . . . Disputes arising because of claims made by a worker after retirement for old-age pension monies, medical expenses, industrial injury insurance benefits and other social insurance expenses against the original employer who does not participate in social insurance pooling' (China Legal Change, no. 9, 2001: 1).
29. 'Other means' usually refer to intervention from the local government (Burell 2001: 313).

To be able to use the formal system in place, information is needed and a system providing legal aid has been established gradually since the Ministry of Justice proposed it for the first time in 1994. A special centre within the Ministry promotes the development of legal aid bodies at the provincial and county level and monitors their operations and a fund has been set up to collect donations from government and other sources. Furthermore, later regulation stipulates that every lawyer has an obligation to provide free legal service once or twice a year, supervised by the Ministry of Justice. Legal advice can also be sought at non-governmental bodies, primarily the so called legal clinics established by law schools at universities. The clinics combine free legal service with education as they are staffed by law students under supervision of teachers, and they are considered to be more independent and also more professional than the Ministry system that uses lawyers who are only assigned a few cases each year. So they receive the lion's share of cases of social complaints or conflicts.

Finally, the traditional mediation function of the neighbourhood committees is still in place and encouraged by the authorities to lessen the pressure on the court system. Mediation at the neighbourhood level is done in civil cases of marriage dispute, individual debt, petty theft, etc. and the number of cases dealt with has declined during the reform period, while the number of cases brought to court or to arbitration committees has been risen (Lubman 1999: 40ff).

Social security reform

Like the economic reforms were prompted by a practical problem of low productivity, the establishment of a new social security system in China after 1979, in turn, was a reaction to problems created by the new economic policies, and it was set up by the leadership with the aim of supporting the transition to market economy and guaranteeing social stability, not as a result of popular demand or a change in social priorities (Gu 2001: 133). The long-term objective of the reforms in social provision was to diversify the burden by moving sources of funding away from the public sphere to other actors, primarily to the family and the market, but also to community and charity activities. The ambition was to change the system, so protection would be structured according to type instead of according to providing unit. Earlier, each person was protected against all risks from one single source; under the new system each person, in principle, should be protected against each single risk for itself, cross-cutting different work units. The focus would change from the work unit to the individual, who would be empowered to diversify his or her own protection with the support of a government-backed basic institution.

The policy was characterized by the two related catchwords of socialization (*shehuihua*) and diversification (*duocengci*), both basically meaning to lift the burden of social expenses from the SOEs or the state and onto other shoulders. The expenses should be diversified into society. Socialization is not necessarily privatization (a word very seldom used) but implies both commodification and decentralization of responsibility from the state to non-state actors, be they local communities (*shequ*), social organizations (*shetuan*) or the family. The role of the state was to be a regulator of private activities, and funding for social security would basically come from the parties involved, i.e. employers and employees, and would be raised as compulsory savings for future (individual) use.

Because the reform of social security was a product of or caused by economic reform, it came later in time and has been slower in implementation. It was inextricably linked to reform of state-owned industry, and therefore did not begin until the middle of the 1980s, when the first signals of urban reform came, as we have seen, with the decision on reform of the economic structure in 1984. The development can roughly be divided into two periods (Wang Mengkui 2001: 57).

From 1984 to 1995, experiments were taking place beginning with pension and unemployment followed by housing. The principle was 'social planning' (*shehui tongchou*), involving collection of funds at a higher – local government – level than the work units, but retaining the principles of PAYG and distribution on a benefit basis.

From 1995 to 2000, experiments continued, now also with health care. The new element was the pairing of social pooling funds with personal accounts (*tongzhang jiehe*, in the following called the Combination System). With this the system was changed from being on benefit basis to being partly on contribution basis, and from being a PAYG system to being partly a savings system. The new principles were for the first time mentioned in the decision of November 1993 (*BR*, vol. 36, no. 47, 1993: 12) and thereafter they became the established model for pension and health care. The party session that year is normally counted by Chinese scholars as the point in time where social security moved several steps up on the priority list of the political reformers to be among the top concerns. While some people and localities are allowed to become prosperous first, income distribution should give 'priority to efficiency while taking fairness into account'. The expression became an abstract of the official view to be repeated in following documents.

But also on this front, reform was no smooth sailing and there appear at times indications that rules were not implemented. For example in Jiang Zemin's report to the 15th Party Congress from September 1997 the paragraph on social security indicated more of a future ambition than an accomplished feat:

> We shall build a social security system, introducing old-age pensions and medical insurance systems by combining social pools with individual accounts, and improve the unemployment insurance and social relief systems so as to provide the basic social security. (*BR*, vol. 40, no. 40, 1997: 20)

The formulation is interesting in light of the fact that in the hour of speaking a new national pension system had already been adopted by the State Council and several decisions had been promulgated on establishment of unemployment and health insurance. The future tense is not in line with the existing regulations, which can be taken as a sign of problems in implementation. This impression is confirmed when one looks at the local level, where we also find that the pace of reform subsequently quickens and important decisions on social welfare reform follow like pearls on a string during the last half of the 1990s.

The process in this area was, like the general economic reforms, managed by 'small groups' formed by the SC with the aim of conducting trials. Pension reform was orchestrated by the Ministry of Labour, which in April 1998 was renamed the Ministry of Labour and Social Security,[30] health care reform was under the Ministry of Health, housing reform under the Ministry of Construction and educational reform under the Ministry of Education. The guidelines for reform from the national level were copied rather closely by the local counterparts, being the local Labour Bureau, the Housing Bureau, etc., as will appear from the local material, showing that the reform process is primarily a top-down endeavour

CONCLUDING REMARKS

One of the main challenges of the economic reform programme, approved in December 1978 and started immediately after, was the tremendous task of separating political and economic power. The state apparatus should be separated from the party, and both should estrange themselves from economic activities. Economic growth and raising living standards were the ultimate goals to be achieved by introducing market mechanisms into the socialist planned economy. In the cities the *work unit* was the pivotal element in the process. The full and sound use of market forces presupposes economic units that are self-sustaining, so 'to be responsible for own profit and loss' became the new guidelines for enterprises. In order to realize the true economic independence of work units it was necessary to relieve them of the social obligations that used to constitute an important part of their expenses. The reasoning goes that if a factory has to pay pensions, medical bills, housing and schooling for all its workers, it cannot possibly produce on market conditions i.e. sell their goods at prices that people can afford or are willing to pay. The responsibilities for social security had to be taken out of the economic entities and placed else-

30. The new ministry collected many social security functions from other agencies, e.g. Ministry of Personnel, Ministry of Civil Affairs, Ministry of Public Health and the State Commission for Economic Reform (Wong and Flynn 2001: 46).

where in the social structure. The protection of basic economic and social rights to work, health care, housing and education were to find funding either with the government, the market, civil society units like community services or, as the ultimate individualization, the family; or, more likely, with some combination of these different actors.

The local material described in this study gives a still-picture, freezing this dynamic process of change at a certain point in time. Looking at a snapshot of the reform process, certain delays are clearly discernible. Social security reform is delayed in relation to economic reform and local implementation is delayed in relation to national policies. There are both a causal and a temporal relationship between the economic reforms as such and the reform of the social security system, and the two processes mutually influence each other. Efforts to make productive units profitable are slowed down by the units' role as safety net. To overcome the hindrance economic reform has to be halted or even reversed for a period until institutions are in place that can make up for the emerging deficiencies.

In the hour of writing the process of change has been going on for two decades. During the first decade – the optimistic and vital boom before the disaster in 1989 – economic efficiency was on the agenda and the public argumentation was that equity would follow development and efficiency. Some would get rich first and then the others would follow. A three-year period of political conflict and economic decline divide the two decades, and from the recovery of the reform spirit in 1992–1993 growing attention was being paid to the equity element of the two social policy contrasts. Except for a non-specific commitment to improve living standards, the fate of disadvantaged groups is not mentioned in official documents until social security is listed as number three of 'important and interrelated tasks' in the report to the 14th Party Congress in October 1992. Social security moves up the list in the subsequent years to be part of both the second and third of the eight points of economic restructuring in the report to the 15th Party Congress in September 1997, and two years later reform of state owned enterprises is subject to a special decision whereby reducing social burdens and maintaining social stability are key points to be achieved by speeding up the building of a social security system.[31]

The growing official recognition of the need for state regulated solutions to problems like unemployment and welfare provision is reflected in the active experimentation going on during the middle of the 1990s orchestrated by the relevant ministries. A provisional conclusion on the character of the new system can be seen in the State Council decisions on the pension, health care and unemployment insurance schemes, consisting of a combination of personal savings and redistributive measures. These decisions have subsequently been realized at the local level gradually and have been met with resistance and inertia. The idea of individual accounts, for example, seems not to be an integrated part of the system as perceived in the individual homes in the local material from 1997 and 1998, when it had been official policy for five years already.

The implementation of reform – the true separation of economy and politics – showed itself to be much more difficult and time-consuming than expected and targets for realization of new policies have been postponed one time after another. The caution and setbacks have in many instances been motivated by social and/or political concerns. Fear of protests and unrest has provided loss-making enterprises with new state subsidies and prevented an explosion of bankruptcies. Factories have been forced to keep people on the payroll even though they do not have the finances to pay them.

The socialization and diversification of social protection has been realized in such a way that individuals now have a much greater choice as to how they want to obtain social services. They can buy insurance in the market, they can choose their own doctor and hospital if they can pay themselves, and they can buy or rent a flat according to their own economic priorities. But as we shall see, the freedom is to some degree won at the expense of a formerly existing social safety net.

---

31. 'The Decision of the Central Committee of the Communist Party of China on Major Issues Concerning the Reform and Development of State-Owned Enterprises' (adopted at the 4th Plenum of the 15th CCP Central Committee on 22 September 1999).

2 只能靠自己

The Human Rights Regime

> *The point of reference, in this discussion as well as in international human rights law, should be the promotion of being human or the capacity to be human.* (Scott 1999: 635)

Human rights have for the last decades occupied a prominent position as a new global discourse, replacing the discourse of political ideologies that dominated the forty-year period of the Cold War. On paper human rights are globally accepted as expressing the basic values of the United Nations with its membership of 191 states, constituting all nations in the world except the Vatican in Rome.[1] The origin of the concept has been placed in European thinking of natural law, even going back to Ancient Greece, but from other cultural settings and from the UN system itself it has been argued that the basic values and ideas behind the idea of human rights are in conformity with all major world religions and thought systems, as expressed by the High Commissioner for Human Rights, Mary Robinson:

> The result (the Universal Declaration of Human Rights, ht) is a distillation of many of the values inherent in the world's major legal systems and religious beliefs including the Buddhist, Christian, Hindu, Islamic and Jewish traditions. (Lassen 2001: 179)

The introduction here will not delve into the philosophical roots of human rights but proceed from the fact that the human rights regime was born in 1948 by the decision of 48 states from five continents[2] to adopt the Universal Declaration, and the ideas contained

1. As one of the last countries, Switzerland voted yes to membership of the UN in a referendum in the beginning of March 2002. Taiwan is also not a member, its 'statehood' contested by the Chinese Mainland claim on the island.
2. Australia, New Zealand, 3 countries from Africa, 10 from Europe, 12 from Asia and 21 from the Americas.

in the Declaration have subsequently been endorsed by almost all countries in the world by their membership of the United Nations. To clarify the basis of this study I will touch slightly upon the doubts raised about the applicability of universal standards in different areas[3] and the motivation behind the widespread support for the UN organization as such.

However, as the only philosophical comment, attention will be drawn to the fact that the rationale behind the concept of human rights rests in the notion of *human dignity*, a non-material quality perceived as being present in every individual human being.[4] According to the basic human rights documents, human dignity consists of or is expressed in the 'reason and conscience' imbedded in each person.[5] This quality is inherent, meaning it is not conditioned by status, gender, nationality, etc., or by any performance or contribution to the common good. Unlike entitlements that can be earned by being born to certain parents in a certain place, the dignity connected to human rights is within or part of the human being from the hour he or she is born. It can be understood as deriving from a divine 'outer' force, like God or Nature or it can be taken as a practical device to prevent people from doing against others, what they do not want done against themselves. No matter from where the quality is derived, the acceptance of it has practical consequences.

> This moral claim (of human dignity, ht) is rightly said to constitute the *normative* premise for the whole system of human rights (Lindholm 1999). Though the article is stated as a simple description, it should rather be read as a normative prescription saying that all human beings *ought* to be recognised and treated as free and equal in dignity and rights. (Brudholm 2001: 26)

Read in this way the Declaration can also be seen merely as a joint decision by states to behave in a certain way. The objective of the nu-

3. The universality of human rights is inter alia discussed in Hastrup 2001.
4. Arthur Chaskalson, President of the South African Constitutional Court, has described the right to human dignity as 'a foundational value of the constitutional order' and 'a value implicit in almost all the rights enumerated in the Universal Declaration' (Odinkalu 2001: 338).
5. UDHR, article 1 reads: 'All human beings are born free and equal in dignity and rights. They are endowed with reason and conscience and should act towards one another in a spirit of brotherhood'.

merous specific rights is to protect this 'humanity' of human beings that is taken for granted and not to be subjected to scientific proof.

Thus, the following is anchored in both a historical and a philosophical premise: human rights is an important part of international law that was initially established by adoption of the Universal Declaration of Human Rights in 1948 and later confirmed by the states ratifying the ensuing legal documents. The regime is based on the conviction that each human being possesses a unique value that deserves protection from the larger community or from the rest of mankind.

THE REGIME[6] – SYSTEM AND MECHANISMS

Before the end of World War II there was no international scrutiny of how governments treated their own citizens. However, the horror of the war created a feeling that some kind of global commitment was necessary to stop the disrespect of human life and dignity that escalated during the 1940s, and the United Nations was born to further that aim (Craven 1995: 6). Human rights standards came to constitute the basic elements of the whole UN system and they are codified in a number of declarations, recommendations and conventions (also called covenants or treaties).[7] The international 'Bill of Rights' is to be seen as an international constitution or an important part of international law, containing the Universal Declaration of Human Rights (UDHR) approved by the UN General Assembly on 10 December 1948, and the two big conventions from 1966, the International Covenant on Civil and Political Rights (ICCPR, the content of which in the following will be called civil rights for short) and the International Covenant on Economic, Social and Cultural Rights (ICESCR, the content of

6. The word 'human rights regime' is used here as a loose term covering both the mechanisms and documents adopted by the UN member states as well as the values and principles behind the concept of human rights. For a discussion of regime theory in general and human rights regime in particular, see Kent 1999: 4–6, where a definition by Stephen Krasner is used of regimes as 'sets of implicit or explicit principles, norms, rules and decision-making procedures around which actors' expectations converge in a given area of international relations'.
7. For a full list of documents see Eide et al. 2001: 767–775.

which in the following will be called social rights for short). Later a number of important conventions were approved by the UN system and gradually signed by an increasing number of member states.[8] The conventions are legally binding documents successively to be ratified by national parliaments, while a declaration is an expression of a political commitment shared by the signatories and adopted once and for all. Declarations, resolutions and recommendations are not open to additional subscription, and they are characterized as 'soft law' in contrast to the 'hard law' of the legally binding conventions. The 'softness' does not imply that declarations are without meaning or legal consequence, but their influence is less direct and touches upon other modes of international communication, notably politics and morality (Koch 2001b: 144).

Apart from the international documents three geographical areas have adopted regional treaties, specifying their understanding of the human rights principles: the European Convention on Human Rights and Fundamental Freedoms from 1953 and the European Social Charter from 1961 parallel to the two big global conventions. Two other important regional instruments are the American Convention on Human Rights from 1969 and the African Charter on Human and People's Rights from 1981. Asia does not have a common regional human rights document, but has adopted several declarations and joint communiques, inter alia in an ASEAN context (Luo Yanhua 1998: 83–84). The Arab world has passed Islamic Declarations in 1981 and 1986 (Cassese 1990: 214). The third kind of actors on the scene are nation-states and, in fact, national governments are the ultimate duty holders in the human rights system.

When the Universal Declaration was to be translated into legally binding instruments soon after its adoption, political and ideological disagreements began to affect the issue, as they have been doing ever since. The socialist states, led by the Soviet Union,

8. Convention of the Elimination of all Forms of Racial Discrimination (CERD) in 1966; Convention on the Elimination of All Forms of Discrimination Against Women (CEDAW) in 1979; Convention Against Torture and Other Cruel, Inhuman, or Degrading Treatment (CAT) in 1984; and Convention on the Rights of the Child (CRC) in 1989. For ratification status see homepage of the Office of the High Commissioner of Human Rights, www.UNHCHR.ch.

stressed social rights as part of their commitment to egalitarian redistributive goals, while the Western world tended to favour civil rights in accordance with their ideals of freedom and democracy. The UN General Assembly insisted in the beginning – 1950[9] – that human rights were interdependent and that all categories of rights should be contained within one document. However, on the basis of Western claims the arguments were ignored by the Economic and Social Council (ECOSOC), which drafted the document and the result became the two conventions separating civil and social rights, adopted in 1966, but only in force from 1976 (Craven 1995: 16–22).[10] However, the idea of the indivisibility and interdependence of all human rights continued to figure in official documents and public rhetoric, most recently confirmed in the Declaration from the World Conference on Human Rights in Vienna in 1993[11] with the wording: 'all human rights are universal, indivisible, interdependent and interrelated'.

Decisive for the division into two categories were arguments for the different nature of the two types of rights, creating different demands on states and different needs of instruments,

> . . . it was expected that states who did not want to undertake the obligations arising from economic, social, and cultural rights would be willing to ratify an instrument which contained only civil and political rights. (Eide et al. 2001: 10)

Civil rights were understood to be 'negative', 'immediate', 'justiciable', 'precise' and not least important, 'cheap'; while social rights were 'positive', 'programmatic', 'non-justiciable', 'vague' and again not least, 'expensive'. In other words, civil rights only demanded of states not to interfere with individual freedom and violations could easily be brought to court. Social rights, on the contrary, obliged governments to provide social services that are costly and viola-

9. General Assembly Resolution 421 E (V) of 4 December 1950: 'When deprived of economic, social and cultural rights, man does not represent the human person whom the Universal Declaration regards as the ideal of the free man'.
10. A certain number of ratifications have to be deposited before a convention enters into force. E.g. for CESCR the 35th ratification, making the Convention effective, came 3 January 1976.
11. The General Assembly convened this second world conference with the aim of reviewing and assessing progress made in the field of human rights since the first global conference on human rights took place in Teheran in 1968.

tions cannot easily be brought to court. The distinctions are contested as will be discussed below, and complaints are made that social rights have received far less attention than civil rights in regard to implementation. The controversy was from the outset, apart from the embryonic Cold War mentality, also prompted by the discussion on how to implement and monitor the new world order, where it was felt that the different rights could not be supervised with the same kinds of instruments.

One indication of the perceived difference in character between the two Covenants lies in the famous article 2(1) of ICESCR saying:

> Each State Party to the present Covenant undertakes to take steps, individually and through international assistance and co-operation, especially economic and technical, to the maximum of its available resources, with a view to achieving progressively the full realisation of the rights recognised in the present Covenant by all appropriate means, including particularly the adoption of legislative measures.

No passage in ICCPR corresponds to the concept of 'progressive realisation' which has been understood as giving more flexibility to the implementation of social rights while civil rights are to be realized right away. However, in spite of the apparent leeway in the formulations of progression and 'to the maximum of its available resources', there are certain limits to state behaviour. An official interpretation of the article confirms core obligations to ensure minimum levels of each right.[12] For example to ensure access to the minimum essential food or freedom from hunger is not to be realized gradually but is an immediate duty. If a state is unable to feed a starving population it is obliged to seek international assistance. The idea of core obligations is related to an internationally accepted notion of a distinction between *obligations of conduct* and *obligations of results.*[13] Some articles in the Covenants demand of states merely to do something in order to fulfill or protect a certain right

12. CESCR General Comment, no. 3, *The Nature of States Parties Obligations*, para. 10. UN doc. E/1991/23.
13. Some authors classify social rights as imposing obligations of conduct on states and not obligations of result (Scheinin 2001b: 30), while the CESCR, General Comment, no. 3, para. 1 includes both kinds of obligations as valid under the ICESCR (Eide et al. 2001: 618).

while others demand a certain result. An example could be article 14 of the ICESCR on the right to education, where free, compulsory primary education is an obligation of result and a core obligation, while the General Comment no.11 upholds an obligation of conduct to *adopt a plan of action* within two years after ratification if a state does not have free primary education (Nowak 2001: 256).

The human rights standards are institutionally based in the UN Economic and Social Council (ECOSOC). Following the picture of human rights standards as an (international) legal system, the question immediately poses itself of the existence of courts and law enforcement personnel. There are no international courts (only regional, like the European Court of Human Rights in Strasbourg, mentioned below) where individuals can send petitions nor any international police capable of enforcing international human rights law, and the effectiveness of human rights standards rests just as much in the political landscape as in the legal realm. No states like to be criticized in international forums for human rights violations.[14] But an elaborate system for monitoring human rights conventions, built largely on voluntary reporting by states parties (i.e. signatories of a convention or covenant) has also been developed since the adoption of the first legally binding documents.

Each member state of a particular convention, i.e. the states that have ratified the convention, are obliged to deliver a report with fixed intervals about the situation in the country concerning the special issue contained in the convention. There are certain standard demands on these reports and they are received and treated by a committee mandated within the specific area, the so-called treaty bodies. The members of the committees are nominated by their governments and elected by the member states according to specific rules for each convention and the members serve in the committee in a personal capacity, rather than as government representatives. Upon receiving the reports the committees after examination and further questioning produce 'concluding observations' on each, containing what the committee sees as deficiencies

---

14. The serious efforts in Geneva during the 1990s of the Chinese government to avoid a critical resolution bear witness to the effectiveness of political pressure (Kent 1999: 49).

in the report or the situation in the country as such, and commenting on how to improve human rights protection related to the specific issue. On the basis of these experiences and the information obtained, the committees can publish 'General Comments'. These comments are to be compared with interpretations of laws in a national system. E.g. the Committee on Economic, Social and Cultural Rights has issued 14 General Comments, among them one on each of the rights to housing, education and health, which will be used below in the analysis of the Chinese situation.[15]

Some conventions have other supervisory mechanisms, and guidelines for state behaviour have been worked out in the general comments of the committees. The European Committee for Prevention of Torture, for example, conducts unannounced state visits. Possibilities for individual complaints are secured for civil rights in the Optional Protocol to ICCPR, according to which persons who claim that their civil rights have been violated, and who have exhausted all domestic channels of complaint, can lodge their case with the Human Rights Committee. Likewise the European Court of Human Rights in Strasbourg receives individual petitions. A corresponding arrangement does not exist for social rights, where individual cases cannot be tried in international forums. An optional protocol with access to individual complaints for violations of social rights has been discussed for years and a proposal for a working group to prepare the protocol has been put forward at the 2003 session of the Human Rights Commission. The European Court and the channel of individual complaints cannot be likened to a national court system and a national police force, as the international institutions do not have the means of physical coercion that the national forces possess.

The Human Rights Commission has 53 voting members, selected by ECOSOC for a three year period according to a principle of regional distribution.[16] The mandate of the Commission is to mon-

15. For the texts of the 14 comments, see Eide et al. 2001: 613–695.

16. 15 from Africa, 12 from Asia, 5 from Eastern Europe (the rules for distribution were made before the collapse of the communist bloc in 1989), 11 from South America and 10 from a group called West European and other states. Some big countries are normally elected each term. Russia, India and the US have been members since 1947, China since 1982. Quite extraordinarily the United States was not re-elected in 2001, but the US regained its seat in 2002.

itor existing international standards and recommend new ones, to investigate violations, to submit proposals for new programs and policies and to provide advisory and technical services to countries needing assistance in protecting human rights. The Commission elects so-called *special rapporteurs* to follow the development within certain subjects, e.g. on torture, violence against women, education, housing, food, etc., or in certain geographic areas, like Iraq, Burundi, Palestine, etc. The Commission meets for six weeks every March/April in Geneva to discuss what is deemed to be important human rights topics and to raise criticism of specific countries if a majority is behind such a discussion. Selected themes and problems will often be put on the agenda after recommendation by the General Assembly.

Protection of specific rights as legal categories is not an end in itself, but instrumental in relation to the perceived higher aim of preserving human dignity. Ultimately, the formal mechanisms have to be seen as useful tools in assessing life situations as a whole. In discussing the interdependence of the different categories of rights, Craig Scott warns of the risk of reifying rights as objectively existing entities and forgetting what they are all about. He reminds himself and his readers that '. . . the idea of rights has been developed not for the sake of rights but for the sake of persons' (Scott 1999: 635).

> Instead general conceptual analysis of human rights . . . should be approached with sustained attention to the underlying humanity of human rights and to the reality that human experience rarely confines itself to neat categories, much less to highly abstract ones. (Scott 1999: 636)[17]

Adopting a holistic approach, an evaluation of rights protection in a specific case can be seen from 'above', focussing on state compliance with the documents, or from 'below', i.e. from the perspective of the individual. Views from 'above' focus on state conduct (Robertson 1994), on how the different mechanisms available to the state interact and support or negate each other. Taking the individual as the centre from 'below' makes it clear how different kinds

17. Scott's article also contains a self-criticism, when he quotes himself for having contributed to this 'rigid legalistic tendency'.

of rights interact and depend on each other, just as a person's different areas of life interact and form a whole. From both perspectives a holistic picture can be sought and an integrative approach has been adopted by various supervisory organs.

Surrounding and continuously refining these more or less juridical instruments are academic debates and legal applications in commissions and treaty bodies. The field is constantly moving and human rights have become one of the dominating global discourses also used to fight political and economic battles. For example, the US for many years made renewal of special preferential trade conditions with China contingent on fulfilment of certain human rights criteria. And China, on the other hand, has lobbied extensively to prevent criticisms of its policies in the Human Rights Commission, while criticism of Saudi Arabia practising physical punishment has neven been proposed in Geneva. Numerous other examples can be mentioned of how human rights have come to be part of political plays and deals all over the world.

QUESTIONING HUMAN RIGHTS

Indivisibility: the civil/social dichotomy

The division of human rights into the two different texts or categories, introduced above, led to a theoretical cleavage formulated as *rights generations.* The French legal thinker Karel Vasak in 1979 developed the idea of a first generation of civil and political rights, a second generation of economic, social and cultural rights; and later was added a third generation of so-called 'solidarity rights', such as the right to a clean environment, the right to peace and the right to development.[18] Another distinction has been suggested, viz. the aforementioned, that civil rights are negative, demanding of states to refrain from interfering, while social rights are positive, i.e. demanding government involvement. Both efforts to divide

18. The last category is also called 'group rights' or 'collective rights'. 'It is often assumed that these rights should benefit not only individuals but also groups and peoples ('collective rights') and that their realisation requires global co-operation based on the notion of international solidarity.' (Eide et al. 2001: 120)

human rights into subgroups in the process of implementation have been met with academic criticism, upholding the principle of indivisibility of all human rights.

Concerning the generation concept, it is worth noting the order of rights. Though it is never openly expressed, the understanding of 'first' as 'most important' lies close at hand, and the priority of civil rights was actually borne out in practice in the decades after WW2, leading to an academic criticism of the typology as such and the arguments for the division.

> In the years that have since (1951, ht) gone by, civil and political rights have attracted much attention in theory and practice, while economic, social and cultural rights have often been neglected. (Eide et al. 2001: 3)

The neglect often concerns the possibilities of bringing social cases to court expressed in what Paul Hunt outright calls a 'juridical marginalisation of social rights' (Hunt 1996: 1). Other scholars see the generation theory as still a valid tool to assist 'in interpreting the exact scope of the right in question, the precise legal claim of the respective holder of the right as well as the corresponding obligations of the state' (Nowak 2001: 252).

One critical comment of the negative/positive distinction has been that not all civil rights are cost-free. Fair trial and the right to free elections are for example rather resource demanding. And not all social rights are non-justiciable; the right to free and compulsory education can for example be legally applied.[19] Some civil rights are also vague; the right to family life for example is not very precise, but it has in Europe been clarified through legal practice in the Court of Human Rights in Strasbourg. The reason civil rights are seen as more justiciable could be that they have been tried in court over the years and gradually have acquired a more precise legal interpretation (Koch 2001a). The statement of the non-justiciability of social rights could be self-fulfilling; believing they cannot be tried, victims of violations will not bring them to court, no practice will evolve, in turn confirming that they are not justiciable.

---

19. See discussion in Martin Scheinin, 'Economic and Social Rights as Legal Rights' in Eide et al. 2001: 41 ff. The justiciability of socio-economic rights is affirmed in the Maastricht Guidelines on Violations of ESCR (Human Rights Quarterly 20, 1998: 726).

In a challenge to the generation thinking Asbjørn Eide in 1987 introduced the idea of different levels of state obligations, viz. to respect, protect and fulfil. To respect is to refrain from interfering, to protect is to defend people against threats from third parties, while to fulfil is to provide or facilitate services. The three-level typology of state obligations cuts across the demarcation line between civil and social rights and thereby confirms the indivisibility of rights.

Opposition to the civil/social dichotomy rests on the practical observation that different rights interact in everyday life, alternately being instruments for or consequences of each other. The right to vote and be elected is linked to the right to education; the right to life is guaranteed through fulfilment of the right to health; the right to assembly is the precondition for enjoyment of the right to join a trade union, etc. As mentioned above this acknowledgment has led human rights bodies to adopt an integrated approach, where especially the European Court of Human Rights has found that social policy measures can be essential for protection of certain civil rights. An example is a dispute in the Netherlands over payment of pensions to a widow, whose husband had been killed in an industrial accident. The court proceedings had taken 11 years and the court found that the length of time was a violation of the right to a fair trial (Scheinin 2001b: 36), confirming that the widow had the right to demand fulfilment of a social right (to her husband's pension) by judicial means. By this the court signals that a social right can and should be enforced as a legal right.

However, critics of the duality do not claim that there are no differences between the two categories, the concern is that social rights receive too little attention from legal circles.

> It is hardly in accordance with the indivisibility of human rights a priori to deny courts any control over half of the fundamental rights. (Koch 2001a: 180)

A societal practice has emerged where social rights to a far lesser degree are tried in courts, partly as they are perceived as closely linked to redistribution and social equality involving policy making. But from the outset human rights should all have the same value and potential effectiveness, as they supplement each other and none of them are meaningful in isolation. The civil/social dichotomy can be understood as the two extremes in the balance between freedom and necessity, philosophically an archetypal dilemma. In a very crude sense civil rights entail freedom from interference while social rights imply security, meaning fulfilment of basic needs. The indivisibility and interdependence of all human rights mean that both freedom and security are necessary to live a life with dignity.

Universality

Application of a common set of norms and standards in different political systems had already posed itself as a problem at the time of drafting the basic UN documents, as we saw in the controversy in the 1950s over whether there should be one or two conventions. Forty years later the fundamental legal texts had been finalized and attention was turned to the problem of realization. The issue of universal implementation of human rights standards was put on the top of the international agenda with the Vienna Conference in 1993. The world was no longer dominated by an East-West political cleavage. New independent states had been established and a North-South divide between rich and poor countries had gradually grown. Economic inequality did not disappear with the decolonization beginning in the 1960s, actually quite the contrary was happening. The change in the nature of global contradictions also influenced the human rights scene, causing among other things developing countries to demand the drafting of a right to development. They had succeeded with the adoption of a Declaration on the Right to Development by the UN Assembly in 1986 and again with inclusion of this right in the Vienna Declaration. The concept keeps provoking discussions and is generally viewed with suspicion by the developed nations (Eide et al. 2001: 119 ff), who fear the right will be used to demand transfer of resources from the rich to the poor countries.

Focus on implementation also raised new questions of how to make the same norms work not only in different political but also in different economic, social and cultural settings. One of the main challenges was – and still is – to develop mechanisms to ensure protection of human rights in a culturally sensitive way, '... bearing in mind the significance of national and regional particularities and various historical, cultural and religious backgrounds ...' as formulated in the Vienna Declaration.[20] Especially non-Western participants expressed doubts about the compatibility between the written standards and the social and cultural reality in large parts of the world. The arguments against universal application of human rights norms can roughly be grouped in three categories following a cultural, an economic and a political logic.

Doubts were strongest and most expediently articulated in relation to restrictions on rights protection on cultural grounds. Indigenous traditions and value systems were seen as impediments or obstacles to the realization of international standards. The most persistent discussion concerns the idea of 'Asian values', implying that values of a traditional social structure can be in opposition to the norms laid down in the international human rights conventions and instruments. In the Bangkok Declaration of 1993[21] Asian nations claimed to possess a unique culture, built on values incompatible with Western norms, and demanded this to be kept in mind when applying human rights standards in Asia. The declaration prompted a vigorous global debate, known as the 'Debate on Asian Values' (Bruun and Jacobsen 2000). The Asian states stressed that human rights must be considered with all the differences mentioned in the Vienna declaration in mind, and subsequent Asian government statements and academic debates alike identified a contradiction between individualism and collectivism as a vital cleavage between Western and Asian social systems. Asian societies were said to build on collective responsibility, duty and consensus, in contrast to a Western culture allegedly focussing on individual rights and conflict stabilization. We could call this the 'cultural argument against human rights'.

In discussing Asia it has to be remembered that this region has astonished the world with high growth rates in some countries for

---

20. The full text is to be found in Tang 1995.
21. Representatives from over 40 Asian governments prepared for the Vienna Conference at a meeting in Bangkok in March–April, 1993. See the text of the declaration from the meeting in Tang 1995: 204–207.

the last three decades and forecasts have proposed Asia as the global economic centre of the 21st century. Some Asian countries indeed seem capable of fundamentally changing their status as low-income, export-oriented zones to fully fledged industrial economies with high living standards. The phenomenon has prompted a large amount of literature on this (until the Asian crisis of 1997 at least) so called *Asian Miracle*,[22] as well as a smaller amount on the question of social security in the New Industrializing Countries[23] and Japan (Leung 1995; Goodman et al. 1998; Lee Ming-kwan 2000; Tang Kwong-leung 2000). Within Asia the new prosperity has led to a certain political assertiveness, manifesting itself, among other things, in the discussed attacks on the concept of human rights in general and criticizing the Western model for social protection, linking the two as expressions of an unhealthy individualism and rights approach as opposed to traditional Eastern, more communitarian, collectivistic social norms (Ghai 1995: 60).

So another element in the demand for adjustment of norms in the implementation process is what could be called the 'economic argument', dealt with in the whole range of literature on the role of the human rights framework in the development process – and basis for the very idea of a right to development (Sano 2000), including the discussion on the possibility of prioritizing the different types of rights on economic grounds. The Chinese government has been especially insistent on linking human rights protection to the issue of economic survival, implying a hierarchy of rights, where the protection of some might be affected by the 'priority to people's right to existence and development' (*BR*, special issue 1996: 4). Together with the other Asian nations China also supported the economic argument in the Bangkok declaration:

> (We, The Ministers and Representatives of Asian States) . . .
>
> 18. Recognise that *the main obstacle* to the realisation of the right to development lies at the international macroeconomic level, as reflected

---

22. From the title of a World Bank report from1993: *The East Asian Miracle: Economic Growth and Public Policy.*
23. NICs is shorthand for the four countries that have developed especially rapidly from the middle of the 1960s: Hong Kong, Singapore, South Korea and Taiwan. They are being followed by a new batch: Thailand, Malaysia and the Philippines.

> in the widening gap between the North and the South, the rich and the poor;
>
> 19. Affirm that *poverty is one of the major obstacles* hindering the full enjoyment of human rights . . . (emphasis added) (Tang 1995: 206)

The argument has been refuted by the rich countries, conditioning aid to the concept of good governance. This measure has met with violent opposition from developing countries as expressed in the Bangkok Declaration:

> (We) Emphasise the principles of respect for national sovereignty and territorial integrity as well as non-interference in the internal affairs of States, and the non-use of human rights as an instrument of political pressure . . . (Tang 1995: 205)

In certain parts of the literature the human rights concept is accused of not only being too expensive for poor countries, but also fostering 'laziness and dependency' (Goodman et al. 1998: 11), echoing the cultural argument of rights thinking as being an expression of excessive individualism, an issue which is especially relevant for the discussion of social policies in the next chapter.

The effects of globalization are closely linked to the economically based criticism of human rights. A trend is to claim that:

> The international economic institutions, through their influence from the Western states, are responsible for human rights abuses by encouraging globalisation through the medium of marketisation. (Ghai 1998: 82)

The reasoning is that a growing dependence on the international market and the rapid commodification of all areas of life are causing more and increasingly severe human rights abuses in Asia, and the same Western institutions and governments that preach human rights and democracy profit by the new economic order. It is a well known concern that commodification of e.g. social services threatens vulnerable groups, and that a certain degree of 'de-commodification' is an integral part of social policy (Philion 1998: 519), and it is a question worth pondering whether the globalization process weakens social rights protection at large. More about that in the next chapter.

Little interest has been shown in a major challenge to the human rights system, what we could call the 'political argument', i.e. rights protection in socialist systems, including the socialist countries' criticism of the ruling paradigm for propagating freedom at the expense of economic security. Manfred Nowak distinguishes between a 'liberal' conception of human rights, marked by minimal state/church intervention and a focus on the right to choose, and a 'socialist' conception characterized by positive state action and a unity of rights and duties (Nowak 2001). A traditional, somewhat sarcastic, remark on human rights in capitalist countries from socialist governments and left-wing parties in the West has been that people 'had the freedom to die from hunger in the streets'. In the international discussion the former socialist states – as do governments in most developing countries – tend to uphold the right to life (meant as a social right) as an ultimate priority, and the obligation of the state to protect that right more than any other right, meaning that economic and social rights take prominence. The argument is the opposite of the free-to-starve provocation that if one is without adequate food the right to free speech or to vote is meaningless. The socialist countries were likewise heavily involved in drafting the ICESCR, as discussed above. An obvious reason for the lack of attention to socialist experiences in rights protection is probably the general idea that socialism is a thing of the past. The end of the Cold War has effectively erased socialism as a political option and thereby also as an interesting object of attention and research, despite the still living remnants of this particular system influencing social development in large parts of the world, and the few pockets of 'real socialism' existing today – Cuba and North Korea. It should also not be forgotten that both China and Vietnam still claim to have socialist systems.

Central to all three arguments is the relation between internationally adopted textual norms and other forces shaping individual lives, such as culturally based value systems, economic level or political system. Focus is on the overlapping of texts and instruments on the one hand and social structures and institutions on the other, both defining the kind of individual protection possible. Law and social practice together underpin individual lives. In this respect the human rights regime is not much different from a national system, where the law might be somewhat ahead or behind people's behaviour; law and moral judgment are seldom totally in tune.

Some laws are not always obeyed and some practices in society might move to the edges of the legal system, but still be within the morally acceptable.

Pursuing the understanding of human rights as an international legal structure, the criticisms of the human rights concept referred to above would correspond to the argument that poor people did not have to be law-abiding, or that a person who finds murder acceptable for cultural reasons should not be punished for that crime. The important difference between national and international laws is of course the wide spectrum the latter has to accommodate and the corresponding difficulties in assuring compliance and acceptance. But maybe the problem is more one of quantity than one of quality. As in a nation-state, the challenge of the human rights regime is to draft laws and to promote practices that can be basically accepted by all members of the (in this case international) community. This has in a formal sense already been done, as almost all countries in the world are now members of the United Nations and thereby have expressed their willingness to abide by human rights standards. Still, the problems raised by the criticism must be taken seriously in the ongoing efforts to refine and adjust the system to social practices all over the world, just as national systems keep changing and adapting to new forms of social practices.

The criticism from the three corners – cultural, economic and political – in relation to the theme of this study, social security, will be elaborated in the following chapter on theories of social policy. The cultural argument is most clearly articulated in the discussions about East Asian welfare models, the economic argument in the problem of social policy in developing countries and the political argument in the scant literature on social policy under socialism.

CHINA'S OFFICIAL STAND ON HUMAN RIGHTS

The human rights regime was not acknowledged, hardly even known, at all levels of Chinese society before well into the reform period.[24] Pre-reform China (i.e. China before 1979) did not accept

24. However, the human rights concept was introduced into China by the turn of the 19th century and discussed in elite circles (Svensson 1996).

the validity of human rights norms, neither in theory nor in practice, though the basic civil and social rights were incorporated into the Constitution from the very beginning of the life of the PRC. The idea of *human* rights were, however, frowned upon as a bourgeois attempt to cover up for repressive use of class power (Svensson 1996: 294). China became a member of the UN in 1971, but only began to be incorporated in the human rights system from 1980 with membership of the Human Rights Commission in 1982 and signing of a number of conventions and protocols in the ensuing years. ICESCR was ratified in 2001, the ICCPR was signed in 1998 and is awaiting ratification.

An awareness of the importance of the human rights regime in international interaction emerged in China during the 1980s, partly because of the increased importance of the concept on the international scene and China's wish to be acknowledged as a full member of the international community, and partly as a result of experiences with total lawlessness during the Cultural Revolution that frightened both leadership and ordinary citizens. Usually mentioned as expressions of the gradual public acceptance of the concept are the commemoration of the 40th anniversary of the Universal Declaration of Human Rights in 1988, the ratification of the Convention against Torture the same year and Chinese participation in working groups on the Convention on the Rights of the Child and the Rights of Migrant Workers (Kent 1999: 45). Ironically, China's human rights activities thus reached a peak just before the fatal Tiananmen crack-down made China a target of human rights criticism. It is worth remembering that before 1989 the Chinese government's violations of human rights did not occupy so prominent a place in the international debate as after, being mostly put forward by the US Taiwan lobby and international human rights organizations. These were easier to neglect as political statements from parties to the case and they did not dominate the general opinion to the same degree.

The strong international reactions to the repression of the student movement in 1989 prompted an 'active defence' line from the Chinese government, which ever since has issued several official explanations of its human rights stand[25] and has lobbied extensively to prevent anti-China resolutions from being put forward in the annual sessions of the Human Rights Commission in Geneva. Fundamental to the Chinese attitude is adherence to state sovereignty and the priority of subsistence rights, within a general acceptance of the indivisibility of all human rights.[26] The government insists on a hierarchy of rights where the protection of some civil rights might be affected by the priority of the right to existence and (economic) development.[27] China, unlike Singapore and Malaysia, has not invoked the cultural argument and has not participated in the demand for the concern of a special Asian culture at odds with human rights standards. Individual Chinese scholars debate and disagree among themselves on the compatibility between Confucianism and human rights, and socialism and human rights, but the debates have not been silenced by an official interpretation.

The stress on social and economic rights is not confined to China, it goes for other poor areas as well. In the preamble to the African Charter on Human and Peoples' Rights, the conviction is expressed that '. . . the satisfaction of economic, social and cultural rights is a guarantee for the enjoyment of civil and political rights' (Odinkalu 2001: 336). There is nothing controversial about the idea that some rights override others. Even the most fundamentalist human rights thinker knows that rights often – everywhere –

25. The first so-called white-paper on human rights was published by the Information Office of the State Council in October 1991. For a collection of white-papers on general human rights and specific topics, like women, Tibet, religious freedom, population policy and reform of criminals until 1998, see *Zhongguo renquan baipishu zonglan*. Beijing: Xinhua chubanshe.

26. Another understanding is argued by Michael Sullivan: 'The two core elements within the CCP's policies are (1) a relativist emphasis on China's *guoqing* (national characteristics, ht) and (2) an instrumentalist perspective on the political use of human rights.' (Ness 1999: 125)

27. The Chinese refer to a right to 'existence' (*shengchunquan*) mentioned in the white-paper of 1991. The term is very often translated as 'right to subsistence', which word is not found in any official human rights document, but it is probably close to the right to life, which is article 6 of the ICCPR. In the Chinese literature the term is connected to the Austrian utopian socialist Anton Menger of the 1880s (Xu Xianming 1992: 39). In Western scholarship it is linked to the much later Western philosopher Henry Shue (Kent 1999: 156–159).

conflict with each other (Bell 1996: 649). The one-child policy in China is one case, where it has been internationally accepted that one (collective) right, e.g. to food, has been allowed to overrule another (individual) right, viz. the right to family life. Excesses in enforcement of the policy have been heavily criticized, but the policy itself is widely recognized both internationally and within the country as a necessary step to protect the common good.

So, in the eyes of this author, the problem with the Chinese stand is not the insistence that some rights can have priority over others, but that one group of rights *generally and in total* is claimed to have priority over another group of rights. The ranking of rights takes the form of a general statement. It is not based on a particular situation other than the argument that China at the present stage needs to prioritize the right to subsistence, which seems to be a rather broad and sweeping statement. Conflicts between rights can occur in narrowly confined areas, where two rights obviously cannot be protected at the same time. The predominance of one right over another cannot be a long-term strategy, but must be a result of a temporary situation in order to live up to the established idea of the indivisibility of the different sets of rights, also supported by the Chinese government in official documents.[28]

As a consequence of the stress on 'subsistence', the different reports from the government have consisted of facts and figures on rising living standards in society and assurances of more law enforcement, more freedom of expression, more democracy, etc. Problems are mentioned but not thoroughly discussed, and the tone is defensive, interspersed with attacks on earlier Western imperialism and contemporary Western hegemony according to which human rights criticism is just a pretext for interference in China's internal affairs. All in all the official Chinese position seems more to constitute political gate-keeping than to contribute to a more appropriate understanding of exactly how cultural differences can be 'borne in mind' at the same time as offences against human dignity are prevented.

---

28. See statement of the head of the Chinese delegation in Vienna: 'The various aspects of human rights are interdependent, equally important, indivisible and indispensable' (Tang 1995: 214).

3 只能靠自己

Social Policy Theory

> *To build and complete a social security system is both an important economic issue and an important social problem. It not only concerns whether China can sustain a rapid development in the new century and realize the grand restoration of the Chinese nation, but to a very large degree it also determines the long-term stability of Chinese society.* (Li Jingwen 2000: 7)

The blooming of the welfare state concept as an ideology and as political practice in the Western world since the mid-1950s created a new social science discipline around state involvement in the provision of social welfare, usually known as social policy or social policy theory. A tradition had emerged in the UK already from the late 19th century integrating empirical studies with policy prescriptions on welfare institutions. In the post-war era British and American universities and research institutions set up academic departments on the issue investigating social legislation, patterns of public expenditure and effects of social services, to mention but a few examples. Schools for training in social work were established to meet the need for qualified personnel dealing with the implementation of state provision of social services.

The field of social policy is concerned with the *role and capacity of the state* as well as with *the needs and properties of individuals* and thus involves a range of disciplines within the social sciences and the humanities, such as sociology, anthropology, economics, law, psychology and history. The discipline is furthermore characterized by strong links to politics and ethics, as it touches upon redistributive justice and fundamental moral questions as the obligation of the rich to help the poor, individual responsibility, compassion and social order.

Two key problem areas will be presented here, defining the crucial distinctions and classifications used in social policy analysis involving both continuities and breaks:

- The balance between state and non-state actors, the latter most typically involving market, civil organizations and family
- Relationship between contribution to society and protection from society

Protection of those who cannot protect themselves is in all modern societies taken care of by a mixture of both the larger community and the closest family. The distribution of responsibility between these entities can be very different, constituting degrees on a scale going from the (almost) total state engagement seen in many socialist countries before 1989 to liberal everyone-for-himself regimes like the US – or the UK in recent years – with limited state engagement. Most societies lie somewhere in between these two extremes. Societies with relatively little public protection are exposed to a danger of creating a huge impoverished class of citizens that in turn can threaten political legitimacy and social stability. Furthermore, they ignore the basic humanistic ideals that in the first place gave rise to social commitment, e.g. in the UK in the 1880s.[1] On the other hand, strong state involvement can impede economic development by creating dependency and pacifying, or even destroying, individual initiative, as has been seen as a result of the highly redistributive mechanisms in socialist systems (Havel 1985). Redistribution is basically a problem of available resources, technical competence and political will, but it can be restricted by and criticized on account of the fear of negative consequences of rising dependency.[2] The criticism has mostly been levelled at so-

1. Beginning with the Fabian Society, established in 1884, which became very influential in shaping concerns of social security in parts of Europe.
2. Dependency is on the one hand treated as an individual problem, where low degrees of participation and influence further passivity and destroy personal initiative. But it is also addressed by neo-Marxist dependency theorists as an international problem of poor countries' ability to develop being destroyed as a result of continued links to former colonial powers.

cialist systems but has also been brought forward in the Western debate on new trends in social protection, as in Denmark, where the social democrats in the 1990s argued for cuts in social spending on exactly these grounds. Furthermore, redistributive strength facilitates *social control*, so obviously prominent in the socialist systems, but also put forth as a criticism of the capitalist welfare regimes (Deacon 1983: 2, n.1; Lee Ming-kwan 2000: 2).

The mix of concerns can be depicted as a triangle of state-market-family or as a continuum from more to less state engagement, both ways it is a question of a flow rather than opposites. The dichotomy of public/private or state/non-state has often been conceived as an absolute question of either or, but this view has been challenged in the last decades during the development of social policy studies, especially in relation to Third World countries (Cook and Cabeer 2000: 3) and the new Asian economies, where the distinction between public and private sectors has been said to be unhelpful or at least irrelevant.

Another crucial distinction, especially pertaining to a human rights approach, is whether social support is contingent on individual contribution, in the form of work or money, or is unconditional. Most societies provide little or no social support without demanding a previous contribution, but here a continuum is also involved, some countries giving more, some less unconditional support. The amount of unconditional support is among other things related to the scale of economic resources controlled by the state, often leading to a perceived *conflict between equity and efficiency*,[3] between social justice and economic development. Social welfare and economic development have often been seen as two irreconcilable entities fighting for scarce resources: the one will gain at the expense of the other. One of the reasons for underprioritizing social rights was exactly their costs, as we saw in the preceding chapter, and this view is the practical background to the discussion of justice *versus* efficiency, where likewise a balance, not mutually reinforcing activities, is sought. This perceived conflict has in recent studies been turned upside down by scholars and policy makers pointing to the dynamic potential of social funds in generating sustainable growth in poor countries (UNRISD 2000: 1; Tang Kwong-leung 2000: 158; Tang Ying 1997: 17).

---

3. See the introduction to Chapter 1.

However, from the very beginning of development studies, pioneers considered economic growth *a means* of alleviating poverty, which function coincides with the ultimate goal of all social policy (UNRISD 2000: 1). Only later the dominant view came to be that development (efficiency) and welfare (justice) were in conflict. It is not new or unknown that savings for pension and health care create fortunes that can be used as investment in housing and productive activities. This is obvious in a social democracy like Denmark. Without having been created for that purpose, e.g. pension or unemployment funds nevertheless play an important role in the national economy. The Central Provident Fund in Singapore is another example. The fund is the main provider of social services with assets worth one-third of total GDP, sourced by compulsory savings of employers and employees (Hort and Kuhnle 2000: 174). It is independent of the state budget and functions according to market mechanisms. In China voices are heard that the housing sector can be a dynamic element spurring economic growth (Tang Ying 1997: 17). The idea constitutes a new variant of integration of economic and social policies, distinct from the former practices of socialist regimes, where it was state-driven.

MODELS

A dominant approach in European and American academic theories of social policy is to use 'models' or 'regimes'[4] as a tool of classification. The literature is permeated with discussions about which models, and how many, are helpful in analysing different kinds of societies. The variables constituting the different elements of a model are usually the respective roles of the state, the market, the family and the individual, i.e. classification is done according to the duty-holders, corresponding to the needs – or rights – of members of the community. Quantitative indicators, like the percentage of GDP used for social services, poverty counts, unemployment rates, Gini coefficients, health standards and many others, can be used to group societies into different types, depending on the the-

4. On welfare *regime* as different from both welfare state and specific social policies, see Esping-Andersen 1999.

oretical approach and purpose of each study.[5] Models can in an abstract way be said to represent different criteria for making choices (Titmuss 1974: 32), or more instrumentally as '. . . referring to the rules and institutions which deal directly with the welfare of the citizens within areas like social security, health and education' (Dalberg-Larsen 1995: 22). They should be seen as ideal types rarely existing in reality, and the usefulness of each model has been contested and discussed as new research reveals empirical evidence falling outside of the set categories. But the approach is still used and has been applied recently to the Far East in the discussion on the existence of a special model of Confucian 'Welfare Orientalism' (Goodman et al. 1998) or even a characteristic 'Chinese Form of Social Protection' (C.L.W. Chan 1993; Yuen-Tsang 1997).

One of the first and most important classification theories dates back to 1965 and consists of a distinction between 'residual' and 'institutional' social policy, based on different roles of the state. The scheme was developed by H.L. Wilensky and C.N. Lebaux on the basis of conceptions of social policy in the US (MacPherson and Midgley 1987: 116). Residual social policy prescribes the state to intervene only in the case of abnormal situations, i.e. if all other actors have failed. Residual social policy is also called a 'safety-net' approach, it accords with privatizing strategies for welfare and is usually linked to conservative or liberal ideologies and regimes which prefer regulating instead of providing social services. Institutional social policy places the state in the front line as the provider of social welfare for everybody. It is not based on an assessment of need, it is tax-funded and often functions on the basis of a PAYG principle. The institutional – or statutory – approach is normally linked to social democratic countries like the Scandinavian ones.

The Wilensky and Lebaux dichotomy was enlarged ten years later with a third element called the 'industrial-achievement' type of social protection (Titmuss 1974: 30–32), which stresses the link between social provision and performance, and which exists in many societies in some form or another. The latter form integrates social end economic policies, and in its most 'pure' form, as seen in

5. For an overview of welfare indicators see Esping-Andersen 2000.

the socialist systems, social services almost disappear as an independent category as they are absorbed into the general economic policy. It shares traits with the institutional protection approach, as the dependence of social protection on performance (read: work) is institutionalized and supervised by state authorities. It is also related to residual social policy, however, in that people unconnected to the labour market are subject to a service system '. . . marked by narrow scope of work and limited direct state involvement', as expressed in a recent analysis of social welfare in China (Wong 1998: 57).

The academic debate and later developments notwithstanding, the distinction between residual and institutional social policy has taken root and has indeed proved helpful in outlining two different ways of perceiving the rights and obligations of the state and the individual, respectively. Like models as such, they must be seen as two extreme positions, materialized in the real world in a wide range of mixtures. The basic distinction is aptly described as one between 'selective' or 'universal' social services, but the two diametrically opposed approaches will not always lead to significantly different outcomes, as the example of the Chinese socialist welfare system will show. In pre-reform China, social security was linked to employment = selective protection, but employment, in turn, was provided to everyone = universal protection resembling the basically universalist Scandinavian systems, like the Danish. But even in the universalized Danish system a meagre state pension has to be supplemented by employment-based insurance schemes to secure an adequate standard of living during old age, showing one among many possible combinations of the two principles.

Mirroring the typology of Richard Titmuss, a distinction between three different social welfare 'regimes' under capitalism was presented in 1990, using a tripartition pertaining to Western political cleavages of a *liberal*, a *conservative* and a *social democratic* welfare regime (Esping-Andersen 1990). The three forms are linked to specific geographical areas, and the key defining variables are degrees of de-commodification (the distribution of engagements between the market and the state) and 'modes of solidarities', i.e. the extent to which the individual is ultimately dependent on the state, the employer/market or the family. The liberal regime is found in the Anglo-Saxon countries (US and UK after Thatcher) and is characterized by a low degree of state intervention, the promotion of market solutions and individual (as opposed to family) responsibility. Typical conservative regimes are found in Continental European countries like Germany, France and Austria, and they build their welfare on compulsory social insurance schemes differentiated between occupational status groups, and responsibility is placed with the family. Social democratic regimes are found in the North European countries that build their welfare on universal coverage based on citizenship and funded by corporate and income taxes. This categorization has been used extensively and was recently re-examined by its author in an analysis of prospects for welfare in the so-called post-industrial economies, his conclusion being that the typology of the 'three worlds' is still valuable, even when considering systems as non-Western as the Japanese (Esping-Andersen 1999).

It has been argued that two distinct models, confined to Europe, developed after World War II, a German (named after Bismarck's social insurance legislation of the 1880s) and a British (named after W.H. Beveridge who in 1942 became the architect behind the post-war British welfare system).[6] In the German system, social protection is linked to employment and funded by employers and employees while the British model is based on universal citizenship rights and funded through taxation, basically like the social democratic regimes, referred to above (Kuhnle 1995: 16).

If the future system in China is further developed in the same direction as the present trend the result will accord with the Industrial Achievement-Performance model of Richard Titmuss and the conservative model of Esping-Andersen. These two models share the stress on merit, work performance and productivity as a basis for the fulfilment of social needs, with a relatively marginal role assigned to redistribution. As social protection is linked to employ-

6. His views, inspired by Keynesian economics, was formulated in his *Social Insurance and Allied Services* from 1942, also known as the Beveridge Report. The system was changed after the Conservatives took over in England in 1979.

Chart 3.1 Rough overview of the described models

Models		
Wilensky/Lebaux (1965)	Institutional	Residual
Titmuss (1974)		Industrial-achievement
Esping-Andersen (1990)	Social-democratic	Liberal and conservative
Characteristics		
Principle of coverage	Universal	Contribution-based / selective
Entitlement	Citizens	Employees
Political system	Social democracies	Liberal and conservative regimes
Goal	Minimum protection	Status preservation
Europe after WW2	Beveridgean/British (1942)	Bismarckian/German (1880s)
Predominant in geographical area	Scandinavia UK before 1979	Continental Europe UK after 1979 USA China and Eastern Europe

ment, family care becomes important: the unemployed and the dependents have to be supported by the breadwinner(s) of the family. So a part of the burden shed by the state in the course of the reform process will no doubt fall on the family whose role as caretaker has grown considerably, which development is problematic in China where the one-child policy already has placed excessive burdens on the only children (in the cities) with two parents and four grandparents to provide for.

The following passages introduce social policy concepts in relation to different cultures, geographical areas and political systems that China is related to one way or another, and the implications for the analysis of Chinese welfare will be discussed. The outset is the Chinese discussion of welfare models, followed by a description of the background of social policies pursued in its culturally and geographically close neighbours in East Asia. China is furthermore economically related to the Third World countries, and politically to the other former socialist countries in Eastern Europe, so it is necessary to include the issues of social policy and development as well as social policy and socialism. All three areas involve specific conditions and potentials for blocking or developing welfare protection and the Chinese reform process is being influenced and inspired by them all to varying degrees.

THE CHINESE DISCUSSION

A study of the Chinese discussions on social security shows a consensus with Western social policy theorists on definitions of key terms and reveals Chinese researchers' basic knowledge of the rationale and background of social policy, historically and geographically.[7] Chinese scholars and policymakers – like their Western colleagues – see the whole concept of social policy as a product of modern industrial civilization and notice that the time sequence and the character of the institutions developed have been different under the various political and economic systems (Hu Xiaoyi 1998: 27). In capitalist countries social security was a result of industrialization, brought about by the workers' movement and their struggle to obtain their share of the surplus, whereas in socialist countries it was 'a prerequisite or a component part of the drive towards industrialisation' (Zhu Ling 2000: 79). In the development of the Western world social security, thus, was a mechanism to repair failures of early capitalism, while in the establishment of the

---

7. The following is based on a general reading of Chinese books and articles on the topic. All references will not necessarily be quoted in the text, but are referred to in the bibliography.

socialist regimes of the East, it was part of a state strategy to reproduce cheap labour power.

The Chinese style socialist welfare system implied a total integration of economic and social policies and has been criticized in the internal Chinese debate, basically because of the imbalance in responsibilities between the state and individuals which led, on the one hand, to heavy dependence on the state and a deprivation of the right to make choices and, on the other, to excessive burdens on the state budget via the work units.

> Such a system eradicates the independent role of social needs, social organizations, social policy, social functions and social mechanisms and mixes the system of social security up with the economic and political system. It was maybe useful in stabilising political power in the past, but at present it exposes weaknesses that are all too easy to see, and it definitely does not comply with the needs of a developing market economy (Yang Tuan et al. 1996: 7).

Furthermore, the social equality granted in the Constitution was not realized due to the increasing difference in the level of services offered by different kinds of work units (Hu Xiaoyi 1998: 28). Income distribution and redistribution are said to have been confused and social security programmes were used to control consumption. This could have been appropriate during a short period of crisis, but turned out to be counter-productive in the longer run, in that it weakens personal initiative and fosters power abuse. What is not so often mentioned is the most glaring inequality of all, i.e. the fact that only employees in urban publicly-owned work units were covered by the relatively generous social protection. Farmers had to make do with far less guaranteed and stable sources of social security in the agricultural collectives.

As opposed to the Western social democratic notion of equal opportunities and social justice as the raison d'etre for state welfare provision, the basic understanding of the relationship between economic development and social protection in China is that, at present, a social security system is necessary as a *means* to sustain economic growth and defend political and social stability. Western advocates of state-slimming in the different European governments argue along the lines of minimizing state expenses and empowering vulnerable groups in order to lessen their dependency on the state and improve their quality of life. Chinese arguments seldom turn to claims for social justice or equality as reasons to establish social protection. New measures to alleviate poverty and bad health are viewed as practical vehicles to safeguard the new economic order.

> To install a social security system is an important frame for guaranteeing economic and social stability. In the period of transition from a planned economy to a market economy people will have an even greater need for this 'safety net' to help alleviate the stress on vulnerable people and maintain social stability. (Wu Jinglian et al. 1998: 229)

This attitude is not only expressed by bureaucrats and policymakers, who are the natural defenders of official policy, but also by scholars and social work practitioners, which latter groups seem to harbour a strong commitment to the goals of economic reform.

A feeling of urgent necessity and the idea of facing a fateful choice are prominent in many texts and are based on a fear of disorder and threats to economic development, not on ideological or humanistic concerns (Wu Jinglian et al. 1998: 231). The dichotomy of equity and efficiency is often used to illustrate the transition from one set of priorities to another. The two concepts are not treated as absolute contradictions, but as matters of degree. It is said that all societies must find a balance between considerations of fairness/justice and the efficient use of resources, as both concerns seldom can be satisfied with the same measures. At present China has to change the balance somewhat, i.e. leave room for economic efficiency at the expense of fairness. From 'first priority to equity' (*gongping youxian*), the new slogan should be 'first priority to efficiency, with due consideration to equity' (*xiaolü youxian, jiangu gongping*) (Li Jingwen 2000: 10; Hu Xiaoyi 1998: 30). The soft formulations about degrees and 'due consideration' cannot hide the fact that the attitude is a radical departure from earlier priorities. It is an expression in the area of social politics of the famous Deng Xiaoping saying 'somebody must get rich first', implying the idea that growth has to precede distribution, a priority which is seldom questioned by Chinese researchers working on resource management. Society has to accumulate wealth before resources can be reallocated to needy groups of people.

A treatise by three prominent social policy scholars is quite clear about the necessity of making a basic choice between the two forms or systems:

> No matter what choice China takes there are basically two roads: either a welfare model, administered by the state and with help from others as the basic principle; or a system dividing social risks using market mechanisms and with self-help as the basic principle. (Yang Tuan et al. 1996: 27).

For the authors in question the choice is clear: China must select a system of division of social risks between many actors based on family support and with reciprocity between rights and duties. The Western, and especially the North European, models are rejected as wasting public resources and hampering economic growth (Lin Ka 2001: 326).[8]

Allusions to 'cultural' explanations are not prominent in the Chinese literature.[9] Most scholars refrain from discussing whether or not their ideas on China's future social protection are related to traditional moral values or philosophical systems. The discussion about a special 'Confucian Welfare Model' has been conducted most actively among Western (or Western educated Asian) scholars dealing with comparative social policy (Goodman et al. 1998; Tang Kwong-leung 2000). Chinese scholars have a much more practical approach, discussing *what* to do, instead of *why* to do it. One scholar, however, discusses and in principle accepts the idea of the importance of the cultural influence, when she 'defends' Confucianism against the Asian Values argumentation of political centralism being especially necessary in an Asian context. She points to the fact that the idea that the state alone defines the interests of the individual is not a Confucian notion, but an idea which was developed after the communist take-over of China in 1949. According to Confucianism, state and individual are two parts of a reciprocal relationship defining the interests of both parties. A culturalistic approach is acknowledged, while the specific content of

8. Lin Ka understands 'the Chinese view' as being that 'the Scandinavian model is on the verge of collapse' (p. 327).
9. For discussions on how cultural arguments are used in debates over different political and social systems and protection of human rights, see Bruun and Jacobsen 2000.

the arguments is questioned: Confucianism is not as autocratic as proponents of the Asian Values argument claim (Yang Tuan et al. 1996: 25).

The reading above shows a Chinese discourse in agreement with the Western concepts and the model thinking of the European theorists. Models are generally not foreign to Chinese thinking, neither to the social sciences nor to the humanities and the philosophical disciplines, so it is apparently not difficult to utilize the approach in the societal setting of a China in transition. Likewise, the dichotomy of equity/efficiency, which is pivotal in the Chinese discussion, is widely used in academic literature on social policy in the West (Brooks and Thant 1998: 416; Esping-Andersen 1999: 37; UNRISD 2000: 1). A difference between Chinese and Western attitudes can be discerned in the strong commitment to economic reform, which manifests itself in the Chinese argumentation. Chinese scholars seem much more 'on the side of' the government than European researchers and social work practitioners would normally be in such a debate. The former tend to support government reform policies and accept the idea that egalitarian goals must not endanger economic growth. Whether this stand amounts to paying lip service to an authoritarian political culture, a genuine belief in the beneficial effect of modernization for all citizens, or a mix of both, will not be discussed here; for most individual scholars it is probably a mixture. Efforts to secure continued economic and political support are mingled with a serious commitment to social change, protection of vulnerable groups, or the like. The blend of self-interest and social commitment is not a special Chinese characteristic. In the Western world academics also have to adapt their research applications by keeping an eye on the priorities of their governments or other funding agencies. Still, without having researched the matter, the impression is that the Chinese scholars are somewhat less independent than their Western counterparts, but ironically also often exhibit a more utilitarian and 'responsible' attitude as they try to find solutions to social problems instead of merely pointing to shortcomings of state policies.

INTERFACES: CULTURAL, ECONOMIC, POLITICAL

Cultural: a welfare model with East Asian characteristics?

The rise of Asian economic power began with Japan after World War II, followed by rapid growth in the 'four little tigers' from the mid-1960s, and further tailed by Malaysia, the Philippines, Indonesia and Thailand from the early 1990s. In these countries spectacular economic growth has been followed by a more equitable income distribution during the last three decades (Xin Meng 2000: 133). The growth has for a large part been export-led with the state in an important role as the regulator of a market economy, and the spending on social welfare has been tightly controlled. In spite of the limited investments in social welfare schemes, the area has seen a high level of political stability and no substantial decline in income equality (Tang Kwong-leung 2000; Goodman et al. 1998). An ideal combination seen from a politician's point of view: peace and prosperity on a small state budget, a fact which invoked the interest of scholars and social policy makers in Western societies, where the existing institutions for the provision of social welfare were being questioned. In the mid-1990s the '. . . low-spending 'welfare states' of East and South East Asia not only attracted increasing attention among Western scholars and politicians, but were actually pointed out as potential welfare models for the West' (Hort and Kuhnle 2000: 164). But the picture changed radically during the Asian crisis of 1997 when the region's economies to various degrees suffered severe setbacks, causing social upheaval throughout the entire region.

In the wake of the discussion on the relationship between Confucianism and economic growth, spurred by the *East Asian Miracle*, an academic debate has focussed on the possible existence of a special form of Asian social protection, named 'Welfare Orientalism' (Goodman et al. 1998); 'Confucian Welfare State' (Jones 1993; Leung and Nann, 1995); 'Social Orientalism' (Tang Kwong-leung, 2000); or other combinations of the concepts of Oriental/Confucian and social policy/welfare.[10] The trend of thought is inspired by the sit-

10. For a creative pun see the title of chapter 10 in Leung and Nann 1995: 'A Confucian Welfare State or a Confused State of Welfare'.

uation referred to above of a seemingly peaceful evolution in Asia of growth without substantial state intervention in social protection, running counter to the accepted idea of a close and necessary correlation between industrialization and the development of welfare policies.[11] The questions asked are whether Asian nations have special (i.e. different from the Western) mechanisms and concepts of social protection and, if so, whether these can be used as a source of inspiration for new thinking in Western welfare states. In a similar vein, with respect to China, several studies address the question of whether a special Chinese concept of social protection exists (C.L.W. Chan 1993, Yuan-Tsang 1997).

In general, the conclusions to the above questions are all in the negative, although almost all scholars agree that there are *common traits* with respect to social protection in the investigated Asian countries. The common elements are based on the strategic priority of rapid industrialization on the one hand and an authoritarian political regime on the other, whereas cultural explanations, like the impact of Confucianism, most often are rejected as unhelpful to the analysis. Welfare policy is more often than not linked to support of the political legitimacy of the regime in question, which coincides with the above mentioned arguments in favour of social stability for the development of welfare mechanisms in China. What exists of social welfare mechanisms in these countries is said to be characterized by:

- An authoritarian or paternalistic political rule
- Low government spending on social welfare
- Attachment to non-statutory welfare, i.e. dependence on family and community
- Weak development of the notion of social rights or entitlements
- Social insurance favoured over tax based pay-as-you-go models
- Exclusive support to elite groups and lack of popular participation

11. On this 'industrialism thesis', see Tang Kwong-leung 2000: 20–21.

In his analysis of Japan, the prominent social policy researcher responsible for the model of the three capitalist welfare regimes, Gøsta Esping-Andersen, concludes that there is nothing 'uniquely Japanese' in the welfare elements of Japanese society; they constitute a – albeit rather peculiar – hybrid between a liberal and a conservative welfare model not worthy of being described as a distinct model in itself (Esping-Andersen 1999: 92). Gordon White and Roger Goodman talk of 'certain key respects' wherein East Asian welfare systems are different from the Western, but they nevertheless warn against the creation of a special new model: '. . . it is misleading to think in terms of one homogenous, overarching "East Asian welfare model" common to these five societies' (Goodman et al. 1998: 14).[12] In an earlier study Goodman and Peng argue for the development of the concept of a 'Japan-focused East Asian social welfare regime' and they criticize the 'Western-focused approach' of applying models based on Western experiences to the Asian scene (Goodman and Peng 1996: 193–194). At the same time they acknowledge that the three countries they have been studying most intensively – Japan, South Korea and Taiwan – have been heavily influenced by the West in the development of their social systems (Goodman and Peng 1996: 211–212).

A different conclusion – that the Asian systems are sufficiently different to warrant a special type or model – is drawn by Catherine Jones in an earlier study from 1993, in which she contends that Japan and the 'four tigers' 'make up an "own brand" of welfare states' (Jones 1993: 199). Jones sees the attachment to non-statutory social welfare as the most important common trait for the Confucian societies, and she finds it useful to define a new type by the name of the Confucian welfare state with the following characteristics:

> Conservative corporatism without (Western-style) worker participation; subsidiarity without the Church; solidarity without equality; laissez-faire without libertarianism: an alternative expression for all this might be 'household economy' welfare state – run in the style of a would-be traditional, Confucian, extended family. (Jones 1993: 214)

---

12. The five societies are Hong Kong, Japan, Singapore, South Korea and Taiwan.

Then how does China compare with Japan and the 'four tigers' with respect to issues of social protection? The picture is mixed. Pre-reform China before 1979 resembled the other Confucian states by its paternalistic rule and low degree of popular participation, but differed by its centrally planned economy, its commitment to full employment and substantial welfare provision, meaning high spending on welfare. In these latter respects the Chinese system was more related to the North-Western institutionalized types of welfare discussed above. Reform China after 1979 still resembles its Asian neighbours in terms of their autocratic political systems, though less so now than before – some of the tigers have gone a long way towards democratic rule. In addition, China and its neighbours now share a focus on economic development and diversification of social provision, as an important goal of the Chinese reforms is to lower government spending on social protection and greatly enhance individual responsibility. The replacement of the former PAYG system with compulsory savings schemes fully accord with the practice in the tiger economies. Furthermore, China has abandoned the adherence to full employment at the expense of economic efficiency. Thus, as we saw above, to study the development of the 'four tigers' seems a sensible and beneficial occupation for Chinese decision makers.

The unique combination of rapid economic growth and authoritarian government in these countries defines their form of social protection and the results will probably yield new insights into the relationship between politics, economics and social welfare. In Western thinking on social policy, industrialization paired with democratic rule has been viewed as a one-way ticket to social welfare, whereas authoritarian rule would be thought to obstruct the building of social security, as the disadvantaged would have no way to claim their rights. But voices have been raised in the debate pointing to a link between welfare and paternalism and arguing that social protection is part of the Confucian legacy (Tang Kwong-leung 2000: 34), and/or that the state in some Asian countries has been successful in passing the responsibility for their own welfare to individuals (Goodman et al. 1998: XV). Jones raises the important question of whether or not the distinction between state and non-state provision is meaningful in an East Asian context, because voluntary social work in Confucian societies to some degree is being directed and orchestrated by the state. According to Confucian ideology the elite has a duty to care for the commoners, just as much as the people have a duty to respect and obey their rulers (Jones 1993: 213).[13] This perceived duty of the state has led to heavy government involvement in private fund raising activities and the organization of charities, which deliver a good deal of social services that would not formally be considered state provision. These trends touch upon a special role of the state that is clearly visible in China as well, and which will be discussed further in the next section.

In the discussions about models it is important to note that models are not chosen strategies but analytical tools to separate already existing systems from each other. A model is no ready-to-use package of relevant political measures; a model is created through ad hoc reactions to specific political and economic situations. The Bismarckian model was constructed to secure sufficient manpower for continued industrialization, and the development of the Scandinavian welfare system was a consequence of the victory of labour movements. The development of the export-led economies in the Asian tigers was not caused by social considerations; and the gradual build-up of public education or health and pension systems was caused by the needs of economic development, not by the choice of a specific model. The Asian nations in question have developed a set of mechanisms, some of which are known and used in other places – as Esping-Andersen points out in the above mentioned study on Western countries – with only a few being innovations. It might be more useful to talk of a special Asian societal variant, which includes the common features of social policy enumerated above combining high growth rates, authoritarian rule and cultural traits normally associated with Confucianism. As it is difficult to separate Asian authoritarian rule and Confucian culture in the countries in question – they seem to be two sides of the same coin – it might suffice to state that if they differ in 'key respects'

13. Jones deals with five tigers: one big – Japan, and four small – Hong Kong, Taiwan, Singapore and South Korea.

from others (Goodman et al. 1998: 13), it could be acceptable to speak of, if not a model, then a *special combination of political, economic and social elements*, or maybe the same as what Esping-Andersen calls a hybrid between two models.

This leads to a discussion of the model concept as such – of how big a difference it takes to require the establishment of a new model, a problem which will not be elaborated further in this context, just raised for future consideration together with the question of whether model thinking is useful or necessary at all. A preliminary conclusion at this point – meagre as it is – could be: there are common elements to the solutions of the problem of social protection in East Asia, including China, but the commonalities can still be contained within the vocabulary of residual and institutional as the two extremes. At a closer look, it seems that only small margins divide the opposing views on whether to create a new model or not: the proponents of a special 'brand' or 'regime' recognize similarities with the Western categories and accept an East Asian debt to Western social policy systems (Jones 1993: 214; Goodman and Peng 1996: 211). And the scholars rejecting the naming of a new model stress that 'East Asian welfare systems do differ from their Western counterparts and to that extent do constitute a distinct welfare experience with shared common elements' (Goodman et.al. 1998: 13).

Economic: social policy and the Third World

China not only belongs to the Confucian civilisation but is economically still to be considered a developing country, part of the Third World or the South, as it is more politically correct to say today. With a GDP per capita at less than 1,000 USD in 2000 (*ZTN* 2001: 49), China belongs to the low income countries according to the World Bank classifications, but to the medium level countries according to the Human Development Index, incorporating social indicators like life expectancy and literacy rate (UNDP 2000: 283). In contrast to most other poor countries, China was not colonized by any single Western country. It has been discussed whether this was good or bad for the country. On the one hand is the rendering that it was plundered by all and taken care of by nobody. On the other hand it has been claimed that the position enabled the Chinese government to play off one power against another, in fact strengthening national sovereignty. Whichever is correct is difficult to measure, but China certainly began its modern nation-building in a most precarious state, economically and socially ruined by aggression and disasters coming from both inside and outside. In that respect it was no better off than the liberated colonies from the 1950s and 1960s, except that it did not preserve a link to any former master who had left, however feeble, a framework of institutions for social protection or on whose ideas a social policy could be built. Instead, the Communist government in 'New China' adopted the Soviet political system, marked by a total integration of economic and social policies.

As has been suggested above, concepts like state welfare and social work are Western creations, which came about in response to specific industrialization processes and popular pressures in Europe and other developed regions. The historical background of most of today's poor countries is very different. Traits like weak reallocation powers, a focus on economic development and/or a lack of political will to redistribute resources of the state have survived in the Third World and also persist in the Asian economies that have been discussed above. State capacity is limited: the government apparatus is generally weak and corrupt, making redistributive policies impossible or at least inefficient. Often it is not the state but different non-state actors, like charity organizations and business corporations, which take on the task of supplementing family care. Thus, diversification of the provision of welfare and blurring of the distinction between public and private delivery become especially relevant when dealing with the problem of social policy in the context of developing countries (Cook and Kabeer 2000: 3). Colonial exploitation has stalled economic development and preserved a traditional lifestyle with the family as the provider of social security. Furthermore, the pattern of state intervention in social welfare was shaped by the colonial powers with the primary aim of *maintaining social order*. Seen in this light the special Asian characteristics, perceived as part of Confucian culture, might also be connected to a colonial past, at least where Taiwan, Singapore and Hong Kong are concerned.

It has long been contested whether Western theories and practices of social policy and social work are appropriate for Third World countries, and it has been lamented that there is a general lack of comparative studies comprising experiences from both the North and the South (Midgley 1981; Moore 2000). The problem is not only that Third World countries have been ignored in spite of their massive social problems, but also that valuable contributions to a generalized theory on social security were lost as experiences of non-Western traditional social protection were not sufficiently acknowledged. This deficiency was the focus of much attention around the late 1980s (MacPherson and Midgley 1987) but since then the situation has been somewhat ameliorated by a growing amount of literature on welfare in specific regions, like the works on East Asia referred to above and general discussions on social policy and development (Cook and Kabeer 2000; UNRISD 2000), as well as on globalization and welfare (Deacon 2000).

The problems of social protection in Third World countries, as discussed here, relate to China as a developing country with a – maybe politically strong but – financially weak state. The role of the state in reform China is strongly debated; the seemingly all-embracing power monopoly of the Communist Party, which may still exist politically, is being questioned as the economic capacity of the state has been eroded. Critics stress the declining economic control and strained state budget as signs of declining reallocative power on the part of the Chinese government. The proportion of central revenue relative to GNP has fallen from 31.2 per cent in 1978 to 14.7 per cent in 1992 and is projected to fall even further (Wang and Hu 1995: 11; Gu 2001: 148). A vital part of the economic reform programme has been decentralization of economic powers to lower administrative levels, draining the central state apparatus of funding as in other transitional economies (Brooks and Thant 1998: 419). The latitude for directly providing social security is minimized accordingly and becoming closer to a situation known in many poor countries. Yet the political hegemony can be an advantage as it enables the state to do a relatively better job at directing resources that are nominally outside of state control towards social goals, e.g. by 'squeezing' money out of private corporations and individual citizens. This practice is seen in China in the form of the establishment of government charity funds, which channel donations from non-state economic entities to needy families or individuals on a more or less compulsory basis (Bruun 1995: 198–200; Wang Zhen 2000: 62; Young and Woo 2000: 23).

In the context of general social policy, this scheme of state-ordered 'voluntary' contributions to social welfare seems unique to East Asia, as it falls outside of the categories of the residual/institutional frame of reference. Its importance could be gauged by statistics on the size of donations, which are difficult to come by, however. During an interview in 1998, a scholar estimated that 25 per cent of social relief – not social insurance – comes from private donations, but the area needs to be studied further.

The possibilities of establishing social protection mechanisms in poor countries are not only constrained by internal state capacity, but also by the structure of the world market, where poor countries depend on favourable investment conditions. The term social dumping has been used for the situation '. . . when jobs and money disappear from high-tax and high-wage economies to less expensive alternatives where the rate of monetary return for investors – or dumpers – looks brighter than elsewhere' (Hort and Kuhnle 1999: 12). In the post-colonial period the movement of labour-intensive production has been from Europe and North America to Asia, Africa and Latin America. After the opening up of China a new link has been added to the chain, as the low wage level on the Mainland has attracted investment from the former 'victims' of social dumping in Southeast Asia. Hort and Kuhnle, however, find that social security has been introduced earlier, relative to economic development, in Southeast Asia than in Europe and this phenomenon could be repeated in China as well (Hort and Kuhnle 2000: 181). If that comes true, social dumping will turn out to be a transitory stage on the road to a modernization including establishment of welfare institutions and programmes.

Political: social policy and socialism

Besides being a culturally Confucian, economically poor country, China in a political sense belongs to the group of former socialist countries that are replacing plan with market economy. China is furthermore joined only by Vietnam in a special category combining economic transformation with an authoritarian political system. In the so-called transitional societies the state has lost or disengaged itself from the reallocative role characteristic of the socialist system. Before the demise of communism, the welfare policies of Eastern Europe, the Soviet Union, including its Central Asian regions, and the communist countries in Southeast Asia, as mentioned before, were characterized by a unity of social and economic policy, linking social protection tightly to a work ethic and thus, strictly speaking, to performance criteria instead of building it on a universalistic rights approach. But occupational welfare in a socialist system differs fundamentally from the same structure under capitalism[14] in the case where the socialist state provides almost everyone with a job. When all people are workers, occupational welfare almost takes the form of institutional social policy – still, of course, notwithstanding the rural population. The systems are characterized by this provision of full employment as well as free health care and other forms of social security, and by at least a theoretical upholding of egalitarian goals. With respect to welfare policies, the socialist countries before 1989 (and China before 1979) in some respects belonged to the same family as the North-European welfare states in terms of the high level of state involvement. In other respects, notably in relation to the eligibility to obtain services, the Eastern systems were closer to the conservative welfare regimes of Continental Europe, but with a much broader coverage due to the commitment to full employment.

Already from the mid-1980s an East–West discussion of what constitutes a *socialist* social policy was initiated by scholars from the UK, soon in collaboration with Eastern European social policy researchers. The field has been growing since then (Deacon 1983;

---

14. For a discussion of the concept of occupational welfare in capitalist countries, see Ming-kwan Lee 2000: 2–7.

Deacon and Szalai 1990) with a focus on questions like the characteristics of social policy in socialist states, and how welfare is defined and institutionalized in the transition from plan to market. Furthermore, UN and OECD agencies have in recent years conducted conferences and established research programmes on social policies in transitional societies with the aim of helping to prevent the most harmful effects of market reform, such as unemployment and the withering away of social safety nets (Fischer and Standing 1993).

The debate with East European scholars showed that the rosy picture of the superiority of socialism advertised by their regimes tended to become more and more misleading as the socialist countries developed. In a dialogue between Eastern and Western European social policy theorists in 1988, a criticism of the implementation of this kind of social policy was put forward, focussing on power abuse and the lack of popular participation (Deacon 1993: 178). Social policy in Eastern Europe before 1989 was said to be marred by

- paternalism, causing insensitivity to the felt needs of the population, also called a 'dictatorship over needs'
- bureaucratic and inflexible service provision
- greater benefits given to (or taken by) managers/party officials. Administrative redistribution tends to favour the redistributors themselves
- small or non-existing benefits to people outside the labour market
- demands on women to bear the double burden of family and wage labour

The flaws of socialist social policy were formulated along the same lines ten years later in a treatise on social sector development in transitional economies of Asia:[15]

> In all transitional economies, there has been a long-standing emphasis on equity in access to health and education services, often at the cost of efficiency. Thus in most of these countries, basic social

15. The countries under scrutiny are China, Kazakhstan, Vietnam, Kyrgyzstan, Mongolia, Cambodia, Laos and Myanmar.

> services are available in greater quantity and sometimes greater quality than in many less planned economies at similar income levels. However, the services provided may not have corresponded to consumer demand, service providers faced few incentives to use resources efficiently, quality control was minimal or non-existent, and financing of the centrally planned social sectors, as of other sectors in transitional economies, proved unsustainable. (Brooks and Thant 1998: 418)

And seen from the perspective of the end user, a Hungarian scholar sums up how the traditional social policy of the planned economy has outlived its usefulness:

> What social policy today gives its subjects are the many irritating, humiliating and painful experiences of unfairness, defencelessness and chronic shortage. Social policy has come to be associated with widely unsatisfied needs, of ununderstandable bureaucratic regulations, of haphazard solutions of services of more and more unacceptable levels. (Szalai 1990: 92).

By the mid 1990s all the former socialist countries in Central/Eastern Europe and Central and Southeast Asia had adopted new legislation on social protection, which was characterized by a diversification of service provision through the devolution of responsibilities to local governments, marketization and support of voluntary charity activities. These countries experienced consequences of the reforms that were similar to those seen in China, i.e. growing inequality, loss-making state enterprises, deteriorating protection of vulnerable groups, discrimination against women, but they also saw an unexpected serious decline in gross domestic product in contrast to the high growth rates in China (Kapstein and Mandelbaum 1997: 175).

The solutions to the reform-related problems in Eastern Europe and China show many similarities and few differences. Just as in China, pension reforms in Central and Eastern Europe have consisted of movements away from redistributive policies towards individualized and contribution-related benefits. The political leaderships plan to establish mixed systems combining a public scheme with a mandatory tier of individual savings, and they struggle with the transitory problems of replacing a PAYG mechanism with a savings system and the separation of social security from the state budget (Fultz and Ruck 2001). The core points in the proposals for new institutions and mechanisms for social security as such in Eastern Europe concern basically the separation of economic and social policies, i.e. a pluralization of service provision and democratic control, making restrictions of the hidden privileges of the former nomenklatura possible and creating space for the articulation of needs. Generally there is a tendency to worry less about the negative effects of market liberalization and the commercialization of social goods than many Western, especially left-wing, analysts do:

> Western Marxists found themselves as the defenders of the equality of social welfare in conditions of poverty and contended with the East Europeans who justified the differentiation and pluralisation of welfare as a conditions of improved welfare for all. (Deacon and Szalai 1990: 16)

Noteworthy is the observation that the dialogue has to be conducted outside of socialist and Marxist phraseology, as 'the language of socialism is simply unusable by Eastern critics where it has been robbed of all subversive and critical content' (Deacon and Szalai 1990: 16).

The same tendency can be found in an interview with the famous Hungarian economist Janos Kornai from 1996, where he stresses the fundamental importance of individual responsibility as a philosophical issue: 'Even prisoners in Auschwitz were responsible for what they did in the specific situation . . .' (Kornai 1997: 221). While in no way denying the impact of social circumstances, it seems important to him to stress that everyone bears responsibility for his or her own life, which was probably a logical reaction to having lived for a long time in a system where individual responsibility and initiative were censured and taken away. Here we are closer to the individual end of the continuum but not in a different category than, for example, in Denmark, where – it has to be remembered – the basic premise of the social system also is that people should take care of themselves. For health care and a meagre pension allowance the state steps in for everyone but in other areas society only intervenes when the personal capacity is exhausted. But in Denmark it is not considered politically correct to stress this fact; it is more acceptable to express solidarity with vulnerable groups and concern for marginalization of deviants, etc.

The picture of the welfare systems in Eastern Europe, the former Soviet Union and the Asian transitional economies before 1989 bears striking similarity with the Chinese work unit form of social protection, and in the discussion about the choice of a new set-up and reactions to the old regime in Eastern Europe likewise the voices of the Chinese debate are resonated. The Chinese share the demands for diversification and even commercialization of social welfare provision, and the priority of free market mechanisms over basic social security, but are far less outspoken with regards to the claims for democratic control and the articulation of needs than their Eastern European colleagues. In view of the different political systems of the two areas this may not be surprising. In China the problem is phrased in terms of complaints that the former statist welfare creates a passive, dependent psychology among ordinary citizens, making them unfit for the challenges of a dynamic market economy and unfit as support for the decentralization to local administrations and the new concept of 'community services'.

Altogether China seems to have just as much in common with the other former socialist countries as it has with its capitalist neighbours in East Asia, with whom the country shares traits of a more cultural and traditional nature. The basic problem in the transitional economies is how to shift the burden of direct social provision away from the shoulders of government, i.e. changing the distribution of responsibility between the state, the family and the market, the same three actors that are dealt with in the model construction referred to in the introduction. In a study from 1993 Bob Deacon tentatively places the Central and Eastern European countries in relation to Esping-Andersens typology of capitalist welfare regimes. He suggests that the different countries develop different types of welfare systems, but places five out of nine countries in a new, what he calls transitory, category of 'Post-communist Conservative Corporatism'. This type resembles the Chinese case to the extent that it would be able to contain the variant of an economic transition led by a single-party government (Deacon 1993: 195–197).

CONCLUSIONS

The application of Western social policy thinking to the reform of the social security system in China has revealed a great deal of congruence with regard to problems and solutions. The existing categorizations can be used with minor adjustments and Esping-Andersen's conservative model is closest to the reality of the new Chinese mechanisms. The adherence to occupational welfare and the close link between employment and social coverage go for both pre- and post-reform China. Other Western scholars, however, have pointed to a need for new models which encapsulate special traits of either a cultural or a political nature. A model of 'Confucian Welfare' or of 'Post-communist Conservative Corporatism' could be possible, but a final choice of one over the other seems premature at the current stage of investigation. The most striking traits of the new structures are the contributory savings scheme, well-known and widely used in Europe for decades. The discussions and ideology behind the creation of a new understanding of social problems, likewise, are conducted along the same lines and circling around the same concepts, e.g. the seeming contradiction between equity and efficiency – between social justice and economic growth and the question of who is ultimately responsible for the individual members of society. The wish to diversify and 'privatize' – or collectivize – social security is also prominent in the globalization process at large.

I have pointed to several important aspects in which Chinese society has interfaces with other countries in the world, as depicted in Chart 3.2: culturally with the Confucian regimes in East and Southeast Asia, economically with the South and politically with the transitional conomies in Central Asia and Eastern Europe. Compared to these other regions China possesses certain peculiarities that are of consequence for the establishment of a viable system of social protection: compared with the four (or five) tigers, China has the legacy of a strong social commitment to egalitarian goals and redistribution of social resources; compared to the rest of the Third World, China has had a stable political history and one legitimate government for the last 50 years, and the country can

Chart 3.2 China's political system and socio-economic policies in relation to global trends and to traits in regions that share a common heritage with China

	CHINA 1949–1979	CHINA AFTER 1979
EAST ASIA	Authoritarian rule Confucian ideology	Authoritarian rule Confucian ideology Restricted social spending Organized charity Focus on economic development
THIRD WORLD	Poverty	Poverty Weak reallocative power of state
CENTRAL AND EASTERN EUROPE, CENTRAL ASIA	Integration of social and economic policy: social protection linked to work Provision of full employment	Diversification Privatizing social policy Occupational social insurance Conditionality of foreign funding
WESTERN EUROPE	Heavy state involvement High social spending	Occupational social insurance
GLOBAL TRENDS	----	Individualization of rights Limitations on central/ national control

refer back to its former days of glory as one of – if not *the* – strongest and most advanced civilization of the pre-industrialized world; and compared to the other transitional economies, China has witnessed a persistent and substantial economic development with an average growth rate of almost 10 per cent over the last two decades. These peculiarities all leave room for cautious optimism, in spite of the apparent dangers and challenges discussed above. The conditions for a *relatively* peaceful and socially acceptable transition process exist, at least in theory.

Particular to China and other East Asian regions is the role of non-state actors based on the idea of charity and benevolence, a concept which for the last centuries have played a minimal role in European thinking but a larger one in the US. The feature is connected to a special view of the social elite as the patriarch caring for its subjects, who are not citizens but subordinates, a view resonant of 19th-century Europe and maybe other Third World countries today. The ideas of charity and donations are not particularly Chinese, but have played just as great a role in our own past as they do in China today. Other special traits could be mentioned – duty means more than right, collective affiliations overrule individual fulfilment, moral persuasion is preferred to legal disciplining – and these will be explored further in the analytical chapters below.

4 只能靠自己

How to Get and Keep a Job

> *To be moved to another work unit? All factories in the town are losing money, where should I go to? To be transferred to another work unit, you need money. Everybody knows that to get into the electricity works you need to pay 50,000 yuan. And then you should know some people working there as well.*[1]

The analysis in this chapter will raise the question of whether the labour allocation system in China, regulating employment in urban areas, complies with article 6 of ICESCR – on the right to work – and how the reforms have affected employment rights. The specific circumstances in China make it relevant to focus on the fulfilment of the right to *get* a job (i.e. to employment), not strictly speaking the right *to* work nor labour issues, like safety regulations and trade unions, being rights *in* work. Chinese scholars, likewise, tend to view the right to employment, the right to *get* a job, as the 'core and basis' of a broader right to work that includes as well freedom of choice, minimum wages, safety regulations, etc. (Li Buyun 1997: 1).

It will be shown how the institutional set-up for job provision under pre-reform Chinese socialism in practice effectively protected some rights and violated others without the support of specific rights normally thought to be an essential prerequisite for the effective protection of the right to work. In addition, the chapter shows how the post-reform employment system protects rights that were violated before, and vice-versa.

1. The quotes beginning each chapter are, unless otherwise indicated, remarks and statements drawn from the interviews.

LOCAL IMPLEMENTATION

The foremost worry in daily life for the workers in Xingtai is not to get a job, as most of the workers have affiliation with a work unit. The source of greatest concern is the delayed and irregular paying of salary and pensions, as well as the widespread practice of 'laying people off' (the practice is called *xiagang* and the system is described later in this chapter) or in other ways depriving them of both work and income. The problems are rooted in difficulties coping with the new economic policies on part of the work units. The bad economic results of many enterprises make it a rule more than an exception that pay is not forthcoming as it should be, causing deep feelings of insecurity, especially among the older people. Eighty per cent of the enterprises referred to in the interviews are classified as having bad economic results and therefore not meeting their obligations in differing degrees, while only a few are said to be economically well-off. By far the greatest number of adults covered in the material are in one way or another not enjoying the benefits they are entitled to, many do not even have suitable possibilities of occupation in the minimal sense of having something to do. In the Guangzhou neighbourhood in the south, the actual underemployment and non-payment seem to be less endemic than in Xingtai though similar situations exist, as also confirmed by Ikels's study (Ikels 1996). But the increasingly bad economic situation described by the interviewed families is not reflected in the official local statistics.

'Real cash income' and 'real cash expenditure' have both increased sixfold in Xingtai between 1985 and 1996 according to published data.[2] The official unemployment rate rose from 0.63 per cent to 2.37 per cent in the whole of Hebei province from 1985 to 1996. No unemployment figures are given in the Xingtai statistics. A comparison between the average income from published material and the income stated by the interviewed – keeping in mind the

2. A sample of 60 households has been selected to represent the urban population. Income increased from 2,443 yuan per family in 1985 to 12,686 yuan in 1996. Expenses increased from 2,547 yuan to 12,906 yuan (*Xingtai shi* 1996: 374 and 1997: 708 and 712.). The figures from Guangzhou in the next note are not directly compatible for technical reasons.

uncertainties surrounding information on personal income, whether official or unofficial – reveals that the interviewed are in a lower income category, the official average being more than 1,000 yuan a month compared with 700 yuan as an average of the interviewed. For Guangzhou, official income has been raised tenfold and expenditures ninefold from 1985 to 1996[3] and the difference between information derived from official sources and interviews is smaller. Interviews show an average monthly income per family at 1,300 yuan, compared to the 1,600 yuan related to in the official material. So the families in Xinjiao neighbourhood are also low-income families, other things being equal. In all, neither under- or unemployment nor increasingly bad household economy are reflected in the official statistics.

The problem of getting paid

The following stories from Xingtai illustrate the problems with arrears. One retired worker, Lao Zhao, has not received his pension for several months. He has visited the leadership of his work unit (which has to pay his pension) several times, only to get the answer that the enterprise does not have money even to pay salary, not to speak of pensions. He is asked to go to the city government, only to be told he has to contact his workplace, where he just come from. So he is sent back and forth between the same few institutions. Four or five retired labourers have tried to go together, but they have not been able to get any information about what they can do or how long they will have to wait. He is living on his savings and help from his daughter. He makes sure always to save enough money to get by for two or three months, which is the period the pension sometimes is delayed. Recently his daughter's salary also started to become unstable and they do not know what to do.

The factory of Lao Zhao sometimes delays payments of one or another kind because it has economic problems and is losing mon-

3. Income rose from 2,088 yuan per family in 1985 to 19,920 yuan in 1996 (*Guangzhou sishinian 1949–1988:* 507). Expenses increased from 2,016 in 1985 to 17,640 yuan per family in 1996 (Guangzhou 1997: 344). The figures from Xingtai are not compatible for technical reasons.

ey. One possible consequence could be to declare the unit bankrupt. In such a situation there seems to be no guarantee of anything. Formally, the unit owes the workers all the missing salaries and pensions, but how much they will get depends on what the enterprise is sold for at auction. If the price is low they might not get anything and no other organization is responsible for covering the individual losses.

As part of the commercialization, factories also get leased out in parts to different contractors:

> One takes one part, another one takes another part. The contractors then have the decision making power and do not follow the rules. Maybe the state rules do not exactly fit with development of the market economy, but they have to be obeyed, nevertheless. We have got a Labour Law but they do not read it. They set their own patterns and stick to these. When somebody mentioned the Labour Law, my manager often said: 'Does the state pay you salary or do I pay you? I contracted this factory and I am responsible for the profit, otherwise there will be no salary at all!' He does not say that in reality the factory belongs to the government, it is the state that invested money in the first place, it was not him. My wife's unit also breaks the law. They often work overtime, their workday is ten hours at least and they do not rest every week. Some managers are very straightforward, I heard one had said 'The Labour Law does not provide me with any goods'. What kind of people are they?

The overall situation of one family, hard hit by a bankruptcy, gives a typical picture of life in that particular neighbourhood. The Yao family consists of ten adults: The old couple in their mid-60s, two sons and two daughters, all four with a spouse. The two old people are retired and get their pensions. They live with an 8-year-old grandchild, daughter of the first son. The first son and his wife both work in a chemical plant, a state-owned enterprise. The factory has very little work to offer and does not pay salary or pension on a regular basis. The wife was forced to retire early (45 years old) but the son is still at the factory where he is employed now and then. Sometimes other enterprises employ him, too. The first daughter was transferred from a switchgear plant to a printing house, because she is allergic to copper. She was employed in a permanent position at this big collective enterprise, but is now laid off and receives no money. She got a poverty card (*tekunzheng*)[4] from her work unit. Her husband was working in a tile factory, which went bankrupt, so the two of them opened a small acupuncture clinic together with the husband's father, who used to be a doctor. The second son replaced his father at the power supply bureau, and his wife works at a community-run workshop, which is in economic trouble, so she is not paid and has not found anything else to do. 'She doesn't know any craft and is not good at trading' according to the old man. The second daughter worked in a garment factory, a big collective enterprise, but has been laid off. So she now works with her mother-in-law, who is also laid off, in a small shop selling clothes. None of them get any benefit from local state authorities. The husband of the second daughter works in a waterworks where the salary is irregular. Thus of eight children and in-laws of the retired couple, only one, the second son, is in a somewhat 'regular' employment situation. The others are laid off, fired, retired at an early age or have only part-time work and unstable income. The situation is not exceptional in the neighbourhood.

When a person tries to get another job or create a new activity to secure a new source of income, the work unit can support her or him more or less in the endeavour. Some enterprises provide unsold goods from their stocks to idle workers and arrange for stalls in the market to sell them. One former cadre worked as an accountant in a shoe factory that had bad economic results. The leadership arranged for a place on the free market in Tangshan, where she could try selling shoes from the stocks. But for an accountant it is not easy to degrade oneself to be a street vendor, so she was not very successful and in other examples as well the effort was not very well received:

> My daughter-in-law was transferred to the textile factory last year. Her pay was delayed, sometimes more, sometimes less. Now they owe her 900 yuan. Once they gave her a bundle of sweaters they had in the storeroom and could not sell. How could she possibly sell them? So now we have a bundle of sweaters at home. We let friends

4. A poverty card can be obtained by recommendation of the work unit when being laid off. It entitles the holder to reduction in prices of essential goods including school fees, as well as tax reductions.

and relatives try to sell them on the street, but they cannot, either ... they have not sold a single one.

To get and keep a job

To get a good job in a state-owned factory in Xingtai today is considered almost impossible, or at least very costly. Only very good relations can secure you a job at the Dyeworks, for instance, or in the cotton textile mill – two of the units still making a profit and paying their workers regularly. The most common knowledge about how to get a job is that it requires 'money and connections', as the statement in the beginning of this chapter indicates. Of the more than 100 persons in the interviews who got new jobs after 1980, not one got a stable position without relying on knowing somebody and giving money and maybe gifts. In fact, very few have got a 'job' in the ordinary sense of the word, but very few have been fired as well. Most are in a kind of limbo between having and not having employment, maybe officially designated as laid off, maybe not.

It is common in the interviews for someone to say he or she belongs to a certain work unit, even though they have not been working there for several years, maybe never. Their exact status seems in many cases unclear to the workers themselves. In the Yao family, described above, the informant – the father of the four grown-up children – at the beginning of the interview says that all the children 'go to work' (*shangban*). Other euphemisms will be used, like 'having holiday' (*fangjia*), 'have gone home' (*huijia*), 'not go to work' (*bu shangban*) or just 'have a rest' (*xie*). Vague answers are given:

Q: This year she has not gone to work, does that mean she is laid off (*shuyu xiagang*)?

A: Hm, this year there is no work, she does not go there.

Or:Now I am at home, I am kind of laid off, I have been resting for half a year.

So not only the ways of getting a permanent job have changed, but a variety of types of affiliation between worker and work unit have emerged to adapt to the changed circumstances.

Some units ask (or force) people to invest money in the enterprise as a precondition for gettig a job or for staying as an employee. The Iron Works in Xingtai asked their employees to buy shares, each should pay 3,600 for 3,000 yuan worth of shares. The enterprise could not go public as the products could not pass a quality test, so the workers were asked to provide some funding. In return the factory would assign a job to one child of each employee as the parent retired – a revival of the old system of 'inheriting jobs', which was forbidden by regulations of 1986 referred to below. In another case a bankrupt factory tried to survive by buying a cold storage warehouse and leasing it to the employees for a considerable amount of money to store goods for sale on the street markets. The cooling system of the warehouse broke down, damaging the products, but the rent was not paid back to the workers. The interviewed person lost 40,000 yuan when his apples rotted away. In the mentioned cases the investment was a precondition to get or preserve the affiliation with the work unit, so workers are forced to find the money, most often using private loans or savings. More instances of paying to get a job at state-owned enterprises are reported in Xingtai, up to several thousand yuan.[5] This practice has reached serious proportions in Guangzhou, too, which can be seen from a notice in the local newspaper, warning with enlarged red types that it is illegal to take money as a deposit when hiring people (*Guangzhou ribao*, 22 May 1998).

Employment status and possibilities can be influenced by one's status in the household registration system. A change in registration from rural to urban (*nongzhuanfei*) is an advantage in the labour market. A woman had been temporarily employed as a school teacher for many years. She had never had an urban registration, but had been living in Xingtai for ten years with a rural status. She claims she does not feel very much affected by the 'wrong' registration status, but it has prevented her from getting the permanent position she wanted in the school where she works. And urban status would double her salary and provide her with social security

5. Similar stories abound in magazines and newspapers, e.g. when a laid-off man tells how his son borrowed 8,000 yuan to pay a middleman to find him a job (*Renmin luntan* no. 10 1998: 37–39).

like pension and health insurance. Also she has had to pay a higher school fee for her daughter than the city dwellers with the correct papers. As a new development, an urban status can now be obtained locally.

The provincial authorities get a quota of transferable registrations every year. They are disseminated down through the system to the Street Office via the local police station. The woman in question managed to get an urban registration in 1996, paying a fee of 5,000 yuan (the corresponding figure in Guangzhou is 10,000 for adults and 5,000 for children). When talking about the price, she adds happily: 'And we did not have to send presents'. She feels she has a good relationship with the leader of the Street Office; she often helps him, which is why she got one of the urban registrations to be transferred that year. The Street Office has the decisive say on who gets a change of status. The woman in question is now in the process of getting her daughter's status changed too (the place of registration follows the mother). That will lower the school fee and she says it worries her daughter not to be like the other kids. Compared to her and her husband's combined income of 800 yuan a month the registration problems seem to be a strain on their economy, though.

Re-employment efforts

Real employment, and not just work unit affiliation, is without doubt *the* biggest social problem in a town like Xingtai. The government has established mechanisms and institutions to solve it, but without great success as the economic development in the city is stagnating. Two tracks have to be followed, one to create new jobs, the other to support the people unable to live off their own income. The latter aim is pursued through social assistance, described in more detail in Chapter 6. To address the former the government tries to motivate enterprises to employ laid off people through tax deductions and preferential treatment. If incentives have no effect, harsher measures take over according to a regulation passed in 1995, which states that all larger enterprises should recruit workers through a labour allocation system belonging to local government. In this way the authorities got more control over the labour allocation process and they can influence it in various ways. The Xingtai City Labour Bureau has also set up two 'employment bases' (*jiuye jidi*), both belonging to the category of township and village enterprises (*xiangzhen qiye*), called the Kang-da group and the Dong'ao group. For each laid off person they employ, the Labour Bureau subsidises between 500 and 1,000 yuan. For the whole city a new regulation promises one year of tax reduction to work units which employ at least 20 per cent laid off people in new positions and the tax reduction increases the more laid off people are admitted into the enterprise. A regulation demanding that all enterprises have at least 20 per cent of their labour force consisting of formerly laid off people already exists, but it is difficult to implement without some kind of incentive.

At a lower level, the Sheepmarket Street Office has established small shops like photographers or hairdressers where they could offer employment for 75 laid off people. And at the very lowest level, the Neighbourhood Committee, the laid off people are offered work in small shops owned by the head of the committee. The story is a bit complicated, though. The head, a woman of 61, claims to have built the shops using her own money and she rents them out at a low price to people in need, so the old and the poor do not have to travel too far to find work or buy things. Activities like food stalls, hairdressers, a pharmacy and a bookstore are organized in nine small rooms, which are labelled the collective property of the Neighbourhood Committee. But among the residents she is accused of cheating by charging high rents from people and pocketing the money herself. She was also said to have rented one stall to her daughter for 40 yuan a month, whereupon the daughter re-rented it to other people for 200 yuan.

Outside the formal hierarchy, independent job information is an option, such as a small company with three staff members called a 'Labour Services Station' (*laodong fuwu zhan*).[6] It is a non-profit en-

6. For the role of Labour Service Companies in the 1970s and 1980s see Gu 2001b: 7.

terprise responsible for its own economy but it has a bureaucratic relationship with the City Labour Bureau. Already since the middle of the 1960s, the company has been involved in employment consultancy, as well as establishing contacts between work units in need of people and job-seekers. Because of its long history it has an extensive network of contacts and a good reputation. It introduces 30 to 40 people each month to new jobs, mostly young people just out of school. The income consists of fees from these introductions, rent from a few apartments they own in the courtyard where their office is, and administration fees from two factories affiliated with the station. The jobs they can introduce are mostly with small collective enterprises.

Thus re-employment efforts are taking place through many different channels, but none of the interviewed families had any useful contact with these organizations, nor did they seem to place much confidence in them or in many cases even to know of their existence.

INTERNATIONAL AND NATIONAL LAW

The right to work is found in article 23 of UDHR, containing free choice, just and equal pay and the right to join trade unions. In ICESCR the different components have separate articles and article 6.1 will be used here:

> The States Parties to the present Covenant recognize the right to work, which includes the right of everyone to the opportunity to gain his living by work which he freely chooses or accepts, and will take appropriate steps to safeguard this right.

Safe working conditions and equal remuneration are the subject of article 7 in ICESCR, and article 8 is about trade unions and freedom of association. There is no General Comment on the right to work from the Committee on Economic, Social and Cultural Rights.

It appears that the right to work includes the right of everyone to 'gain his living by work', hinting that to gain a living is not the only reason for working. Curiously enough the text refrains from attempting to define *work*. One would assume work to mean wage labour, connecting the right to work with the right to subsistence, food, clothing, etc. And the right to life is surely a vital component of the right to work, but ostensibly there is more to it than that. As gaining a living is only part of the aim of working, the article must include a right to work without getting paid, which seems meaningless as long as work is not defined more closely. So the phrasing of the article could be aimed at stressing that, apart from a source of income, work is an important element in the constitution of personality and self-esteem and thereby also an end in itself. This interpretation accords with new trends in the understanding of labour as such:

> In its traditional, but narrow sense, labour has been perceived as a means of earning a livelihood, in other words a means for economic survival solely. As early as the dawn of the twentieth century two other important perspectives of more global and humane dimension gained ground. The first stressed an interdependence between labour conditions, social justice and universal peace. The second trend in modern perceptions has commendably enhanced the concept of labour as a human value, social need and a means for self-realisation and development of human personality. (Drzewicki 2001: 223)

Historically, international agreements on labour issues preceded the establishment of the present human rights norms, born out of World War II, and labour conditions as an international concern was a reaction to the World War I, with the establishment of the ILO in 1919 (Eide et al. 1995: 169). Discussion about phrasing a right to work in conjunction with human rights instruments began in 1950 on the initiative of the socialist states, and the final version of article 6 was adopted in 1956 after a lengthy negotiation process (Craven 1995: 194–203).

In practice the right to work has often been understood negatively as freedom from forced or slave labour, freedom of association in work, non-discrimination in employment and a guarantee of basic conditions for earning a living. The most elaborate domestic codifications of the article probably concern conditions in work, whereas the right to have or to get a job is poorly described in most domestic laws. Drzewicki talks of a whole cluster of work-related rights divided into four sub-categories, of which only one has a few (two out of a total of seven) separate dimensions regarding the problem of getting a job, namely, a right to employment that is typical for socialist countries but 'without significant legal remedies'. A right to protection against unemployment is not found in any of the core Covenants but only in the non-binding UDHR (Drzewicki 2001: 227–239). All other work-related rights concern the conditions for people in employment or people about to be assigned a job.

As we have seen, the text of article 6 is also vague on guarantees of the right to employment, reflecting that the formulation is a compromise between differing attitudes of the socialist and capitalist countries. During the drafting of the text, one sensitive part of the discussion was the obligation to provide jobs for everybody, where the Western nations were not willing to commit themselves to such a restriction of the free market forces.

> It soon became apparent that many states would not accept an obligation to 'guarantee' the right to work in the sense of ensuring full employment or eliminating unemployment. In particular it was feared that such a guarantee would bind states to a centralised system of government and require that all labour be under the direct control of the state. (Craven 1995: 195)

The socialist/capitalist dichotomy (discussed in Chapter 2 as the 'political argument') is manifest in the disagreement over the right to employment and the corresponding state obligation to create jobs.

Other elements in the text of relevance for the difference between socialist and liberal ideology is the implicit notion in the text of the right *not* to work as well as the wording that state parties have to achieve, among many other items, ' . . . full and *productive* employment . . .'. The possibility of choosing *not* to work opposes many socialist countries' stress on an individual obligation to contribute to society. In fact the worship of labour is an integral part of socialist ideology built upon a moral claim to a connection between contribution and enjoyment. As shall be discussed below, in the Chinese case work is an individual obligation towards the state as much as a right – not only as a duty to sustain oneself, as in the Western systems, but in a more general moral sense as a duty to carry one's share of the burden of producing resources for society. In theory this obligation persists even in the case where a person has other means of livelihood than wage labour. The conflict between the free choice of work and the duty to work was discussed at some length in drafting the document, and there seemed to be agreement not to encourage 'social parasitism', why a proposal for including the following formulation '. . . recognize the right . . . of everyone, *who so desires*, to the opportunity to gain his living by work' was rejected and the wording became the present ' . . . work, which he *freely chooses or accepts* . . .' (Craven 1995: 198). The whole idea of including an article on the right to work came, as mentioned above, from the socialist states themselves, and the topic of a duty to work draws a great deal of attention in the Commission of Economic and Social Rights, as this duty is constitutionally defined in some socialist countries, which is interpreted as being in accordance with the Covenant.

> There is no evidence as yet that the mere existence of such provisions [i.e. a duty to work] will be considered to be contrary to the provisions of the Covenant. (Craven 1995: 221)

The obligation to provide for *productive* employment also addresses practices of socialist systems, including China, formerly valuing full employment more than economic efficiency. The inclusion of the wording aroused little discussion, but it is very likely a comment on the differences between socialist and non-socialist employment policies. In all, the process of drafting the article reflects a dynamic interaction between representatives of different political and economic systems, and it seems that no one part was able to dominate the whole process.

All four Chinese constitutions[7] have codified a right to work for every citizen. Only in the latest version from 1982 has a duty to work been added after the right, followed by the admonition in article 42 that 'Work is a matter of honour for every citizen who is able to work'. It is interesting that a duty to work is included only as late as 1982, in light of the common idea that the concept of du-

7. From 1954, 1975, 1978 and 1982. The interim constitution, 'the Common Programme', in force from proclamation of the People's Republic in 1949 to 1954, contained no right to work, only 'a duty to observe labour discipline'.

ties is part of Confucian legacy[8] and as such actually could be expected to be excluded in future versions in the name of modernization. In order to guarantee the right to work, the state is at the same time in all the PRC constitutions obliged to create more employment and better working conditions and wages. In the wording of the first constitution of 1954, article 15:

> By economic planning, the state directs the growth and transformation of the national economy to bring about the constant increase of productive forces, in this way enriching the material and cultural life of the people and consolidating the independence and security of the country.[9]

The clause of 'progressive realization' is thus built into the Constitution from the very beginning, preceding the adoption of the principle in article 2 of the ICESCR (see introduction to Chapter 2).

Apart from the Constitution, work rights are specified in the Chinese Labour Law of 1994,[10] where article 3 includes the right (*quanli*) to choose an occupation:

> Labourers shall have equal rights to employment and choice of occupation, remuneration for labour, rest and vacations, protection of occupational safety and health, training in vocational skills, social insurance and welfare, submission of labour disputes for settlements, and other rights related to labour stipulated by law.

An analysis of the development of the law by comparing two earlier drafts, from 1983 and 1991 respectively, with the final version concludes that there has been a tendency towards more and more compatibility with international standards, e.g. in terms of fixing working hours, and the stipulation of a social insurance system also mirrors the ILO standards as will be explained in Chapter 6. Other trends are clarifying the word labourer as meaning employed people and not every able-bodied person, as earlier was the ideologically motivated understanding; more focus on protecting workers' rights instead of disciplining them; and a reduction of state intervention (Kinglun 2000: 19). All the discussed tendencies

---

8. See Peerenboom 1993: 43; Ghai, 1995: 8; Tu and Bary 1998: 145.
9. The same content in different wording is found in the last constitution (adopted 1982, amended 1988 and 1993), article 14.
10. The law was adopted by the Standing Committee of the NPC, promulgated on 5 July 1994 and became effective from 1 January 1995.

reflect the new needs of a market economy and point to a growing awareness of state obligations in protection of individuals' rights. The ILO standards are explicitly mentioned several times in the explanatory notes given by the minister of labour to the NPC in March 1994 (Kinglun 2000: 79).

URBAN LABOUR ALLOCATION UNDER SOCIALIST ECONOMY 1949–1979

Principles

What is not reflected in the earlier PRC constitutions and laws is the close relation between the right to work and the right to social security that became a result of the actual design of the different mechanisms to guarantee the right to work.[11] Basic social protection came to depend upon access to employment. The relation between work and social security in the Chinese system was no coincidence, but in close conformity with both the Marxist contribution principle during the first stage of communism and the moral socialist ethic of labour as a token of commitment to community. The Chinese communists adhered to distribution according to contribution as the guiding principle that was laid down by Marx in *Critique of the Gotha programme*:

> The contribution principle justifies the allocation of resources, including wages, according to the labour theory of value; the equality inherent in the contribution principle is the formal acknowledgment of the measurement of the contribution by the standard of labour. (Quoted in Lo and Cheng 1996: 31)

From this grew the moral attitude that care should be weighed against contribution; those who did not work, neither should they enjoy the fruits of labour. The right to subsistence was in theory and practice *earned*, not inherent in human nature, as expressed in the UDHR.

The value attributed to labour takes different forms throughout the history of the People's Republic. One form appeared in one of

11. In all the constitutions the right to work and the right to social security are two different unrelated articles.

the first and most important laws after the Communist take-over in 1949, the Land Reform Law, in which the crucial element in determining individual status was whether the person in question worked the land him- or herself or not. Those not working were put in the landlord category, stigmatizing themselves and their descendants for generations. Those working and hiring labour at the same time could get away with having the part of the land they did not work themselves seized.

In another manifestation, punishment has allways been connected with work. The whole prison system is called 'reform through labour', where work is meant to function as the means to change criminals into good people. Victims of the Cultural Revolution were forced to perform menial chores, implying that hard, physical labour in itself had a purifying effect, doing away with evil forces.[12] In general propaganda, hard work, linked to sacrifice, was elevated as the most sacred virtue. Labour models were praised as heroes; leisure was subordinated to work and any free time was strictly regulated; laziness and sometimes even rest became a taboo (Wang and Hu 1995: 152–156).[13]

Institutions

During the first decade of socialist rule the peasants in the countryside were gradually integrated into agricultural collectives of varying size and structure, granting employment and nearly equal social benefits at a very low level. What materialized for the urban population was a guarantee of the right to be employed, though, as

12. 'Mao sought to implant in the Chinese people a way of thinking imbued with a socialist consciousness that would be immediately practical yet relevant to the future achievement of communism. He recognized that the transformation of his social vision into reality was a most precarious task, involving both personal sacrifice and hard work.' (Dixon 1981: 5)
13. A similar line of thought is found in other socialist systems, e.g. as expressed by a Czechoslovakian dissident in an essay on Charter 77: 'There was a time when the bloc of states to which Czechoslovakia belongs could boast of a great innovation: legislating the right of every citizen to work. But from the start this legal guarantee was used, to an enormous extent, in a way quite opposite from the way in which it was presented to the world. Viz. as social control and coercion granting or denying people work within their profession as a political reward or as a punishment.' (Havel 1985: 200)

would later become apparent, not necessarily in 'productive work'. Economic efficiency was subsumed under social stability and political legitimacy, created by full urban employment. The institutional set-up around the state guarantee of employment was, apart from the centralized planned economy, the household registration system (*hukou zhidu*) and the work unit system (*danwei zhidu*).

Labour allocation became highly centralized. The *state plan* assigned each enterprise a labour quota, specifying the total number of employees and the wage bill at the end of the year (Eckstein 1977: 101). This money could not be diverted for other uses, so the employing work unit would be sure to employ exactly the number stipulated, whether they needed them or not. In the beginning it was easy to get a permanent job in the cities. The work units were hiring people on a large scale through announcements in the streets or through papers and information to the urban residential organizations, the Street Offices. In the first years after establishment of the PRC in 1949, work unit representatives would even come to the villages and recruit farmers directly from the fields. 'It was not necessary to know somebody. They just made a health check and then you would have the job' as one interviewed person recounted. Everybody could get information on which work units needed more people and every urban resident could freely go and apply for a vacant position. The Street Office would write a letter of introduction and the only criteria were a physical check-up and the presentation of diverse official documents stating educational level, household registration and confirming status of 'waiting for job' (*daiye*), which was the only word used for being out of work until 1994, when the term unemployment was formally adopted (Wang Feiling 1998: 27).[14]

But gradually employment opportunities were curtailed by development of the system of *household registration*. Just after 1949, China witnessed high levels of migration from the countryside to the cities, where life was easier and state-owned work units provided social benefits of a magnitude unseen in the villages. At that time people moved around a lot and could take a job, when work

14. Gu dates the use of the term unemployment to 1999 (Gu 2001 b: 9).

units were recruiting people as described above. Aware of the social dangers associated with uncontrolled migration experienced in other Third World countries, the state chose to limit the inflow of peasants by implementing a state monopoly for purchase of grain and other daily necessities. The rationing coupons were distributed by means of a registration system, originally established in the early 1950s as a device to monitor, not to control population movements (Chan and Zhang 1999: 820).

Everyone had to register with the authorities at the place of permanent residence through his or her household. The main tool became the household register, the small book that each family head had to keep up-dated on changes in number or composition of the family, i.e. at any given time it should be possible to check if all permanent residents of the household were in their right place. It was forbidden to move or travel without written permission from one's place of residence. The control in general only hit a small number of targeted people, usually those called 'bad elements' or suspects during the Cultural Revolution; ordinary people did not experience having their registration checked by the police. The registration card was also used to buy – with money and coupons – certain daily necessities such as cereals, coal and other things.[15]

The household registration became effective in controlling migration by being linked with employment possibilities and the rationing of daily goods. The registration status followed the place of residence, so it became impossible to get a job in the city without an urban registration, and coupons for grain and other necessities were distributed by neighbourhood committees[16] and agricultural collectives, only to local residents. Living without formal registration in the cities meant no access to work, housing, food or clothes, and a black market never evolved due to harsh measures and effective internal supervision. After a period of escalating inflow of peasants from the cities the first set of household registration legi-

15. As one interviewee from Xingtai tells, 'Before the reform period one could not buy anything without a household registration card. In the beginning (1976) I was not registered here and could not buy meat, coal, sugar, wheat or anything. Now it is better, if one only has money one can buy everything.'
16. People who did not have their own dwelling, like university students or unmarried young people, got their coupons through their work units.

slation in 1958 was used to force wandering farmers back to their villages and the system quickly developed into an effective instrument for controlling growth of the urban population (Chan and Zhang 1999: 820). In the next two decades Chinese society was divided into two segments – town and countryside – totally isolated from each other. The urban part of the population was taken care of by the state in almost every aspect of daily life – it was called 'to eat the emperor's grain' – while the peasants were 'eating their own grain', depending on the size of each year's harvest for basic social security.

Institutionally, local governments from the middle of the 1950s got more and more responsibility for labour allocation in tune with the general nationalization of urban industry and commerce. Labour bureaus at provincial and county levels were in charge of distributing the young school graduates to local enterprises or institutions and a job was theoretically assigned to everyone. A job assignment could in practice not be rejected, nor could it normally be altered, as labour mobility became extremely restricted due to the introduction of the household registration system. Informal networking and the use of social positions of friends and relatives could influence the choice of employer at the level of local government. But the final decision lay with the authorities, not with the individual in question.

The system placed the work unit as the core agent, administering funds from the central state apparatus for health and old-age care, maternity protection, housing, education, protection against work-related injuries, etc. When the Chinese Communist Party in 1956 declared that 'A decisive victory has now been won in the socialist transformation' (Resolution . . . 1971: 31), the basis of a social security system was included. The state had become the sole provider of social and economic protection, replacing the family and the frail market structures that had born the burden hitherto (Wang Feiling 1998: 14–17). [17] As the state had delegated social

17. Wang characterizes the employment system in China as an 'authoritarian state labour allocation pattern', in his view a variety of the family based traditional labour allocation pattern. In this interpretation the state substitutes for the family.

welfare down to enterprises and institutions, individual social security came to depend on relation to the labour market and no protection was available for people without a job. However, those were few in number.

The equality embedded in the central labour allocation in the urban areas, securing almost everyone a job, was limited by the different status and wealth of the different work units. There were 'good' and 'bad' units, and job assignment depended ostensibly both on the educational level and social connections of the person in question. The biggest difference concerned the distinction between state-owned and collective enterprises or institutions, with the former providing far more benefits than the latter; 'good', state-owned, units provided e.g. bigger apartments, better health services and more recreation facilities than 'bad', collectively owned, ones (Lü and Perry 1997: 7–8).

The economic consequences of the labour allocation pattern described above was serious overstaffing of work units caused by the lack of relationship between the number of employees and the economic needs of production. During the first decades the system created virtually full employment, but with the 1970s it became more difficult to get a permanent position and people tended more often to be hired on a temporary basis. Underemployment became rampant, leading to a strengthening of the practice of 'inheriting jobs' (*dingti*),[18] literally meaning that one young person in a family could get one parent's job when he or she retired. The urban unemployment rate grew high for a socialist country, 5.3 per cent in 1978, almost double the official rate in 1995 (*ZLTN* 1996: 10), which in turn was influenced by the rapid population growth of 13 per thousand in the last two decades of the 20th century (*ZTN* 2001: 91). Furthermore, state and collective enterprises could not generate a profit as social security constituted a heavy burden on enterprise budgets.[19] The social consequences were a factual protection of some basic economic and social rights, like health care,

18. *Dingti* is also referred to as *neizhao*: internal recruitment, or *jieban*: to take over.
19. Around 25 per cent of total salary expenses was used for welfare items like health care, pensions, etc. (Zhu Ling 2000: 86).

housing and education, at a low level, coupled with severe restrictions on movement and freedom of choice. Some civil rights were sacrificed for social security and political stability.

Reform trends

Reform entered the urban sectors in 1984 with policies aimed at making enterprises and institutions economically independent of the state coffers. Work units were first given decision-making power over part of their profits, and the direct transfer of surplus to the central level was gradually replaced by taxation (Cheung 1997: 511). The commercialization process included labour as well. Four important State Council provisions from 1986 introduced a labour contract system which opened the possibilities of hiring and firing workers and set up rules for a 'waiting-for-job' insurance (*GWYGB*, no. 25, 1986: 739–750). The practices of 'inheriting' jobs and allowing other kinds of 'internal recruitment' were officially forbidden.

One respondent from Guangzhou told that her son got into a department store in 1990 because of an advertisement he saw on TV, he just registered by himself and had to pass a simple test. This way of getting a job was new to urban residents. All newcomers to the labour market should enter into contractual relationships, fixing rights and duties of the two parties with their employers while people already employed preserved their former status. The contract workers were to have the same entitlements in terms of social welfare as colleagues employed within the life-tenure system had had. In 1992 the application of the Labour Contract System was extended to all employees and the autonomy of work units was confirmed in a series of new policies to reform enterprise management (Gu 2001b: 6). The system of life tenure was in the process of being abolished, metaphorically ingrained in China research as 'the smashing of the iron rice bowl'.

The adherence to the Marxist distribution system based on contribution was explicitly reconfirmed and egalitarianism condemned in the important decision on establishing a socialist market economy from November 1993:

> In the distribution of incomes to individuals, it is necessary to adhere to the system which takes the principle of 'to each according to his work' as its mainstay and facilitates the coexistence of multiple distribution methods, and to implement the principle of giving priority to efficiency while taking fairness into account. It is necessary to introduce competitive mechanisms for rewarding individual labour and break away from egalitarianism, so as to implement the principle of more pay for more work and rationally widen the income gap. (*BR*, vol. 36,no. 47, 1993: 22)

The same commitment was made in the new Labour Law to be enforced in January 1995, further regulating working conditions like time, salary, holidays, training, arbitration, security and containing non-discrimination clauses (*Shehui baozhang zhidu*, 1998: 87–91). Working time was fixed to 44 hours a week and lowered to 40 in May 1995 (*GWYGB*, no. 7, 1995: 222). Provincial governments were given the authority, and the duty, to fix a minimum wage based on local economic indicators.

The state was active on the job market in new ways by trying to create jobs for the many surplus workers, especially since efforts at reform of the state industry intensified with the 15th Party Congress in late 1997. A 'Re-employment Project' was initiated already in September 1994 when local government were called upon to launch a series of active labour market policies, such as subsidies to start up new businesses, development of job training programmes and tax exemption by employment of the surplus workers. Labour bureaus at all levels conducted re-employment campaigns and supported the establishment of job introduction centres at the community level, in big work units, and through mass organizations like the Women's Federation or the Youth League (*Minzhu yu fazhi*, 1998, no. 22: 20–21; *FEER*, 6 August 1998: 61 and 25 February 1999: 47). Efforts were made to introduce new forms of employment, for instance in relation to primary care at the level of street offices or neighbourhood committees (Yang Yiyong 1997: 215). The employment models seen in TV news programmes were mostly in the service sector and very small-scale, like a woman (the examples mainly concern women between 35 and 50, by far the most vulnerable group) serving breakfast on the street for busy families or repairing clothes in her home in one hour's time. This type of new employment solved the problem for some people. In 2000, 4.2 million people are said to have been re-employed through these measures. Many difficulties plagued the job introduction centres though, like lack of funds, new jobs and social security opportunities, low qualifications of the applicants and what in the media were called conservative and backwards attitudes to employment. The 'backward attitudes' probably point to the often reported fact that former state employees tended to be rather choosy with what kind of work they would do. The status difference between being part of the heroic working class and being a street sweeper was hard to accept for some people. The re-employment project was a temporary measure and will disappear by the end of 2003. In 1998, 8 billion yuan from the central government were allocated to support localities in introducing surplus workers to new employment opportunities, but central funding was planned to be phased out rather quickly (*China Daily*, 11 November 1998).

These documents and new policies created the legal and political foundations for a more flexible labour force moving around in a gradually developing free market. In theory at least it was now possible to get rid of surplus manpower and to select the most qualified person for any given task. Much evidence exists, though, that the new rules were not always implemented, and the new restrictions were ignored, like the prohibition on promising employee's children a job, which we saw was circumvented in Xingtai when enterprises promised jobs to children of employees who were willing to buy shares.

Reforms had bright and dark sides. The emergence of a private economy and the steadily increasing migration began to generate employment opportunities and a mobile labour force outside the state sector, while the ensuing competition created and exacerbated open and hidden unemployment. Jobs became advertised in papers and on billboards; employment markets and job introduction meetings were held in public places; new concepts such as job-seeking and head-hunting were introduced. People were allowed to travel and move within certain administrative restrictions and to set up their own workshops and companies, competing for manpower and customers. The demand for economic efficiency, on the other hand, compelled units to slim their work force and employees ended up with too little or no secure source of income. To prevent and remedy social instability produced by the reforms, the government allowed policies of controlled down-sizing of work unit personnel, coupled with efforts at creating new job opportunities like the ones sketched above and new ways of thinking about work and employment in society. The practice of laying off people that is used so much in both Xingtai and Guangzhou should be seen in this context.

The number of people employed in units other than state or collectively owned units increased from none in 1978 to almost 20 million in 1995, or 13 per cent of all urban employees (*ZLTN* 1996: 11 and 18). Real unemployment in China is hard to measure as the unemployed registered in the statistics are only a fraction of the people actually without any stable source of income or employment. The official unemployment rate has been lingering around 3 per cent, or 6 million people, but estimates by Chinese economists in 1998 are at least 8 per cent, or 16 million people.[20] Registered as unemployed are persons without jobs from 16 years of age just out of school to 59-year-old men or 49-year-old women or drop-outs from educational institutions, as well as persons fired or for any other reason without formal relation to a work unit. They must be registered with the street office and they are entitled to unemployment insurance, in Beijing ranging from 189 to 230 yuan a month, but no other social benefits.

The statistical uncertainty surrounding unemployment rates is partly due to the practice of laying off people. To alleviate the burden of surplus manpower, work units began to send people home while preserving the formal employment relationship with its attached social benefits. The practice became official policy in 'Regulations on the Placement of Surplus Workers and Staff of State Owned Enterprises' from 1993 using the designation 'waiting for a position' (*daigang*) or 'leave for limited periods' (*xianqi fangjia*)

---

20. See for example Hu Angang quoted in *FEER*, 25 February 1999: 47.

(*GWYGB*, 1993: 299).[21] According to the regulations the work units were still responsible for surplus workers and staff. Preferrably the enterprises should place them in productive activities but they were also allowed to grant leave to workers. Especially mentioned in the regulations were pregnant women who could get leave for a period of up to two years, and people about to retire who could be let off within five years before the formal retirement age. In all cases units should pay a 'livelihood allowance' to be decided by themselves, but in principle not lower than the lowest standard of the provincial government. It should be more than unemployment benefit, but in real life it can be less; it can even be zero, without any effective repercussions against the enterprise. The laid off worker will not be registered as unemployed and his/her file (*dang'an*)[22] will be kept in the work unit. The worker could get a 'laid off' certificate (*xiagang zheng*), implying that he or she was entitled to the same welfare benefits, in terms of health care and pensions, as other workers, but no salary, only the livelihood allowance, in the English literature often called a basic living subsidy (BLS) (Saunders and Shang 2001: 284). Obligations on the part of the employee are, at regular intervals, to report to a job introduction centre at the work unit and to receive training and job-seeking information when offered. The centre is responsible for paying health and pension insurance fees for the laid off workers in their registers. A survey done by the Ministry of Labour and Social Security in 1999 showed that future income and social security were the greatest worry of most laid-off workers; this helps explain why they were not willing to sever the contact with their former work unit, as we have seen with many examples in the interview materials. The respondents in the survey had low-level income from service jobs of short duration, but the new practice consti-

21. In SC Decree no. 111 of 20 April 1993 'Guoyou qiye fuyu zhigong anzhi guiding' [Provisions on surplus workers in state owned enterprises]. Translated into English in *Chinese Law & Government* (2001) vol. 34, no. 1: 70–73.

22. Each employee has an individual file recording her or his past. Information on political, professional and family history is kept in this document by the work unit and the material has in the past been widely used to identify victims of political campaigns. The person is not informed about the content of the file.

tuted both a stress factor and a challenge to people used to relying on their work units for everything (Ru et al. 2000: 351–352).[23]

For 2000 the official figure of laid off workers is 9.4 million people (*ZLTN* 2001: 401). The basic difference between being unemployed and being laid off is that the former is taken care of by government agencies through their residence units, the street offices or neighbourhood committees, while the latter is the responsibility of the work units. Both systems have their own job introduction centres and training facilities. Laid off persons are entitled to the basic subsidy, unemployed to unemployment relief usually of lesser value, and the laid off have social benefits like health care and pensions on top of their allowance. At least they are entitled to these subsidies, though they sometimes do not get them, as we have seen.

It can be asked why the government has chosen to introduce this transitional form of laying off instead of accepting the fact that it is not possible to employ everyone in productive jobs, so part of the labour force has to be unemployed for shorter or longer periods. The choice is obviously connected to the fear of social unrest if large groups of workers are left without a stable source of income as well as a recognition of debt owed to those employed during the period of central planning. The accumulation of resources during that period was built on the policy of low salary and part of the wealth thus created in reality 'belongs' to the workers. The excessive labour force is one of many legacies of the past and the government is reluctant to alienate the former core group supporting the communist leadership (Wang Mengkui 2001: 35).

Apart from laying off, other forms of affiliation with a work unit have been introduced, like 'stop of salary, continuation of employment' (*tingxin liuzhi*), meaning unpaid leave, giving the worker the possibility of creating a new job for him- or herself, or 'internal retirement' (*neitui*), which is a kind of early retirement used instead of laying off. In some places the allowance under this category is smaller than the ordinary pension, but it is still attached to seniority (*gongling*) and it is better than being laid off. Still another option

23. These findings correspond very well with the interview material.

is sick leave (*bingtui*), which is the most difficult to get, as one case referred to in Chapter 8 shows, because it counts as retirement, i.e. the unit has to pay for an unknown length of time. In a study from Wuhan, Solinger differentiates between seven different tiers of treatment depending on the ownership and economic situation of the work unit (Solinger 2001: 684–688).

The entitlement to different benefits and job training described above only reflects the formal situation written down in the laws and regulations. Implementation still varies from place to place and increased social unrest has been reported over issues of daily bread and testifies to serious shortcomings and deficiencies in the implementation of the system, as is also documented in the interview material. Arrears of pensions, laid off subsidies and even salary are pervasive problems. An amount of 400–500 million yuan in pensions missing every month was mentioned by an influential scholar from the Ministry of Labour and Social Security.[24] The political recognition of a need to ease the problems can be seen in the slogan emanating from a work meeting called by the SC and the Party Central in May 1998. According to the 'two guarantees' (*liangge quebao*) the basic livelihood of laid off workers and pensions of workers and cadres must be secured.

> Every social security agency should do their best not to owe even one person money, not to be late in payment even one day, and not to pay even one fen [1/100 of a yuan] too little. (Hu Xiaoyi 2001: 16)

The government has put 80 billion yuan into a fund especially meant to realise these goals. During the three years from 1998 to 2001, 21 million persons have been enrolled in re-employment centres, and 20 billion yuan in missing pensions have been paid according to the same source (Hu Xiaoyi 2001). These figures show that more than 20 million people must have been laid off, and on average each retired person was owed more than 600 yuan (the same article mentions a number of 30 million retirees in state enterprises alone).

---

24. In a report from Asia Development Bank, almost 200 billion yuan is mentioned as missing from individual pensions accounts (ADB 2001: 1).

To mobilize and appease the workers the household registration system had to be abolished or at least modified, a process that began in 1985 when regulations on migration to urban areas were changed and a range of different openings between countryside and town were created. Registration became personal when an individual ID card was introduced instead of the former household registration books – administered at the household level – and it became possible for peasants to get a temporary registration in the cities and rent housing from private landlords (Chan and Zhang, 1999: 832). This liberalization set in motion a steady human flow from countryside to town, and at least 100 million people are now believed to be living elsewhere than where they are permanently registered. In metropolises like Beijing and Shanghai and other provincial capitals in the eastern part of the country one third of the population has for many years been part of this 'floating population', creating an endless number of difficulties for local authorities in terms of town planning, sanitation, taxation, crime, job competition, etc. Social tensions are growing as migrants are regarded as dirty and criminal elements by the permanent urbanites, and they easily become scape-goats for all kinds of irregularities in daily life, almost creating a 'neo-apartheid' system (A. Chan 1998: 890).

The migrants belong to different categories (Solinger 1997: 114). At the bottom are destitute beggars and rubbish collectors without papers (China Perspectives, May–June 1999). Further up in the hierarchy we find construction workers living under appalling conditions in dormitories, formally hired by companies that do not live up to any security standards. Or we find young girls doing housework for rich families, often without official permits. And at the top reside business people, who may have bought a permanent residence permit. As jobs can be bought, so can the right to residence in the city, many big cities having fixed prices on residence permits. Abolishment of the registration system as such has been discussed and is demanded by certain groups, but it probably has some way to go. Officially no intentions have been expressed to altogether do away with this tested mechanism for controlling population movements, though changes have been accepted by the authorities.

The former employment system has not been easily up-rooted. After ten years of reform, job mobility had in practice not increased very much (Davis 1992: 1064), and in the middle of the 1990s 70 per cent of the work force was still allocated jobs by the state (Wang Feiling 1998: 100) or got jobs by other extra-market forces (i.e. not by supply and demand) like the use of good relationships (*guanxi*) and money purchase as instruments in obtaining much-coveted positions (Bian 1997: 367). The problem of economic efficiency of the work units has not been solved because the problems with unemployment and lack of social security outside the traditional system impeded the units in getting rid of surplus manpower. Seen from the angle of the individual state employee, the changes that have occurred have given more freedom of choice and movement, but far less stable protection of the right to work, health care, housing, etc.

CONCLUSION

The labour reforms that have had the most effect in Xingtai are the negative elements like the practice of laying off staff and workers, not always formally, but in reality work units have stopped paying salary and encouraged people to stay at home and find something else to do. In Guangzhou the problems with arrears are not so bad and the opportunities of finding jobs are better. The labour allocation system have been replaced by freedom to hire labour and apply for jobs but this freedom is difficult to utilize in the economic climate of stagnation and lack of new job openings. The violent competition for the few good positions have caused a widespread use of irregular, if not outright illegal, measures like taking deposits for getting a job, demanding payment for keeping the personal file or dumping unsaleable goods to employees. The intention to free the labour force from the work units have also not been realised, as the units ostensibly play almost as dominant a role as they used to before the reforms began.

The question raised in the introduction, whether the Chinese work unit system complies with article 6 of the ICESCR, can thus be answered with a mix of 'yes' and 'no'. A comparison between the international standards and the job allocation system, concerning the situation before 1979, gives the conclusion that the system did not comply with the text of the Covenant. The most manifest protection of the right to work in pre-reform China was the provision of a job for every urbanite, a guarantee that deliberately was left out of article 6 of the Covenant during the drafting process. So providing everyone with a job is neither in compliance with nor in violation of the Covenant. Furthermore, it can be discussed how the serious overstaffing in public enterprises influenced the self-esteem and perceptions of human dignity connected with the right to work in the Covenant. To be under-occupied could lead to lack of self-respect and feelings of personal uselessness. To go to work every morning and not have anything to do would for some people be worse than not having a job. To my knowledge, no investigation has been made of this aspect, but it could be an interesting topic for future research.

On the other hand, state policy in practice *did* guarantee almost every urbanite the right to work and with that the basic means of subsistence, constituting an improvement of social conditions before 1949. The new employment system after the introduction of reforms, in contrast, does not guarantee employment but complies with article 6 on the guarantee to 'freely choose or accept' work. System transformation includes a clear trend away from state provision of jobs to individual job-seeking on market conditions, more in conformity with the international standard. At the present stage a progressive realization of article 6 can thus be confirmed for the latter part of the 1990s, but the greater degree of compliance with the Covenant seems at the moment of writing not to have improved protection of the right to employment for the kind of people interviewed in this study.

5 只能靠自己

Welfare Benefit or Investment Object: Housing Reform

One of my friends lives with her husband and daughter in a flat allocated to them by her husband's work unit. She is working in one of the big universities and has got allocated a small flat there, where her parents live, because her brother lives in the flat allocated to her father by her father's work unit. The brother is a private entrepreneur and therefore has no possibility of getting subsidised housing.

Housing is both a basic human need and an important player in the national economy. Adequate shelter is a social right, stipulated in international human rights conventions as necessary for survival, and housing conditions are important ingredients in individual perceptions of life quality as well as status objects in more affluent circles of society. Mirroring the right, the social responsibility for the state is to regulate conditions for construction of residential areas which activity in turn most often is carried out by private commercial enterprises providing jobs and generating profit. Provision of housing necessitates the establishment of a whole range of institutional support mechanisms, like real estate companies, credit associations, mortgage deed systems, etc. The housing market thus plays an important role in the national economy at large, influencing the rate of interest, inflation, employment as well as the family economy.

In socialist China before 1979 urban housing became a welfare benefit in line with health care, maternity leave, etc. Construction was done by work units or local government housing bureaus that also owned and administered residential blocks in all towns and cities. Very little private housing survived the nationalization policy of the late 1950s. Most urban workers lived in flats allocated by their work units, they paid a very small rent, they did not have any responsibility to maintain their living quarters and they could not move. At the same time housing was in short supply, newly-weds had to wait years before they could get their own apartment, and most residences were in bad shape.

OUTLINE OF HOUSING REFORM IN CHINA (1980–2000)

One of the important aims of economic reform in China was to raise living standards, and public spending on housing construction increased rapidly after the initiation of the reform programme. Total housing investment more than doubled during the first half of the 1980s (Wang and Murie 1999: 103), and 2.8 billion square metres of new housing have been built since then, five times the amount built in the 30 years before reform, raising the average floor space per person from 3.6 square metres in 1978 to 8.8 square metres in 1997 (State Council Information Office 1999: 1). The added space is still not sufficient for what could be called a reasonable modern living standard and it is unevenly distributed, as the housing conditions of 3 million families are still characterized as 'wanting', i.e. under 4 square metres per person (*Banyue tan*, no. 7 1998: 10).

Not only living standards but also future economic growth could be supported by capital accumulation generated by housing funds. In a macro-economic context a new concept is emerging for the construction sector and the establishment of a corresponding credit system as a growth point in national economy:

> Development of the housing sector is beneficial for adjusting consumption patterns, and it can spur on a group of related sectors. Housing demand in China is big and can become a pillar of production; it has the potential for turning into a new growth point for economic development. (Tang Ying 1997: 17)

Likewise, prime minister Zhu Rongji in March 1998 characterized the housing market as 'a key engine of growth' when he announced a new step forward in reform implementation (*SCMP*, 20 March

1998). In its own way housing reform, thus, could contribute to two macro-economic aims of the whole reform project, i.e. raising consumption and stimulating growth.

To reach these goals the institutional framework surrounding housing provision had to be changed. In December 1979 the government urged work units and individuals to contribute to housing construction. As an important element it was stipulated in 1980 that individuals were allowed to own, build and purchase their own housing (Zhang 1993: 33), a measure backed up by law in 1983 (Lee 1995: 116). The reform of housing provision in urban China has been going on ever since and is conducted according to the same principle as other parts of the reform programme, viz. via a gradual transition to distribution via market mechanisms instead of administrative decree. Focus and overall aim of housing reform is to convert so-called welfare housing allocation to commercial housing, also called to 'marketize' (*shangpinhua*) or 'socialize' (*shehuihua*) housing. The word 'privatization' (*siyouhua*) is rarely used. It still seems to be politically unacceptable to talk about privatization, though the goal clearly is private ownership of flats, with renting as a subsidiary measure.[1] If residential units are going to be distributed via the market – supply and demand – and not via bureaucratic interference, the establishment of a financial system with bank loans and mortgage is necessary and families need a salary high enough to pay up to 15 per cent of their income for housing purposes in contrast to the pre-reform proportion of around 2 per cent. Housing will no longer be related to work units, contributing to the project of freeing the worker from the work place, enabling her or him to respond effectively to rapidly changing market needs.

The transition from the old system to the new is explained as a change to a principle of allocation in accordance with work contribution, as formulated in one of the important official decisions on housing reform:

> The basic content of the housing reform is . . . to change the form of welfare allocation in kind (*shiwu fuli fenpei*) to the form of salary

1. See the title of a chapter on housing reform giving a name to the new hybrid: 'Housing Privatisation with Chinese Characteristics' (Lee 1995: 113).

> allocation in cash (*huobi gongzi fenpei*) based on the principle of to each according to work contribution (*anlao fenpei*). (*ZZZG* 1996: 133)

The socialist central-planning idea pops up in the formulation of 'salary allocation in cash', giving the impression that some central power is still allocating resources, now by the means of money instead of by administrative decision. The way of phrasing conveys the idea that we deal with two different ways of distributing resources, not with two fundamentally different economic systems. A simple propaganda effort – to sell a new system as if it is the old one in disguise – could be the background, but maybe also a genuine belief that central power is still in control.

Marketization of housing was basically done by two means: home purchase and rent increase. Both methods had been mentioned and put through trial implementation from the end of the 1970s. Experiments of selling new houses to citizens were carried out in the two provincial capitals of Xi'an and Nanning from 1980 to1982, while a transition to private ownership of existing residences was tried out from 1982 to 1985 in four cities (Zhengzhou, Changzhou, Siping, Shashi), where a home purchase scheme allowed local government or work units to try to sell apartments to the people who lived in them.

In 1982 a conference was convened to approve experiments with a 'three-thirds' system, included in a proposal issued by the State Council in April (*ZZZG* 1996: 111–112). Work units in the selected cities should sell new flats to people instead of allocating them and should strive to motivate people already living in public housing to buy their flats. Individuals only had to pay one-third of the outlay, including construction, land rent and depreciation, while the work unit or local construction bureau, which owned or had just built the residential units, paid the other two-thirds. Work units should save the income from sale in housing funds in a commercial bank, earmarked for housing purposes. Despite a report from the Ministry of Construction from September 1984, where it was recommended to expand the trial implementation to Beijing, Shanghai and Tianjin, authorities in 1985 called for the termination of these experiments. The reason given for cancellation was that the incentive to buy was too weak, as the existing – extremely low – rent was not touched and the subsidies were too costly for the work units, as they, with one stroke, lost two-thirds of their investment (Zhang 1993: 26–30 and 34).

More focus on housing reform came in 1985 with the establishment of the 'Housing Reform Leadership Small Group'[2] under the State Council with members from the different institutions involved in the sector: the Ministries of Construction, Finance, Labour and Civil Affairs; the Commissions of System Reform, Economy and Planning; various banks and the Trade Union, in total 25 different departments and organs. The group had the mandate to coordinate housing reform activities and has subsequently been the most important organ directing the course of reform.

Experiments were again conducted in selected cities, now with rent increase and attempts to render the housing subsidies 'visible' as important elements. The experiments of the previous years had shown that rent was still far too low to make home purchase economically reasonable for families, so increase in housing expenses was concluded to be the pivotal element. To prepare people psychologically for dramatic rent increases, measures were designed to heighten awareness of the cost of housing. In a document from November 1986, drafted by the Housing Reform Leadership Small Group, five cities – Yantai, Tangshan, Bengbu, Changzhou and Jiangmen – were singled out as experimental plots, where the increase of rent was carried out through the issuance of vouchers or payment of a cash allowance to make the housing subsidy 'open' instead of hidden (Zhang 1993: 42ff). This measure constituted at the outset an 'artificial circulation', where housing vouchers were issued to residents by work units. The value of each family's voucher (i.e. their rent increase) was calculated on the basis of a coefficient of its present floor space, its income and previous rent compared to an average floor space and income. That meant people with more than average space did not get enough vouchers and had to make up the difference in cash, while people with less room than average got too much value on their vouchers and the difference would be

2. The group was originally called 'Rental Reform Leadership Small Group', but was renamed in 1986 (Lee 1995: 126).

placed in a bank, from where it could be drawn for future housing consumption. A market mechanism was played out in an indirect fashion, softening the immediate effect of the rent increase.

Following the above mentioned experiments, a National Conference on Housing Reform was convened in January 1988, resulting in the promulgation of a national policy paper called 'The Proposal to Implement the Nationwide Urban Housing Reform by Groups and by Stages'. The tone in the first paragraph is surprisingly determined and outspoken, claiming that 'Serious malpractices exist in our country's housing system ... Unfair housing distribution is a serious social problem' (*ZZZG* 1996: 126–131). The elements in the reform were still centred around adjustment of rent by issuance of vouchers, home purchase by preferential policies and the establishment of public housing funds (*zhufang gongjijin*) financed jointly by work units and individuals. This document marks a new emphasis on housing reform, causing some Western scholars to state the beginning of a new housing policy in 1988:

> This marked the turning point of housing reform from pilot tests and experiments in selected cities to overall implementation in all urban areas and was the most important policy document on housing reform. (Wang and Murie 1999: 148)[3]

The changes in the proposal were scheduled to be carried out in no more than five years, but political instability in the wake of the Tiananmen crackdown on 4 June 1989 and the ensuing economic stabilisation programme slowed down the process, only to be restarted in 1993 after Deng Xiaoping's famous Southern Tour (*nanxun*) of the previous year.

The reactivation of housing reform took shape in the next important document, 'Decision on Deepening the Urban Housing Reform' from July 1994 (*ZZZG* 1996: 133–138), focusing on adjustment of prices of housing units and the establishment of public housing funds. More places – 3 cities, 35 towns and 200 middle-sized towns – were this time selected as experimental sites for housing reform (Lu et al. 1997: 650).

Pricing policies were specified. When work units sold flats to employees a subsidy, tied to the number of years of employment,

3. See also Pudney and Wang 1994: 4.

was deducted from the cost price. It amounted to a gradual declining per cent[4] of the cost price per year of seniority. If one family had two employees in a work unit, their combined seniority decided the price deduction with a ceiling of 65 years – 30 years seniority for a woman and 35 for a man.[5] An example: a couple lives in an apartment of 60 square metres in Beijing. They want to buy in 1998 and the cost price is 1,450 yuan per square metre, i. e. the flat costs 87,000 yuan. They have a combined seniority of 55 years, and for each year they can deduct 14.50 yuan per square metre (= 1 per cent) equalling 47,850 in all. So they have to pay 39,150 yuan for a flat of 60 square metres. Using the preferential system the buyer does not immediately acquire full ownership rights as he or she cannot sell the apartment again within five years.[6] If the family does not want it anymore, the flat will have to be sold back to the work unit – which very seldom happens, and why it is difficult to get an answer to to what price. One source claims that the work unit has the right to receive part of the income from sale in any case. This has not been confirmed by my investigation, but could be an example of the variety of practices among different work units (Scott 1994: 26). The preferential price can only be used once by each family, but it is personal in the way that it can be used by an occupant to buy any flat he lives in, not just a flat belonging to his own work unit. Further purchases of new housing or more space have to be done at market prices (*Banyue tan*, no. 7, 1998: 14, 20).

Another new measure was public funds that were introduced in Shanghai in 1991, modelled on Singaporean experiences, and four years later 95 per cent of the work units in the metropolis, including 4 million employees, participated in the scheme. The sources of the public funds are monthly contributions from the participating work units and workers as well as income from the sale of flats to employees (Jacobs 1997: 177–178). Their foremost aim is to con-

---

4. In the 1994 decision it was fixed to 5 per cent, declining one point each year (*ZZZG* 1996: 136).
5. The retirement age for women is five years below that for men, 50 and 55 respectively for workers, 55 and 60 for cadres.
6. As of 2002 this time limit has been shortened to two or three years and in Beijing the limit is no longer valid.

centrate housing capital and secure that the gains from trade in housing are used for housing construction and maintenance. Under the traditional work unit system, housing investment and expenses were not separated from other expenses, making it difficult to calculate the real cost. Now several components like the municipal and enterprise capital earmarked for housing construction and maintenance and for housing subsidies, funds derived from sales of new and old houses, as well as surplus from individual's housing vouchers were to be kept in separate bank accounts serving as resources for new construction and as mortgage in securing bank loans, both for individuals and for the work units. Participation in the fund is voluntary for both work units and individuals, but when a work unit enters the system, it commits itself to contribute a monthly amount to each employee's individual account corresponding to the individual contribution. So most employees want to join if they have the possibility, as the set-up from their point of view constitutes a housing subsidy.

Establishment of housing funds spread rapidly to reach 31 counties and 36 big and middle-sized towns altogether in 1998. On a national level their value doubled from 40 billion yuan in 1996 to 80 billion in 1998, of which 18 billion yuan were in Shanghai alone (*FEER*, 30 July 1998: 45). One example of the procedure for using public funds is explained in the magazine 'Fortnight Talks' (*Banyue tan*, no. 7, 1998: 22–23). A person employed at a Beijing company wants to buy himself a flat. He contacts the Beijing City Housing Fund Administration Centre, which provides him with capital for buying a 90 square metres flat for the price of 520,000 yuan – 5,777 yuan per square metre. The financial arrangements of the purchase are explained as follows: he pays one-third, around 170,000 yuan, himself, probably from personal savings or private loans. He borrows 250,000 yuan for five years from the fund with permission from his work unit. The Administration Centres have a quota for how much each work unit can approve, which cannot be higher than double the amount the work unit has put into the public fund. The work unit thus guarantees the payment of that loan. He gets 100,000 yuan as a personal loan for three years from a bank with the flat as mortgage. This part of the loan is also connected with the work unit as it has to issue a license, stating that his personal contributions to the fund covers the amount, which he is going to borrow. Normally two-thirds of the value of the flat will be recognized as mortgage. In this instance, of the 520,000 yuan sale price 320,000 yuan were mortgage. Interest on the public fund loan is 4.7 per cent, on the bank loan 9 per cent, and he ends up paying 7,800 yuan a month, which he can afford because his salary is high. Ownership certificate of the flat rests in the bank until he has repaid the loan. His flat is built by a private construction bureau, and he naturally faces the risk, as in any other market economy, that it is not worth the price when he wants to resell it.

The proposed measures from the 1994 decision did not sufficiently speed up the process of selling public housing to individuals. In the middle of the 1990s, 75 per cent of all state employees were said to live in public housing – state or collectively owned and managed (Lu et al. 1997: 653). This last figure is high in light of fifteen years of effort to make an end to work unit housing. According to figures from the Ministry of Construction in 1996, still more than 75 per cent of marketized housing was bought by work units, a year later only 1 per cent of total public housing had actually been sold to inhabitants. Even in a progressive city like Shanghai almost half (6 out of 14 million residents) lived in work unit housing in the middle of 1998 (*FEER*, 30 July 1998: 45). The sale of housing at market price was equally difficult. A real estate fever in 1991–1993 had led to oversupply, primarily of houses for luxury consumption but also of office space (Chen 1998: 53). Much housing was built that people could not afford to buy, and worse, the area of unsold space was on a steep rising curve from 1995 onwards. The contradiction between relatively cramped housing conditions and unsold square metres was especially manifest in well-off places like Shanghai, Guangdong, Jiangsu and Zhejiang, where half of the unsold space was located (Jiang 1998: 299; Tian 1997: 76).

The reason for the difficulties in selling flats at subsidised prices is not only lack of economic means, but also still a lack of incentives because of the low rent in public housing (Li Shuzhi 1996: 209–210).[7] A typical example of the difference in price between buying

7. Interview, Li Shuzhi, 11 November 1997.

and renting, seen from the side of a family economy, was given in April 1997. A three-person family buying a 55 square metres flat has to pay 33,000 yuan (at the 'cost price' of 600 yuan per square metre). They get a bank loan with 7.5 per cent interest, this alone giving an annual expense of 2,500 yuan. A rented flat at the highest rate in 1996 is 1.5 yuan per square metre a month, giving a yearly cost of 990 yuan for the family. Just to pay interest on the loan they have to spend 1,510 yuan more a year if they buy instead of rent their apartment (*Jingji cankao bao*, 22 April 1997). The gap between rent and purchase expenses had actually been widened in the course of reform in direct opposition to the declared intent of the reform programme. By the end of the 1980s the proportion was 1:120 as opposed to 1:140 in 1998 (Jiang 1998: 300), and three-fourths of all employees, as mentioned above, still lived in work unit housing.

Huge local variations exist, as we shall also see in the interview material. In Shanghai rent was 6.54 yuan a square metre, equal to 13 per cent of an average income, while it was 0.5 yuan a square metre in Yinchuan, equalling 3 per cent of average income. In Tianjin 18 per cent of total public housing had been sold, in Shanghai 52 per cent, while in the whole of Shandong province 25 per cent of housing was privatized (*Jingji cankao bao*, 22 April 1997). The big proportions of privately owned housing in these East Coast capitals point to an almost non-existent market for housing in the interior provinces, if the average has to come down to the 1 per cent mentioned above.

In the eyes of the reformers, residents' reluctance to buy housing[8] necessitated stronger pressure, either drastic rent increases or bureaucratic interference, which latter option was selected. On 19 March 1998 Prime Minister Zhu Rongji outlined an ambitious reform programme of his new government including an end to subsidised housing already by 1 July of the same year (*SCMP*, 20 March 1998). This measure ostensibly created many problems, as the first deadline was postponed till the end of the year (*FEER*, 30

8. On individual deliberations about whether to buy or not see for example *Fangdichan shijie* (Real Estate World) 10, 1997: 3–5.

July 1998: 45) and eventually the abolition of the subsidised sale was executed by 1 April 2000.

The continuing problems of housing shortage and workers' inability to buy existing empty flats led the government to initiate a special plan for low-income families and families with less than 4.5 square metres per person. On the basis of experiments in several cities that on their own had started to invest in low-cost housing construction, the State Council in January 1995 issued an 'Implementation Plan for Peaceful Residence State Project' (*ZZZG* 1996: 162–164). The Chinese name '*anju*' has also been translated as 'comfort housing' (China Daily, 24 November 1997), and the plan promises state loans to cities that will build cheap apartments and guarantee to sell them to families with severe housing shortage. The national target is to invest in another 150 million square metres on top of the original construction plans within five years. Eligible for the subsidy are cities that have already implemented certain elements of housing reform, like the establishment of housing funds for no less than 60 per cent of their employees, and are willing and capable to raise their own funds in the proportion of four to six as well as to provide favourable conditions for land use and decide on other relevant policies. The project will be managed by the Housing Reform Leadership Small Group of the State Council.

Affordable housing projects had begun in Beijing, Guangzhou, Shanghai, Yantai and other big cities already from the beginning of the 1990s, where local authorities had found the funds to construct cheap residences (Wang and Murie 1999: 195 ff.). In Guangzhou the city had already provided flats to 26,000 families whose living space was less than five square metres per person before the local government in 1997 was allowed to start a three-year Peaceful Living project, sourced by the city's housing funds, public housing funds, potential buyers' advancement payment as well as low-interest bank loans. These efforts mix a welfare concept with marketization, as they both help needy families and assure that housing is brought into the market, as a Guangzhou official explains it: 'the project is expected to play a significant role in commercializing and socialising the city's housing' (China Daily, 24 November 1997: 7).

To sum up, the marketisation process began with efforts to sell new housing and raise rent at the same time. Later, housing funds were established as a motivating factor to be followed by a decision, postponed several times, to administratively solve the matter by abolishing the system of work unit housing. The potential harmful effects of abolishing welfare housing was mitigated by price subsidies to residents in work unit housing and by construction of special housing for low-income families.

LOCAL IMPLEMENTATION

The interview data from the two surveyed neighbourhood committees show that housing reform has progressed further in the community of the 'backward' northern town than in the district of the more developed southern city. 'Reform progress' is here measured as the enduring degree of dependence on the work unit for housing, as work unit separation from housing provision is taken as the immediate goal of the reform programme, followed by longer term goals of the establishment of a genuine housing market and supporting financial institutions.

Xingtai, Hebei

Central decisions have had a strong influence on local regulations in the area of housing reform.[9] The July 1994 decision, mentioned above, was in Hebei province and Xingtai city followed by similar decisions the year after. The government of Hebei in February 1995 promulgated a 'Circular on Deepening the Reform of the Urban Housing System' (*Fanggai wenjian xuanbian* 1997: 49–59) and a Xingtai circular with the same title was published in June 1995 (*Fanggai wenjian xuanbian* 1997: 116–126). The provincial circular refers to the 'spirit' of the central decision and is directed to cities,

9. For a discussion of the relation between central and local legislation, see 'Provincial Laws on the Protection of Women and Children', *Chinese Law and Government* 1994, vol. 27, no. 1: 3–9.

districts and counties with the demand to forward plans for implementation to the provincial government for approval before 1 July the same year. The two local documents are almost identical and contain the same three main elements as the national decision: housing funds, rent increase and housing purchase. Where the national decision leaves room for local interpretation and calls for local specifications, the limits are the same for the two local regulations, for instance that the figure for rent increase by the time of promulgation shall be 0.4 yuan per square metre.

In the local decisions a guarantee fund (*zulin baozhangjin*) is stipulated as a means of promoting rent increase, and it is given much more attention than in the national document, where the item is only mentioned under the paragraph about rent reform as a possibility local levels can use. The guarantee fund is a deposit paid as a lump sum by the employee to the owner of the flat – typically the work unit – as a guarantee for the rent. It is paid into an individual account in the Housing Fund Administration Centre and should be no less than one-seventh of the cost price of (an average) flat. The fund can be used by the resident as mortgage for obtaining a loan for housing purposes and of the work unit as investment in housing construction. This measure has a transitional character as it is meant to exist only until the rent of the family has reached the level of the cost price and it replaces the housing vouchers established before. Funds remaining from saving of vouchers will be transferred to the guarantee funds. These funds are not to be confused with the public housing funds, consisting of accumulated savings withheld over time from both employer and employee. None of these measures are mentioned in the interviews, though, so it is doubtful whether they have been implemented to any considerable degree.

Only four of the 41 families from Sheepmarket Street Neighbourhood Committee live in work unit housing, and of those three are demobilized army personnel, who are treated according to special procedures. Of the rest – 37 cases – two-thirds have bought their house at a preferential price either by pooling capital for new housing or buying the dwelling they live in, and the last third live in private housing mostly inherited from parents or built by themselves on inherited land. Not a few live in housing allocated during land reform or even inherited from pre-liberation landlords. These arrangements survived the Cultural Revolution without the houses being confiscated, which would not have been the case in many other parts of the country. None of the respondents report to live in 'peaceful residence' housing (also called 'economic housing': *jingji zhufang*), which are flats built especially for low-income families. Xingtai had such a programme financed jointly by the City Government, the Construction Bureau and a commercial housing company.

Twelve of the 41 Xingtai families (30 per cent) have bought their house by pooling funds (*jizi jianfang*), i.e. they participate in investment in new housing by paying a sum to the work unit, which then builds the house. Usually the unit will invest half or two-thirds and the family has to contribute the rest. This concept is not given much attention in the official documents or the public debate. In the locality studied not everyone is qualified for pooling money; the criteria used resembles the criteria used in the traditional allocation system, seniority especially is important to be allowed to contribute to construction. Also, like the traditional system, the Trade Union and the Workers Representative Meetings are active in laying down the rules and approving applicants for investment. The preferential price notwithstanding, houses acquired this way can be sold for less than the cost price as the work unit usually does not pay for the use of land and gets cheap energy. The investment is subsidized according to a 40–60 proportion so the work unit pays 40 per cent and has a corresponding share of ownership rights within the first five years, in some instances longer, while the family buys and possesses the remaining 60 per cent. The family has the right to buy the remaining 40 per cent at a subsidised price, adjusted according to seniority. The exact percentage of sharing is not mentioned in the local Xingtai decision on housing reform, where units are called upon to 'continue to implement the methods of pooling money for housing investment, cooperative construction and strengthen the management of housing funds' (*Fanggai wenjian xuanbian* 1997: 117). But informants consider the 40–60 sharing as part of local policy:

> According to the regulations buyers get 60 per cent ownership and the work unit gets 40 per cent. The 60 per cent includes the right to reside in the flat. We do not pay rent. The national policy is privatisation, so gradually we will acquire the remaining 40 per cent ownership, at a subsidised price. We cannot re-sell the apartment within three years, unless it is to someone in our own work unit. In that case we can sell at a negotiated price.

Apart from the outright share of investment, the arrangement includes a whole range of benefits, which explains why the right to invest is restricted and a certain contribution to the work unit – in the form of years of employment – is required to get a permission. The flats are maintained by the work unit, usually through a service company, and even though the investment is modest the families concerned do not pay rent, only electricity, water and heating (gas). Some families even report that the work unit provides cheap gas for heating.

The policy of pooling money for housing construction was started in Xingtai around 1990 and the prices vary widely with a typical price quoted as 35,000 yuan for a flat of 60 square metres, equalling 583 yuan per square metre. In one case a construction price of 700 yuan per square metre is quoted, with 2.5 yuan per square metre deducted for each year of seniority. The highest seniority you can get is 60 years (for two persons in the family), which gives a deduction of 150 yuan, leaving a price of 550 yuan per square metre. Some of the families took loans from relatives or friends to cover the original investment and they thus pay 'rent' in the form of installments on the debt.

The other system to purchase a house is the buying of present housing at subsidised prices in accordance with national policies. Again, the conditions for buying resemble the conditions for getting house allocation in the traditional way, but the connection to the work unit is not so close. Apart from restrictions on re-selling, the work unit does not support expenses to maintenance or energy. The prices vary greatly between the different work units and the housing bureau, ranging from less than 200 to almost 800 yuan per square metre. The difference is not connected to the time of the deal; one could expect earlier transactions would have been cheaper, but they are not.

The neighbourhood is in the old centre of town, some houses are dilapidated and the future demolishing of part of the area attracts a lot of attention and worry from the residents. A city plan stipulates that the core of the old centre shall be demolished and rebuilt within five years. The existing houses will be graded according to quality and a family will be compensated by – in principle – 1 square metre new housing for 1 square metre old, minus deduction in accordance with the grading of the present building. If the old house originally had earthen walls and not concrete, for instance, the grading will be lower, and the square metres will be exchanged with 1 to, for example, 0.8. Thus a family is not compensated for actual outlays in renovating old roofs and walls, only in relation to space and grading. Conditions are the same for inherited property or recently bought allocated housing Many agree that it is necessary to pull down the old houses because they are dangerous to live in and lack sanitary installations, but most worry that they will have to pay a lot of money before they are able to move into the new houses. Few of the existing square metres will be exchanged on a one-to-one basis and even if they were, the new houses will consist of bigger apartments than most people have now, so to move into a new flat they will have to make up for the space difference by buying at market prices. Furthermore, some – especially older – people dislike the thought of not living on the ground and having a courtyard to store bicycles and goods in protection against perceived growing social unrest and rising crime rates. And some feel emotionally attached to houses, inherited from their ancestors and renovated and invested in by themselves and their children.

In general, though, family members accept the new housing policy but they worry about failing economic resources. Their biggest problems with the new system lie in their employment situation, with many laid off workers from insolvent factories having very small and unstable income. Their complaints, consequently, do not question the new rules, but their generally weakened economic position.

Guangzhou

In Guangzhou the housing reform gained momentum from the promulgation of a plan for housing reform on 1 October 1989 – one year after the important 1988 proposal at the national level. The plan includes home purchase at subsidised prices, rent increase and guarantee funds (*Guangzhou shi zhi* 1995: 459–462), and detailed regulations are given for subsidy conditions and rules for allowable incremental rent increases. In the whole of Guangzhou, living space per person has been raised from 4.5 square metres in 1949 to 8.5 square metres in 1993 (Ikels 1996: 55), very close to the national average.

Xinjiao Neighbourhood has, as mentioned, a large migrant population. These 'people from outside' ostensibly rent rooms and houses from landlords living in the area but their situation is not within the scope of this study, which deals only with the permanent residents.

Of the 42 families interviewed only eight households have their own dwelling independent of any relation to a work unit. These private houses were mostly inherited from parents or built on farmland, made possible by the fact that at least one of the family members has an agricultural registration status. To be allowed to build a private house a family will need – apart from farmer status – land points (*di fen*) as well as money points (*qian fen*); i.e. they need to have a peasant background. With the present land shortage, especially in this area, it is difficult to solve housing problems that way. As land points are in short demand the prestige of peasant status is on the rise.

It is usually taken for granted that everybody wants an urban registration status (Chan and Zhang 1999) but in the vicinity of Guangzhou as well as in the whole of the Pearl River Delta this seems not always to be the case. The mentioned possibility of getting land to build housing is one advantage, others mentioned are dividends from land requisition for industrial use or collective economic activities like investment in foreign-funded enterprises. Furthermore, the one-child policy is not enforced so strictly on farmers and they have cheaper access to food than city dwellers.

Coupled with the explosive modernization of the area, which makes village life just as – or even more – comfortable than life in the big cities, the balance easily tips in favour of trying to keep an agricultural status, if you have one. Several people complain of having to change their status, because the village they live in is administratively redefined as urban area, as one interviewee tells:

> I have a rural household registration in Lujiang village. My sister already had her registration changed to an urban one against her own will. If you have a rural registration you enjoy the collective profit from the village and you get land to build a house.

Apart from the few privately owned houses, four out of five families in the researched neighbourhood still depend to a bigger or lesser degree on their work units for residence. Almost half are still in the traditional system, where they get allocated a flat from their work unit after application. Between the two extremes of the few totally privately owned dwellings and the many families still living within the traditional unit allocation system, we see three different transitional forms, each one connected to one special work unit, showing the limits within which the individual units can define their own policies: one is the three-thirds system touched upon earlier; a second is transition to private ownership within 15 years; and a third is a mixed, unclear ownership situation, of which one is stated as half and half ownership.

The three-thirds system is used in five cases, contradicting the claim that it was given up because it was too expensive for the work units. According to a Chinese source a circular was issued in 1985 calling for termination of experiments with the three-thirds system (Zhang 1993: 34) and the concept is not mentioned in the 1994 decision even though subsidised home purchase is still one of the core elements in the document. But in both surveyed sites the seven-three formula (work unit pays 70 per cent and the family pays 30 per cent) is used when explaining the conditions for buying houses. In Guangzhou especially many instances occur in 1995. There seems to be almost a standard price of 40,000 yuan for the employee part of the price of an apartment of around 70 square metres, giving a little more than 570 yuan per square metre. Other expenses average 150 yuan a month, which amount is often deducted from their salary by the work unit and the unit is still partly responsible for maintenance (some state also on a 7–3 basis). That means the work unit is still in charge of important resources connected with the housing situation.

The average rent – or expense on housing – for the interviewed families in Guangzhou is 215 yuan a month, equalling 16 per cent of stated income. This is a high percentage in relation to the traditional proportion of a few per cent and it is equal to the goal of the whole housing reform programme of rent being 15 per cent of income stated in the decision of 1994. But the proportion of rent to income is probably lower in reality than this picture as income is almost sure to be understated, while the rent expense is more probably not. In Guangzhou it seems the pure rent is often deducted from the salary. So an interviewed person is not necessarily aware of the amount of rent he or she pays.

A general impression from the two sets of interviews is that ownership rights and duties are in a state of flux as seen from the side of the family members. Other sources, e.g. more informal talks in other places, confirm that the housing reform and especially the issue of ownership rights is confusing and complicated (China Daily, 30 November 1998). Similar conditions – for instance buying a house at a subsidised price with the permission to sell after five years – is characterized respectively as individual ownership and work unit ownership by different people. In the interviews ownership is almost always mixed, apart from cases of inherited housing and separated into different kinds: the right to live in the place is the first acquired right; the right to sell to 'outsiders' is something other than the right to sell back to work unit or to work unit employees, and the right to sell is often restricted by time limits. Adding to the confusion is probably the fact that the work unit in some places seems to be rather involved in daily housing affairs of maintenance, payment of energy and the like, as discussed above. Thus, you can hear people say seemingly illogical sentences like: 'This house belongs to the Housing Bureau, we bought it last year'.

INTERNATIONAL AND NATIONAL LAW

Housing rights do not have an independent article in the IESCR but appear in article 11 (1) of the Covenant as part of an adequate standard of living.

> The States Parties to the present Covenant recognize the right of everyone to an adequate standard of living for himself and his family, including adequate food, clothing, and *housing*, and to the continuous improvement of living conditions. The States Parties will take appropriate steps to ensure the realisation of this right, recognizing to this effect the essential importance of international cooperation based on free consent. (Emphasis added)

The right to housing has received more attention from the international system than many other economic and social rights, partly because it is more regulated by national law in many countries, in some even a constitutional right (Craven 1995: 347) and is thus considered more directly justiciable. At the same time it is relatively easy to measure in physical and legal terms, like square metre per person, construction expenses in the national budget, regulations in relation to land use and distribution, building codes and property speculation. The Committee on Economic, Social and Cultural Rights published a General Comment, no. 4, on the right to adequate housing in 1991,[10] from which the following observations are seen to be relevant in the Chinese context:

Interpretation should not be in the narrow sense of having a roof over one's head, but rather in the comprehensive sense of 'the right to live somewhere in security, peace and dignity' (para. 7). Furthermore, it is stressed that the right to adequate housing cannot be isolated from other human rights, explicitly mentioning freedom of expression, association, residence and public participation as *indispensable* for realization and maintenance of adequate housing (para. 9).

Adequacy is, thus, a central concept. Acknowledging the influence of different social and climatic factors the Committee, nevertheless, identifies six aspects to be addressed in any particular context (para.

10. The right to adequate housing (Art. 11.1.): 13/12/91. CESCR General Comment 4.' Another General Comment from 1997, related to housing rights, addresses the problem of forced evictions. 'The right to adequate housing (Art. 11.1.): forced eviction: 20/05/97. CESCR General Comment 7.'

8). The house must be legally secured, material services shall be available, price be commensurate with income, adequate space and protection from natural elements be provided, access for vulnerable groups be guaranteed, location be within reach of employment opportunities and social services, and the building materials 'enable the expression of cultural identity' (Leckie 1991: 4–5).

State obligations are *not* to provide housing for everyone. Total direct government involvement is even discouraged, with the commentary that 'experience has shown the inability of Government to fully satisfy housing deficits with publicly built housing' (para.14). The right to housing may be satisfied through 'whatever mix of public and private sector considered appropriate' by the government. The role of the state is crucial, though, by on the one hand refraining from depriving people of the opportunity to find or keep a house, on the other hand by adopting a national strategy, and guaranteeing the most disadvantaged groups a reasonable shelter (Craven 1995: 333).

External factors affecting the ability of the state to improve or uphold living conditions are not viable grounds to free the government from its responsibility, and 'a general decline in living and housing conditions, directly attributable to policy and legislative decisions by States parties, and in the absence of accompanying compensatory measures, would be inconsistent with the obligations under the Covenant' (para. 12).

To sum up, the international provisions stipulate that the state is ultimately responsible for housing of its citizens, either by directly providing housing or by supporting private sector provision; by avoiding interfering in or blocking peoples' access to housing; and by taking specific measures to secure adequate dwellings for disadvantaged groups. As noticed before, the international regime is not concerned with the character of the economic system, i.e. whether public or private funding is dominant, though it tends to warn against direct state construction of all new housing. But it addresses the political context by declaring certain civil and political rights for indispensable to the full enjoyment of the right to housing.

In the Chinese Constitution of 1982, residence is only mentioned in article 39, stating that 'The home of citizens of the PRC is inviolable. Unlawful search in, or intrusion into, a citizen's home is prohibited'. In the Constitution of 1954, article 90 sounds 'Citizens of the PRC enjoy freedom of residence and freedom to change their residence', but this guarantee was taken out in the next version of the Constitution from 1975, following the fact that freedom of movement was severely restricted from 1958 and until the reforms began. And the right to freely change residence has not returned to the new Constitution of 1982. Even in 2000 moving around is still surrounded by cumbersome regulations, as was discussed in Chapter 4 in more detail. This means that the right to housing and free movement is not constitutionally codified, nor are these subject to a specific law. The area is regulated by directives and decisions from the NPC and the SC as well as local governments.

The shift in Chinese economic policy has forced a massive decline in direct state involvement in housing, which does not violate the ICESCR, as shown above, under the condition that remedial measures are taken (Craven 1995: 331). Urban housing is in a process of being commercialized and the former state monopoly has been dismantled. The changed conditions for acquiring a house must be said to be 'directly attributable' to policy decisions by the state and compensation is needed to live up to the international obligations (which is now legally binding for China with ratification of the Covenant). To solve the problems created by the perceived need for cutting state expenditure on housing, the Chinese government from the very beginning of the reform period began discussions and experiments on reforming the housing allocation system, which at that time was regulated by a monopolistic structure.

PRE-REFORM HOUSING ALLOCATION, 1949–1979

The socialist nationalization of the urban housing sector after the Communist victory in 1949 was a gradual process, mainly taking place after the establishment of public ownership over industry and commerce was completed in 1956. The following decade saw the transfer of private housing to public control, culminating in the abolition of landlord ownership and private ownership of urban land in 1967. Only a small number of private owner-occupied houses survived the massive expropriations during the Cultural Revolution at the end of the 1960s, amounting to an estimated 10 per cent of housing in China's largest cities being privately owned in the mid-1970s (Wang and Murie 1999: 86–88).

When the reforms began, most urban housing investment came from the state budget, and flats were distributed to families by the work units or housing bureaus belonging to local government. The budget of central government was the source of 95 per cent of housing construction at the end of the 1970s (Wang and Murie 1999: 105), but central state organs only directly controlled less than 25 per cent, the rest being distributed through and managed by work units (Lee 1995). Very little money was changing hands between the owners: work units or housing bureaus on the one hand and the resident on the other hand in the process of getting and maintaining a place to live. Rent was usually less than 2 per cent of individual income, maintenance was the responsibility of the owner and most often of very bad quality. Housing had become a welfare benefit paid by central government, administered by the work units and provided for employees almost for free.

The state was capable of covering nearly all expenses in the housing sector because of a correspondingly low wage level. Seen in another way, the state controlled the part of profit used for housing on behalf of the worker. In this area, as in many others, the alleged housing security was exchanged for freedom of choice and prioritization on the part of the individual. Families had a good chance of getting a shelter, but they were incapable of influencing what size, where and when.

Housing committees of the work units were in charge of distributing flats according to more or less open rules. Only permanent employees qualified for this so-called welfare housing (*fuli fenfang*); temporary workers had to find other ways of getting a flat. Distribution criteria varied from place to place and over time within the same unit, but it was always closely related to contribution to the work unit. As housing was scarce, it was used by work unit leaderships as a reward to high ranking or otherwise outstanding employees. So not only was it necessary to have a job to get a house at all, the quality of housing depended on relations with members of the work unit housing committee or other kinds of highly personalized factors.[11]

Criteria for allocation of a flat were typically a mixture of the following elements: first of all, one had to be married and it was a rule in most places that the work unit of the male would offer housing to a couple. A single person would not be able to get housing allocation but had to stay with parents or in dormitories at the work place. Secondly, position at the job and seniority counted; then that both husband and wife were employed by the unit; and finally present housing conditions consisting of number of family members and available space. Despite variations in the importance attached to the different 'assets', a pattern emerges where position very often ranked highest – cadres were served first – interchangeably with seniority. The mentioned criteria may not always have been the decisive ones, as the selection practices of the different housing committees were not transparent.[12] The demand for seniority places the relationship with the work unit, and thereby the contribution to production, as the most important asset. Many units counted only time working in the same enterprise as relevant for housing allocation, while others used a conversion figure, where work years in other units counted for less than one year. For instance, a conversion figure of 8:1 would mean that 8 years working in another place counted as 1 year in the new unit. In this way only little credit was given for work years not spent in the unit that now was to pay for the housing of the worker. The next important criterion seemed often to be that of the family having two jobs in the same work unit, sometimes referred to as an absolute criterion, while a third was position in the hierarchy of the enterprise. Some units

---

11. The working of the housing allocation system is not extensively researched in Western literature. The above interpretation is confirmed by other scholars (Walder 1986: 185; Bian 1997: 231) as well as a majority of the people interviewed in the present study. The details of the following description of the system are mostly based on information from the interviews in Xingtai and Guangzhou, supplemented by informal talks mostly in Northern China.
12. The interview material does not give examples of hidden criteriae, most likely because the majority of the interviewed were far removed from the process and only had vague ideas about the procedures in choosing among applicants for a dwelling. Other sources and anecdotal evidence indicate instances of the use of housing as bait for attracting persons with certain qualifications.

only allocated houses to families with at least two members employed and a cadre status was ostensibly very useful, too.

Each criterion gave a certain amount of points (*fen*); applicants queued up, those with most points got first choice. The allocation by a certain unit was performed in groups or rounds with intervals of often many years. Before an allocation round was going to take place a notice could be sent out informing about the conditions for applying. The housing committee had the decision-making power, its members often included Trade Union (*gonghui*) cadres or delegates to the Workers' Representative Meetings (*zhigong daibiao dahui*), and its rules were sanctioned by the Trade Union. In other places the decision of the Housing Committee had to get the approval of the Workers' Meetings or the local Trade Union. Some units were very strict on checking the information of the applicants and asked for a deposit, which would not be paid back if the applicant had submitted false information. This safety measure can be explained by fear of families getting housing allocated from more than one work unit, a misuse seen in some places,[13] aggravating existing housing shortage.

After allocation the family usually stayed in the flat and paid a very low rent and no maintenance fee, until natural growth demanded that somebody, typically grown-up children, moved out. A family very seldom gave up an allocated dwelling returning it to the work unit; some of its members would stay there, not necessarily those whose work unit affiliation provided the flat in the first place, so the place could be 'inherited' and even rented out . The arrangement thus had a private-ownership-like character. More recently, the right to buy a certain flat at a subsidised price, included in the reform programme, likewise belongs to those who live in it, no matter how they got it.

13. Personal information on this concerns one case in Beijing, where the head of the household is with the Foreign Ministry and the wife is employed in a big university. They have two flats allocated by their respective work units. They live in the big (Ministry) flat, and have a smaller flat at the University for the daughter to eat lunch and sleep, when she does not care to go home. This is not called 'illegal' by the informant, only something not everybody should know! See also the quote beginning this chapter.

In principle and official rhetoric, the above described system was designed as an egalitarian distribution mechanism based on the socialist principle 'to each according to need', though this never worked out in the pure sense. For one thing urban housing provision was in fact always linked to a position in the labour market in the sense that housing distribution presupposed job allocation. For another thing the distribution within the unit was not always shaped by need, but as we have seen, conducted according to rank and seniority.

In spite of the theoretical element of even distribution embedded in the old system, reality became an uneven distribution of housing between people in different kinds of work units and between people within the same unit (Bian 1997: 230–231). The high-status work units were for instance allowed to build higher buildings and provide more space per person than less centrally placed units. State owned enterprises could more easily than collective units provide housing to their employees (Chen 1998: 45–46). Cadres got flats before ordinary workers, and leading cadres got the best. Elements of the socialist egalitarian principle can be said to exist, as it was the duty of the state to allocate everyone a job or it was the right of every urban individual to get a job allocation from the state, and thereby to earn the right to housing by marriage. So different principles – to each according to need and to each depending on work contribution – were integrated, and the different rights were closely interlinked. In the egalitarian principle of a job for everyone was embedded the right to housing, which in practice became relative to a mixture of contribution and status because of an insufficient amount of square metres.

The Chinese debates on the issue and opinions from people after 1979 time and again repeat the defects of the pre-reform housing distribution system. The former welfare housing system is said to be both irrational and unfair. The irrationality of the ownership situation of most urban housing under the traditional work unit system was thus described in a Chinese report on social development:

> The present state-controlled housing system in China is an empty name, officially 3 billion square metres of housing is owned by the

> whole people, but they are scattered among all kinds of work units; ownership by work units is also empty, housing is paid, allocated and controlled by work units, but as soon as flats are distributed to the employees (citizens), the unit loses any right to them. Individuals have in name no rights, but in reality they have all rights, officially housing is public, but in reality the people can stay for an infinite period of time and even confer the house on their children. (Lu et al. 1997: 641)

In the course of bureaucratic allocation the economic dynamic of the housing sector disappears, because the link between housing space and costs for the end-user is severed. As the individual family experiences no connection between the square metres occupied and housing expenses, everyone will strive to get as much space as possible. Extra space does not cost extra for the residents, and the allocation of it can be sought by extra-monetary means like use of political power or job position. A World Bank study puts it this way: 'The link between the value that people place on housing, and the cost to the economy of China fails to be established' (World Bank 1991: 4).

Furthermore it is economically irrational, as it does not support the vitality of the financial institutions necessary to build and maintain investment in residential construction. Without the prospects of a reasonable profit, investors (be they state or non-state) will strive to minimize outlays, causing bad-quality building and poor maintenance (*Jingji cankao bao*, 22 April 1997). Addressing the social effect, the administrative distribution method is called unjust in the sense that it is not transparent, and it favours people with the right status and good connections. The unfairness is summed up in the words of one interviewee:

> Pooling money (*jizi*) to buy housing is a fine way, allocation of housing is not fair. The bureaucrats always get too much. When pooling is used, even the bureaucrats have to come up with some money.

The perceived unjust distribution mechanism as well as the widespread lack of housing space were blamed on welfare housing, which is the reason experiments with new mechanisms began early in the reform period, as shown above.

REFORM PROBLEMS

Discussions and criticism of the reforms are widespread in the media, though the new policies seem to be rather well received by the public, probably not least on account of the relatively free choice surrounding the implementation. The time span of trial and experimentation – 20 years – has been long, which also furthers the acceptance by the population at large. One problem with implementation of the reform scheme is that urban people are not used to thinking of housing as an investment object or a substantial expense due to the traditional work unit allocation system, so a change in attitude is constantly called for in official discussions on the subject. Citizens should develop the same psychological attachment to their homes as farmers have for the land: as basic security and an asset important for future survival (Lu et al. 1997: 634). The weakening of the old institutions of basic social security, especially for urban people, creates a need for a new safety net in the form of real estate, both materially and psychologically. This may be the reason for the strong political preference for an owner-occupied system instead of a rent system. It would have been simpler to raise the rent to cost price and let the original owners – the work units – continue with letting the flats to employees facing competition from commercial housing companies. But I have not seen official arguments for the choice of home-ownership instead of renting.

The most common complaint in the debate is the persisting inconsistency between prices and salary. To purchase a house is considered unreasonably costly for people not used to counting rent as any burden to family economy. But doubts are also expressed concerning the principle of preferential prices and the role of public funds.

One of the core problems has been the exact calculation of the price of a housing unit and the system for fixing the size of the subsidy. The 1988 decision stipulated different kinds of prices to be used when trading flats: 'Market price' (*shichang jia*) used in few cases where private housing companies sell to well-off families, like the Beijing example above. For work units sale of housing to employees the 'standard price' (*biaozhun jia*) or 'cost price' (*chengben jia*) was to be calculated on the basis of the actual costs (Lu et al. 1997: 658).[14] The difference between the market price and the various forms of 'artificial' prices is substantial. For 1997 a national average cost price of 600 yuan per square metre is to be compared to a market price of more than 1,000 yuan per square metre (Jiang 1998: 298). For comparison, the cost price in Beijing in 1997 was 1,450 yuan per square metre, while as much as 8,000 yuan per square metre is mentioned as market price (*Funü bao*, 9 October 1997: 2).

Time and again the fact is stressed in the media that still more new housing is being constructed in the old system than on market conditions. The work units still constructed their own housing and sold or rented them out or even allocated them in the old way up until 2000. The subsidized pricing and attached restrictions of ownership rights are seen as a continuation of the old – unfair – distribution mechanism. The policy is not fair and the methods are not 'scientific', with the typical Chinese equation of science and marketization. The point is that an 'artificial' market – in the Chinese literature often called a 'second' market – is created, where prices are fixed according to the buyer's ability to pay, not on the basis of supply and demand. The existence of the 'second market' hinders the vitality of the market, according to the critical voices, and the proposed solution is to promote a genuine market for housing (*Banyue tan*, no. 7, 1998: 12; *Jingji cankao bao*, 22 April 1997). The stumbling block, the 'unscientific element', is the still close correlation between position in the labour market and possibilities at the housing market. The work units are too deeply involved in the implementation of the new policies, and their activities are viewed with suspicion by some citizens, not only regarding the fairness in housing distribution, but also in management of what in reality can be seen as withheld salary in the housing funds.

The funds can be misused by work units with bad economic performance. An experience of some state and collective employees is that money disappears in the units without a trace. Bad manage-

14. The term low-interest price (*weili jia*) is also mentioned for the subsidised price. There is a slight difference between the calculation of the standard price and the cost price, which will not be dealt with here.

ment or direct fraud is not dealt with by legal authorities, so the popular trust in safe management of funds is weak (*Banyue tan*, no. 7, 1998: 18). Even when the funds are used for their purpose, bad management causes huge losses to home buyers, endangering popular support for private ownership of housing. In Shanghai cases of poor construction with shoddy materials have been reported more than once, dampening buyers' enthusiasm (*FEER*, 30 July 1998).

The usefulness of funds in speeding up the commercialization of housing is also contested. The capital actually accumulated in the funds is far from sufficient to reach its goals, as one calculation referred to in the 'Economic Reference Daily' points out: with the existing rate of 5 per cent of individual salary and 5 per cent of total wage sum going into the housing fund a work unit with 100 workers will need seven or eight years to be able to buy one flat! An additional problem is the principle of low interest connected with the funds, which means that to get the benefit people are forced to invest their savings in low-interest ventures, causing them economic losses. Another way proposed is to open a special housing bank operating on market conditions, i.e. charging higher interest, and therefore accumulating capital faster (*Jingji cankao bao*, 24 April 1997).

One radical solution to these problems could be just to transfer ownership rights to the residents. As recorded, this option has not been chosen by the authorities, presumably for fear of widespread dissatisfaction.

> This 'overnight privatisation' intensifies the inequality developed under the traditional housing allotment system, since urban residents who missed the opportunity to savor the provision of low-rent public housing will be even worse off for not being able to enjoy the one-time capital gain. (Chen 1998: 58)

Both state and people are aware of the debt owed after many years of capital accumulation at the expense of consumers. It seems that the recognition of this debt is prioritised higher than the establishment of more 'sound' economic mechanisms overnight.

The core of the reform under debate is a transition from welfare housing to commodified housing. The change is taking the form of a gradual process, where the two distribution mechanisms exist side by side, for example when a deposit can be required to get allocation of a flat, meaning money helps get a certain bureaucratic decision. Or when housing funds and pooling are instituted to relieve the burden of the state and families are motivated to support the reform process with their individual monetary contribution releasing a public allowance. The individual share is gradually increasing, as the public share is decreasing. The role of market mechanisms is introduced and strengthened as bureaucratic allocation is weakened; the role of the families is getting more important as state intervention declines. The transition from bureaucratic allocation to distribution via market mechanisms is, thus, a gradual process where the old system prevails for a certain period of time while the new is instituted.

As the administrative distribution to a large part rested in the work unit, one would presume to see a weakening of work unit power in the course of reform. But on the contrary, the transition seems – in the short run at least – to have strengthened the role of the work unit, which is a general observation by many different observers and not confined to the area of housing policy (Gaubatz 1995; Lü and Perry 1997; Sun 1996; Lai 2000).

The continuing dependence on the work unit in the process of housing reform is shown by the fact that former contribution to the work unit determines the amount of benefit anyone enjoys from the reform measures, supporting the principle of 'remuneration according to work'. Subsidized prices are attached to *seniority*, i.e. the years one has worked in the same unit add up to an 'asset' with a very concrete monetary form. Each year of employment has a certain value which the worker can profit from later on as money (in the form of subsidized goods) or as access to scarce resources (like square metres) or as property to transfer to children or other family members. Like money, the years of work can be used only once, but invested in real estate they become a lasting asset of the family. As the relation with the work unit in itself has become 'monetized', real money is also gradually being introduced between the family and the dwelling in the form of vouchers and contributions to public funds, so the possibilities of a certain worker are still, to a large degree, influenced by the social status of his or her work unit. Earlier inequalities, thus, persist to the degree that marketization is connected with the work unit.

As in the area of social security, the principle chosen to create a sustainable environment for fulfilment of housing needs is that of personal savings. The essence of home purchase via financial institutions is the gradual build-up of resources in the individual family, instead of in public authorities as under the old system. Ownership of a flat or a house will make people feel more secure in what they feel to be an unstable transformation process. The reform serves a double purpose by securing a basic feeling of safety among the population and supporting the accumulation of the necessary capital funds through individual and collective savings.

Housing reform has created a mixed picture with different structures coexisting, probably for a long time to come. True privatization is not around the corner. The market price of housing is still beyond reach of an average urban employee, though the expansion of the private sector naturally will create more and more incomes compatible with commercial housing. The different transition forms will automatically disappear as options, because preferential prices can only be used once. But it remains to be seen whether traces of them will persevere as a continued work unit involvement in designing housing solutions for employees.

The snapshot taken here of the housing reform shows a situation where the work unit is still active in the housing area, both as provider of welfare and as investor, in spite of the described efforts to reform the system, culminating in the decision published in March 1998 to abolish 'welfare housing'. The role as provider of welfare housing will probably be phased out, though it may take longer than envisaged. But the work unit as investor in housing is a long-term commitment that may run counter to the intention of separating worker and work place. As long as the work unit is an active investor in housing, special treatment of its own employees is likely and makes economic sense, both for the employer and the employee. But just as likely it will be difficult for the worker to carry this preferential treatment with her to another job; the old dependency persists and has reproduced itself in a way suited to the market but not encouraging the free movement of the labour force.

CONCLUSION: THE RIGHT TO HOUSING

The drive to marketize urban housing and shift the burden of housing expenses from the state or work unit to the family has been implemented through a variety of means, used at the same time or overlapping. Marketization meant trying to sell – and not allocate – new flats, and to sell existing flats to the people who already lived in them. The selling of public housing fulfilled two purposes; it helped accumulate capital for new investment and maintenance of existing constructions and it supported the ongoing separation of the worker from her or his workplace, being a vital rationale behind the whole reform programme.

The motivation to buy was created by a combination of stick and carrot. The stick was a gradual increase in the rent of public housing, while the carrot was a (gradually declining) subsidy of home purchase. The two methods depended on each other as the reform was build on a free choice on the part of the families, not on bureaucratic decree. As long as freedom of choice was upheld, the families would only buy if the transaction was economically profitable. Ideally a balance had to be obtained, where the price of buying was as near the future expected rent as possible without harming the income of the seller (the work unit or the state) unbearably. The de facto selling out of state assets had to yield a reasonable income if the reforms were to have any meaning at all. The pricing, naturally, was a key issue that came to create many problems in the process.

The policy of housing reform in China complies with some principles of international law and has problems with others. The drastic decline in housing provision on the part of the state is not in itself a violation of the Covenant, as governments do not have to shoulder housing construction. They only have to take remedial measures in case of policy changes that affect housing conditions, which is done through the different policy measures described in this chapter. The principle of progressive realization of the right to housing can be measured by statistics on square metres per person, which shows a doubling during the reform period. A pending problem is the three million families officially without an adequate roof over their heads. Besides, official statistics tend to under-represent the most needy groups, like migrants.

Not only a place to live, but the adequacy of it, has to be taken into account and certain aspects of this adequacy in China can be discussed: on affordability the discrepancy between income level and market price of housing is still very high. On legal security the concepts and understanding of ownership rights are still weakly ingrained and institutionalized. However, these aspects are likely to be addressed with the ongoing reforms, as establishment of financial institutions is already part of the programme and salaries generally are rising rapidly.

The most important challenge probably comes from the access of vulnerable groups to adequate housing. The growing inequality creates exclusion of certain groups, such as people outside the labour market or laid off people from state owned enterprises, migrants from the countryside and elderly people. Protection of social security, including affordable housing, is still very much linked to connection to the labour market, where competition gets more and more tough and squeezes people out. Projects providing cheap housing are remedies targeted at these groups, but it is difficult at the moment to assess how much these efforts have influenced the unequal distribution of housing. The protection of housing rights for the people in need is likely to be the most serious problem in relation to compliance with the international norms in the coming decades.

6 只能靠自己

Social Security

A salesman from Pacific Insurance often comes to see me to sell a pension insurance. He says they also have other laid off workers as customers. An insurance costs 100 yuan a month, more than 1,000 a year, where shall we get the money from? Think about in 10 or 20 years time, who knows what the situation will be? The salesman talks to me for half a day, saying in some years' time I will get 300 yuan a month. Now 300 yuan is some kind of money, but what will it be in the future? Now it will be enough for food, but can it solve the problem of eating in 20 years from now on?

Social security as a designation is part of a terminological complex pointing to the mechanisms of governments protecting people against risks in daily life. The different concepts and definitions used in this study are introduced in Chapter 3. Here will only be repeated one distinction between different forms of social security, that is, the distinction between on the one hand protection linked to a labour relation and thus depending on a previous contribution, and on the other hand support provided by society based on an assessment of a need that the person is unable to satisfy by her or his own means. Social security is achieved through different social policies where the labour related (or contributory) form is often associated with social insurance schemes, while the latter (benefit based) are obtained through establishment of public institutions that can assess need and distribute benefits. Both forms are backed juridically by laws and administrative redistributive mechanisms adopted by governments, and both these forms are used in the Chinese reform process.

In the Chinese Constitution of 1982 there is no single right to social security but article 43 covers workers' (*laodongzhe*) right to rest, article 44 guarantees workers (*zhigong*) and staff (*renyuan*) livelihood in retirement, while article 45 covers the right of citizens (*gongmin*) to 'material assistance from the state and society when they are old, ill or disabled'. So only a rather vague right to 'material assistance' (*wuzhi bangzhu*) is a right for every citizen. Health care and pension are only constitutional rights for the working part of the population. The right to social security for employees is, furthermore, clearly defined as a legal right in the Labour Law of 1994, according to which labourers shall enjoy social insurance benefits in cases of old-age, illness, work injury, unemployment, child birth or death of breadwinner (articles 70 to 76). The standards for social benefits shall be stipulated by laws, rules and regulations, which will appear in the following overview. The right to social protection for people outside the labour market is not regulated by law but only by Regulations and Decisions, like e.g. 'Regulations on Minimum Living Standards for Urban People' from 1999 and many others.

LOCAL IMPLEMENTATION

The laws and regulations of social security ostensibly did not have a substantial influence in the two researched communities. It proved difficult to make the work units participate in the insurance schemes and comply with their obligations. Enforcement problems consequently loomed large on the horizon of local authorities, and worsened due to the restricted economic leeway possessed by the enterprises, especially in Xingtai. Poor knowledge of the new schemes was also instrumental in curtailing their influence. People not knowing their rights or not believing they will be respected are not in a good position vis-a-vis civil servants and politicians sending them back and forth in the bureaucratic systems.

Xingtai, Hebei

In Xingtai a pension insurance system with social pooling funds based on different trades (light industry, mining, etc.) was established 'somewhat hastily' in the 1980s, while the individual accounts only were about to be introduced at the time of the investigation in late 1997. The size of an average pension is around 300 yuan a month. When reforms were initiated in the first place, work units were full of vitality but later the enterprises suffered losses and became unwilling to participate. In 1997 they had accumulated great debts to the social insurance agency that was established in 1986 to collect pension funds, and the local government budget had insufficient funding to compensate for the delayed contributions, even though they were legally obliged to cover up for arrears. In August 1997 the City Government invited all work unit managers to a social security meeting, caused by the fact that the the debt had reached 100 million yuan. As a result of the pressure at the meeting some of the units paid part (around 10 per cent) of their arrears. Other measures to force the units to pay their social security contributions were to distribute responsibility to the staff of the social security agency, so each person would be responsible for getting the contribution out of specific units. If they succeeded they would get a bonus, if they failed their salary would be cut.[1] Or the social security agencies could refuse to grant employees of non-complying work units permission for sick leave or early retirement, which the local government and not the work units has to pay. Sometimes an employee and a unit can agree to apply for sick leave even though the employee is not sick. This arrangement allows the worker to draw allowances from the social security agency, which lessens the burden on the work unit (and maybe enables the worker to earn money in private activities, supplementing his or her illness subsidy). The authorities would also decline the request of noncomplying enterprises to buy cars or to go abroad, measures that have been reported from other places, too (*Yiliao baoxian zhoukan*, 1 November 2001: 1).

The problem was both that the work units did not take the matter seriously, and that the social security agencies did not have administrative power and possibilities of sanctions, being non-profit

1. The method to implement policy by assigning quotas to individual civil servants is common in China, used e.g. also in population control and crime prevention. See also Corinna-Barbara Francis on the tendency for social entities to be held responsible by the state for the behaviour of their members (Francis 1996: 842).

units and not government organs. Some scholars contend that even government organs lack enforcement mechanisms because the system is not backed by law, but only by 'decisions' and 'regulations'.[2] More problems are awaiting, since the social agencies according to the new rules of 1999 have to forward or compensate the benefit directly to the person instead of paying to the work unit as before. Then there will be problems because when the system is more open, everybody will be able to find out that his or her account is 'empty'.[3]

Furthermore, the idea of individual accounts is new and sufficient information to citizens has not been disseminated, as explained by a staff member of the City Labour Bureau:

> Each year a list of the individual accounts will be made, and it will be adjusted four times a year, employees should pay attention to that. Today most workers do not even know they have an account, only when they are moved to another job or when they retire, they find out about it.

This understanding is confirmed by the family interviews, where most respondents knew nothing about any pension scheme, and if they knew something it was vaguely formulated and the family did not know the percentage, where to get information or who in fact was covered. Only one in five of the interviewed had actually seen the book where their contributions were recorded, and most did not have confidence in the system because they suspected the work unit did not pay its due into the fund. As a worker in a coal pit formulated it:

> The work unit takes part in a pension scheme; they deduct five per cent from our salary and pay it to the Labour Bureau. Or at least they did when they were paying salary. Now I am not quite sure about it, I think they stopped paying. We have no personal account, nobody has any money, it is the same for all of us. The Workers' Representative Meetings are held every year, but they will not discuss these matters. The management decides what to discuss and that is all.

For health care, the basic rule was in conformity with the national rule that temporary workers were not covered at all, while the wel-

---

2. Interview at Institute of Sociology, People's University, Beijing, November 1997.
3. Interview with Xingtai City Government, November 1997.

fare of contract workers was the responsibility of the work unit. School children were usually covered by the insurance of the school. Enterprises run by villages (*cunban qiye*) did not cover health care, only work injury. But as there were not many examples in the material, it is difficult to say whether rules vary between different villages.

The traditional system with 100 per cent reimbursement of medical primary care costs from the work units stopped in Xingtai at different times in the different units, ranging from 1991 to 1997. It was replaced by the introduction of a ceiling on how much the work unit would reimburse, usually ranging from 8 to 15 yuan a month, or between 100 and 200 a year.[4] The figure depended on seniority. By showing receipts the workers could get refunded up to that amount. If their expenses were higher they had to pay themselves, if they were lower they should in principle be given back the difference, which seems to have happened rarely. Some also had an upper limit of 3,000 yuan, over which they would be reimbursed with 80 or 90 per cent. Almost half of the families reported to have been enrolled in that system. Visits to work unit clinics or hospitals were free of charge and not related to the ceiling on reimbursement.

For hospitalization outside the work unit, refunding also depended upon seniority, one example given that persons with 8 years of seniority were refunded 30 per cent; with 14 years 50 per cent; and with 20 years 90 per cent; and the hospital had to be chosen by the work unit. It was a common understanding (or complaint) that cadres were reimbursed 100 per cent and retired cadres were given nurses for free, but as few of the respondents were cadres this was difficult to verify. The Serious Illness Scheme was mentioned by a minority as something they had heard about, but none had actually benefited from it, and the Combination System was not mentioned as a health care insurance, but by one-third of the interviewees as a new measure of pension insurance.

4. There seems to be (at least!) two ways to practice a small monthly subsidy ear-marked for health expenses. One is the way described above appearing in some of the interviews; another, described by Linda Wong is just a part of the paid salary, which can be pocketed and used for other purposes if medical treatment is not needed (Wong 2001: 44). It seems some of the interviewees also are under that kind of system.

We here see the problem of low coverage through the ceiling on reimbursement, and benefits were also clearly unequally distributed because of the close relation to seniority. But the biggest problem was that as enterprises were getting less and less profit even this reimbursement tended to disappear, so an employee in a loss-making enterprise (whether formally laid off or not) would most often not have any coverage of health care expenses at all. The many different forms of relationship with a work place that emerged during the reform process could also affect health care protection. By placing people in certain categories, the leadership could reduce their expenses.[5] Internal retirement (*neitui*) was granted instead of sick retirement (*bing tui*) or a regular pension, because the first category does not formally guarantee a benefit graded after seniority, like the last two categories do. For an internal retiree the work unit has less formal obligations and in reality they only pay when they have money.[6] A 51-year-old man had permanent work-related health problems, but found it impossible to get a sickness pension because it was more expensive for the factory. He was designated internally retired and would be so until they had to give him a pension certificate at the age of 60.

For the groups hardest hit by the economic recession, the City Labour Bureau in 1994 established a temporary organ to manage people with 'difficulties' (*jiekun*). The targets were defined as employees who for six months in a row had had an income of less than 210 yuan a month; laid off people with less than 157 yuan a month; and 'special households' with less than 80 yuan a month. Funding of 1 million yuan was set aside from the local budget to cover the expenses. The people to be helped were chosen by the Trade Union from 50 poor work units in the city. These were given a 'poverty card' (*tekun zheng*) promising preferential prices on daily necessities like coal and cabbage up to a certain amount, e.g. 50 pounds of white cabbage, exemption from certain school fees, etc. Private

5. According to Ikels's study, bureaucratic categorization can also be used the other way around; to keep a worker the unit can or will not do without (Ikels 1996: 215).
6. For an overview of the different forms see Chapter 4.

companies were also urged to give donations to the fund. The system with poverty cards is not to be confused with the minimum living standard (MLS), which was 120 yuan per person per month in Xingtai. This allowance is administered by the Neighbourhood Committee, funded by the Civil Affairs Department and is not related to the labour market.

Below the City Government, the Street Office, which is the lowest extension of the state apparatus, can perform a coordinating and monitoring role between state and citizens. It can also identify people eligible for a 'poverty card', and a staff member reported that since 1992 the number of poor families as defined by the Labour Bureau had risen from 4 to 116. After being identified, the poor families have to go through their work units, or, if they do not have any, the Neighbourhood Committee, to arrange the formalities. The Street Office does not have many economic resources of its own, but it can make assessments and provide a link between the state administration and the Neighbourhood Committee, which last unit is closest to the everyday life of the people.

Guangzhou

The local government in Guangzhou city had since 1983 been engaged in different forms of social security reform beginning as a first step with collection of pension funds at the level of the city and gradually expanding as a second step into the areas of unemployment and occupational injury, to be followed by health and maternity care. In June 1993 a 'Decision on Social Insurance for Employees in Guangzhou City' and other specialized provisions were promulgated, summing up experiences of the previous years (*Guangzhou shi tigaiwei* 1994: 30). Social pooling funds had been one of the key elements since the beginning but individual accounts had not yet reached the area at the time of investigation. In the middle of the 1990s the local government received a proposal from the State Council on establishing the system with combining social pooling funds and individual accounts for health care, and the Guangzhou Academy for Social Sciences was asked to prepare the details.[7] So naturally none of the respondents mentioned individual accounts. Some general principles resembled the Xingtai rules, such as that children were insured for health hazards through their schools and that temporary workers were not covered by any social security schemes at all. The minimum living standard in Guangzhou was 288 yuan a month (compared to the 120 yuan a month in Xingtai), eligible were only persons with no family. The money were granted through the Neighbourhood Committee.

Most of the respondents in the Xinjiao Neighbourhood had a stable relation with a state owned unit, meaning that their coverage was relatively high, the most commonly used arrangement for health care being that the work unit paid (or refunded) 80 per cent of documented health care expenses and the families paid the rest themselves. Attached was a ceiling, so expenses above a certain amount would be covered with a certain percentage, e.g. the work unit paid 80 per cent of expenses upon presentation of a receipt, up to 500 yuan a year, while costs over 500 yuan were refunded 100 per cent. The ceilings differed a great deal among the work units, from 500 to 4,000 a year, and the proportions of reimbursement above the ceiling ranged from 45 per cent to 100 per cent. Hospital stays were covered by specific rules; the work unit would pay from 80 per cent to 100 per cent given that they agreed to the proposed treatment and a hospital designated by them was used, a rule that could impede the usefulness of the benefit.

> My mother had to go to the hospital and it cost 50,000 yuan, but the work unit would only refund 1,000, because they did not agree to the treatment. And to get the 1,000 yuan was very troublesome with all kinds of procedures and negotiations.

7. Interview with Guangzhou Academy of Social Sciences, October 1997. The city caught up quickly. In September 2000 it is reported that in the whole of Guangzhou City, 93 per cent of urban workers participate in the pension scheme, 94 per cent in unemployment insurance, 91 per cent in occupational injury and maternity leave insurance, and the city is the first in the country to reach the goal of pension payment 100 per cent on time (*Yangcheng wanbao*, 9 December 2000). Note that the percentages designate the people formally participating; if a unit in reality is not paying its contribution it would not be visible in these figures.

For pensions the most typical system was 50 per cent from the employer and 50 per cent from the employee, each month an equal amount was paid by the work unit and deducted from the individual salary. Figures like 40 or 50 yuan are mentioned as the total contributions. Pensions were generally higher – 700 to 800 yuan – than in Xingtai, reflecting the different economic levels of the two places.[8]

The interviewed persons lacked confidence in commercial insurance so only a few had bought any. One person is very blunt on the matter:

> Nobody believes in them. They can close down, like banks can go bankrupt. Many people have tried that. We do not believe in them.

The general attitude was that social security is more or less a personal matter. It is better to rely on oneself (*kao ziji*) or friends and family, and the knowledge about the entitlements and the new systems under way was very small.

> I have health insurance but I do not really understand how expenses are covered. This is a question of management policy. We ordinary people have no possibility of understanding it, and if we understand it we cannot change it. But I think the work units should not deduct from our salary without our permission, as they do now.

One important difference between the two places investigated was that missing payments and arrears were not considered serious issues in Guangzhou, probably because the general economic development of the whole city was much more dynamic. This clearly affects social policy, as people generally were better off and better able to support themselves. Loss-making enterprises were not mentioned, and people from outside being hired to work in factories were not seen as unfair competition,[9] as their salaries were way below the permanent residents. The presence of the migrants was only questioned as a matter of safety, where they were mentioned in connection with general and vague perceptions of rising crime rates and moral decay.

---

8. As seen in Chapter 4 the average income pr. family in Xingtai was 700 yuan and in Xinjiao it was 1,300 yuan a month.
9. Note that the number of inhabitants in the Xinjiao Neighbourhood as 1,437 permanent residents to about 20,000 migrants.

OUTLINE OF NATIONAL REFORM

The system of social security in China before 1979 has been described in Chapter 1 and shall not be repeated here. In the following will be given an overview of the post-1980 reform of social security generally, followed by a special treatment of health care and pensions, which have been singled out for study among the items traditionally considered parts of social security. Health and pension insurance are the really costly and vital welfare programs everywhere, so the existence and character of these are crucial in understanding and evaluating the protection of social rights in any country (Hort and Kuhnle 2000: 80).

As in other areas social security reform was carried out in a gradual and exploratory manner. It was rather late in coming on a substantial scale, until the early 1990s the work-unit-based welfare system was still basically intact; new schemes began to take real effect only from 1995. The economic reform programme formally entered the cities from the countryside with the 'Decision of Economic System Reform' from the 12th Central Committees 3rd Plenary Session in October 1984, when the self-sufficiency or economic independence of work units became one of the most important political goals. A consequence was the important State Council provisions of 1986 (*GWYGB*, 10 October 1986: 739–750), meant to make enterprises responsible for their own profits and losses (*zifu yingkui*), among other things by forbidding life-long employment and allowing work units to fire superfluous workers. The regulations paved the way for – or rather necessitated – the establishment of mechanisms of social protection outside the work units and addressed the issue of unemployment that was an unavoidable consequence of making enterprises profitable. But in spite of the Bankruptcy Law from the same year, which in theory made it possible to close loss making units, the obligations of social provision continued to rest with the work units. The right to fire superfluous workers was restricted by continued insistence in rules and regulations that responsibility for basic subsistence for employees still belonged to the work units, even those that were on the verge of bankruptcy (*GWYGB*, 27 December 1993: 1278–1280). It was considered too early to really meet the challenge of throwing industry into the market.

From 1984 onwards scattered experiments with diversification of social services began with pension pilot schemes in urban areas, but they were kept within the overall division between urbanites and farmers and between people with or without a job. The traditional watertight division between the different kinds of citizens persisted and social protection was kept divided between two different administrative systems, the Ministry of Labour and the Ministry of Civil Affairs. The system treated in detail below was developed from the former *laobao* system, managed by the Ministry of Labour (in 1998 to be renamed the Ministry of Labour and Social Security) and designed for people having an affiliation with a work unit, as already described. Other groups – marginalized people both in the cities and in the countryside – remained under the authority of the Ministry of Civil Affairs, with a different tradition of social protection, which instituted other forms of social assistance, poverty and catastrophe relief, as well as community services during the same period. For an overview, see Chart 6.1.

The reforms of the Ministry of Labour were authorized by the State Council and conducted in collaboration with other relevant institutions, like the System Reform Commission, the Planning Commission, the Ministry of Health, etc. Health care, pension and unemployment had high priority and each area underwent separate experimentations. Other items, like maternity care and work injury, were included in the trials in some places, not in others. However, the reform efforts in the different areas were based on the same fundamental principles. The transition mechanisms were designed to address the most important problems of the old system: one was the strong link between enterprises and workers, restricting the latter's mobility. In the traditional system, where social benefits were paid by the work unit, shifting job was a complicated process as there were no established procedures to transfer the money for social benefits 'belonging' to an employee from one unit to another. Another problem was a drastic increase in expenses. Concerning old-age care, an ageing work force raised the expenses of pensions rapidly. Concerning health care, there was no real incentive for either work units or medical institutions to curb expenses as overspending by enterprises and institutions in a planned economy is covered by the state budget. A third problem was the narrow coverage and the unfair distribution of social services. Apart from being economically unsustainable, the inequality of the system was stressed by scholars and politicians as a reason for change. The former socialist type of protection was not only too costly, it was also unfair.

The aims of reform were accordingly to raise the level of redistribution from work units to local government in order to facilitate the mobility of workers, to guarantee basic coverage to more people by distributing risks among employers and employees – the move towards welfare pluralism – and to keep expenses within state capacity by controlling the heavenward flight of expenses and outlays (Hu Xiaoyi 1998: 33). To further these ends, it was contended by both scholars and politicians that the PAYG principle had to be replaced by a savings system and that responsibility had to be diversified to more actors. Out of the experimentation process a system for employees gradually grew based on the following characteristics:

1. Low level. One basic ambition expressed was that benefits granted to workers had to be in conformity with the development of the economy,[10] meaning that a basic low protection, equal for all, should be compulsory and backed by law. Further protection had to be obtained from commercial insurances on a private or collective (in practice mostly work unit) basis.

2. Broader coverage. The group of beneficiaries should be enlarged to cover all workers, permanent as well as temporary, in productive state and collective enterprises and administrative organs, and the scope should gradually be broadened to include all urban employees, e.g. also workers in private industries, non-profit and social organizations and foreign funded enterprises.

3. Shared burden. Work units and workers should contribute jointly by paying a certain per cent of salary into a social pooling fund at the level of local government that in turn contributed with management funds and tax exemptions.

10. This aim is given legal value in article 71 of the Labour Law: 'The level of social insurance shall be in proportion to the level of social and economic development and social affordability.'

4. Combination of collective and individual provision. Basic coverage should come from two sources: a social pooling fund and an individual account. The individual contribution goes into the individual account while the enterprise contribution is divided between the individual accounts and a social pooling fund. Funds should be distributed from both sources after certain criteria worked out during the trial period.

As an example of the experiments could be mentioned those in Shenzhen, a totally new town, developed since 1979 from a sleeping fishing village with 30,000 inhabitants to a modern city with a population of over 3 million[11] and an average annual growth rate of 35 per cent. Already from the beginning of the 1980s the Shenzhen government had introduced a free labour market, pension funds, work injury and unemployment insurance, and in August 1992 the different elements of social protection were integrated into a unified insurance system with five components: pension, work injury, unemployment, housing and health insurance. Special committees were set up at the level of the City Government to oversee the transition process and guarantee the sound management of funds, sourced from employers and employees and supported by tax exemption from the government. Payment from each worker and from the work unit were via the latter, transferred partly to two social pooling funds and partly to personal accounts for each worker. A Health Insurance Fund managed health care and a Social Insurance Fund was responsible for pensions, housing and work injury compensation programmes. Coverage was not total for all items: the health insurance part of the system applied to all permanent, contract and temporary workers employed in Shenzhen, the retirement scheme covered permanent staff in enterprises and temporary workers in other units, while housing only covered people with a permanent household registration (Wong and Lee 1996: 220).

With the Shenzhen trials and a similar pilot scheme on pensions in Shanghai in 1993, the system with a 'Combination of Social Pooling Funds and Individual Accounts' was born[12], and it was el-

11. 1 million registered and 2 million transients in 1994 (Wong and Lee 1996: 210).
12. The systems were inspired by Chilean pension reforms.

evated as a cornerstone of official policy in the decision from the 3rd Plenary Session of the 14th Central Committee in November 1993 (*BR*, vol. 36, no. 47 1993: 23). And throughout the 1990s experiments continued in cities and localities, initiated and evaluated by the relevant ministries and commissions. Experiences from trials gave input to new experiments, the whole process resulting in broad national policy frameworks concerning pensions, health care and unemployment insurance to be adopted in 1997, 1998 and 1999 respectively. For support and further implementation, regulations on administration of social security funds were promulgated in the beginning of 1999 after previous preliminary proposals (*ZRGLSBFQ* 1999: 387–392; 395–398).

However, all problems had not been solved with adoption of nationwide systems; implementation takes time and creates problems of its own. In Shenzhen joint ventures and privately owned companies refused to obey the regulations, and many work units continued working as before. In Guangzhou only one-third of the enterprises payed their due to the social security agencies in 1998.[13] As we shall see later, health care is by far the most difficult item as it involves the vested interests of many different institutions and groups of people (World Bank 1997: 56). A more detailed overview of the content of the new health care and pension schemes will be given below, after a survey of where urban people without a job can go in case of insurmountable social problems.

For social protection of people not affiliated with the labour market an important development was the establishment of minimum living standards (MLS) (*zuidi shenghuo baozhang xian*), giving local government a legal responsibility towards basic livelihood guarantees to urban people. However, the obligation was restricted to the so-called 'three no' people, that is people with no children or other close relatives, with no working ability and with no other source of income. Shanghai made the first trials in 1993, stipulating a minimum income level of 120 yuan a month, under which people would be given social relief (*jiuji*). The State Council published a circular in 1997 setting time limits for the local govern-

13. Interview at Guangzhou Academy of Social Sciences, 21 May 1998.

ments to establish schemes for minimum living standards, followed by a circular from the Ministry of Civil Affairs in the beginning of 1999 formalized in State Council Regulations (the most authoritative document before an actual law is passed) in October the same year. At that time all urban areas had a system in place, but the minimum standard was low, varying from 91 yuan a month in Dexing in Jiangxi Province to 280 in Beijing (Lin Lihong et al. 2001).[14]

The MLS rules are that if the average per capita monthly income in the family is lower than the limit, the family can apply for help from the local Civil Affairs Bureau and will get a minimum living standard card (*zuidi shenghuo baozhang jin lingqu ka*). The application goes through the Neighbourhood Committee of the family and the Committee has the duty to supervise that the family is entitled to the subsidy. Every half year the application will be re-considered. The support is most often in the form of a monthly cash subsidy, providing the difference between the family income and the minimum standard. Besides, some localities – especially more wealthy ones – provide goods for free or at deducted prices, and offer subsidized medical services and schooling.

The minimum standard is appraised as being barely enough to survive on but surely insufficient to meet any special social event which this group of people is more likely to meet than the average population. Local government can have a tendency to decide the amount of the subsidy more with an eye to its own financial capacity than to living expenses in the specific environment.[15] According to a white-paper on Labour and Social Security issued by the Ministry of Foreign Affairs, 12 million people were drawing the mini-

14. Starting from 1 July 2002, the local governments in 36 cities have readjusted their minimum living standards. E.g. Shenzhen is the highest between 290 and 344 yuan, Nanchang (capital of Jiangxi Province) with 143 yuan is the lowest. Other cities include: Beijing 290 yuan; Shanghai 280 yuan; Tianjin 241 yuan; Chongqing 185 yuan; Guangzhou 300 yuan (Beijing Youth Daily, 7 July 2002, p.6).
15. Personal communication contradicting the official explanation that 'Funds for this purpose are included in the fiscal budgets of the local people's governments, which determine the minimum living standard according to the cost necessary for maintaining the basic livelihood of the local urbanites' (Ministry of Foreign Affairs 2002: 12).

mum living subsidy in 2001. The use of the programme has expanded considerably during the foregoing half decade as only 850,000 people are reported as recipients in 1995; from 1999 to 2000 alone the proportion of people under this scheme in relation to all persons covered by MOCA rose from 10 per cent to 57 per cent (*ZMTN* 2001: 99 and 102). However, more people are thought to be entitled to the subsidy than actually get it. According to estimates from academics, around 30 million meet the qualifications and even MOCA itself, as result of a survey, found that 19 million people were entitled to get it.[16] Lack of information, low administrative capacity in the localities and traditional ideas stigmatizing receivers of social assistance are given as reasons for people being hesitant to use the system (Lin Lihong et al. 2001: 38).

Another support available to every urban citizen with an urban household registration is community services, a new and much publicized concept by the Central Government since 1986 (C. L. W. Chan 1993). The propaganda for this concept does not really match the resources allocated to implementation of the idea. A community (*shequ*) is a geographical designation sometimes covering the area of a street office or a neighbourhood committee, sometimes not. In big and affluent cities like Beijing, Shanghai and Nanjing, this unit organizes volunteers to help elderly people with daily necessities, takes care of young children after school, establishes centres with recreational or informative functions, like computer rooms for job searching, and runs evening schools or similar low budget support for local residents. The service can be given on an exchange basis, i.e. a person provides free service and then receives free service back when in need. The service given is recorded by the Neighbourhood Committee on an hourly basis. Funding comes from taxation of activities within the community or sometimes from small allocations from the higher administrative level, usually the district. Linda Wong views the system as a form of privatization or at least non-state (Wong 1998: 45, 73–74), which latter designation is formally correct in as much as the community is situated below the lowest level in the state apparatus – the city district

16. Talk by Prof. Zhou Hanhua, August 2002.

– but to call it privatization grates a bit on the ear. On the one hand the Street Offices have direct links to government administration and receive some funds from the district level, on the other hand their leadership are chosen by the residents themselves and they can 'encourage' businesses to donate funds they then will administer on behalf of the community. So if/when the community assumes duties from the state level, 'collectivization' might be a more precise term. Commercialization of community services has been debated during the 1990s as neighbourhoods are more interested in running these types of services on a profit basis, but then they are not helpful to the really needy poor people (Wong and Flynn 2001: 54). To (re)vitalize community health care services, especially in poor urban neighbourhoods, is in perfect accordance with recommendations from the World Bank, among other things in order to downsize the tendency in the Chinese health care practice of visiting the more expensive hospitals instead of the cheaper clinics (World Bank 1997a: 39).

The system also seems to be meant to foster a feeling of citizenship or fellowship within the residential areas. At a conference in Nanjing in 1999 this trend was manifest in a video shown, where well-clad happy youngsters sang the special song made for this community and smiling elderly people were shown exercising together to the tunes of martial music. The aim seemed to be to instil a feeling of togetherness and belonging from above, maybe in recognition of the low esteem held of Communist Party committees in many places.[17]

An overview of the relative weight of the two different systems is given in Chart 6.1, using the number of people covered as a yardstick. Note that while this shows formal protection under existing schemes, it does not necessarily address real needs. Many more people may need social support, but their numbers will be very difficult to estimate.

17. Personal experience, June 1999.

Chart 6.1 Insured or receiving social relief in urban China, 2000

Total population 1.265 billion people, of these 458 million (36 %) living in towns and 807 million (64 %) living in the countryside (*ZMTN* 2001: 82).
Unit: persons

Kind of Protection \ Provider system	Ministry of Labour and Social Security	Ministry of Civil Affairs
Pension insurance (*yanglao baoxian*)	104 mill contributors plus 32 mill retirees (*ZLTN* 2001: 438)	230,000 (primarily military personnel) (*ZMTN* 2001: 83)
Labour health insurance (*qiye danwei laobao yiliao*)	129 mill (1999) covered (*ZLTN* 2001: 483)	
Basic medical insurance (*jiben yiliao baoxian*)	18 mill contributors plus 5 mill retirees (*CSISY*, 2001: 65)	
Serious illness scheme (*dabing tongchou*)	10 mill contributors plus 4 mill retirees (*CSISY*, 2001: 65)	
Work injury (*gong-shang*)	44 mill (*ZLTN* 2001: 444)	
Unemployment (*shiye*)	103 mill (*ZLTN* 2001: 442)	
Maternity (*shengyu*)	30 mill (*ZLTN* 2001: 444)	
Laid off (*BLS*) (xia-gang)	9 mill (*ZLTN* 2001: 401)	
Social relief (*jiuji*)		59 mill (*ZMTN* 2001: 83)
MLS (*zuidi sheng-huo baozhang*)		11 mill (*MOFA* 2002) 4 mill (*ZMTN* 2001: 85)
Community service centres (*shequ fuwu zhongxin*)		14 mill (*ZMTN* 2001: 155) 12,674 centres (*ZMTN* 2001: 89)
Welfare lottery (*fuli caipiao*)		1253 agencies spent 3.6 billion yuan (*ZMTN* 2001: 265)
Charity (*cishan*)		110 agencies spent 419 mill yuan (*ZMTN* 2001: 267)

Health care

In 1997 the total expenses on public health reached 77 billion yuan, constituting an increase of 28 times in relation to 1978. On average, annual growth was 19 per cent, to be compared with a GDP growth rate of 9.7 per cent. Another calculation shows that average pr. capita income rose by 6.5 per cent from 1992 to 1997, while the average cost of a visit to a clinic or stay in a hospital rose by 10 and 14 per cent respectively (Bloom et al. 2001). Comparing the figures with pre-reform statistics is difficult, as these are full of problems, making it difficult to estimate the actual expenses on health care (Wong 1998: 59). But there is no doubt that expenses went out of control and rationalising the whole system became a high political priority from the 15th Party Congress in 1997, where reform of the state-owned sector was put at the top of the agenda of the government.

In 1989 sites for trials on new mechanisms for collecting funds and for paying and administering health care services were selected, but the experiments were restricted to controlling expenses and they never became effective. A more comprehensive effort did not begin until 1992 when the Commission for Economic System Reform was put in charge of a Health Insurance Reform Small Group, created to oversee, coordinate and not least design policies for reform. The group included members from all possible stakeholders, ministries as well as financial institutions and other parties (*GWYGB*, no.13, 1992: 456).[18]

Two approaches were tried out together, separately, and mixed until the nationwide system was approved in December 1998. One approach was the Combination System, mentioned above, based on the principle of joint contributions by employers and employees and a combination of redistribution via social pooling funds and savings in individual accounts. The other approach was based on the idea that serious health situations should be separated from more everyday events and the two should be treated via different

18. Stakeholders were besides Economic System Reform Commission, Ministry of Health, Labour, Internal Affairs and Finance, the Pharmaceutical Drug Bureau, the Price Bureau and the Trade Union.

mechanisms, so a 'Serious Illness Scheme' (*dabing tongchou*) was established covering high health costs.

Experiments with social pooling funds and individual accounts were done in Zhenjiang in Jiangsu province and Zhujiang in Jiangxi province from 1994 (later to be called the 'two Jiangs' model') and the following year spread to cover 57 other cities. The concrete mechanisms differed in the different places. Some cities began enrolling only some kinds of work units, others made participation voluntary; the percentages of contributions varied and the compliance rate was very uneven. But all measures were kept within the overall principles of tripartite sourcing – contributions from employers and employees and administration expenses and tax exemption from the local government – and a combination of social pooling funds and individual accounts. In 1998 a total of 100 million were participating in one or another version of the Combination System (Hu Xiaoyi 1998: 38).

At the same time other localities – among them Chengdu and Beijing – experimented with taking serious illnesses out and creating a fund to cover these, also with contributions from both employer and employee, 6 per cent and 1 per cent respectively. The scheme for serious illnesses was meant to cover expenses above a certain amount. Serious illness was defined according to kinds of illness and/or level of expenses. The higher the expenses, the higher proportion was reimbursed. Expenses under 1,000 yuan were reimbursed with 80 per cent, above 3,000 yuan were reimbursed with 95 per cent, and in between a gradual increase. Chengdu in Sichuan province began trials in 1989, a circular was issued by the Ministry of Labour in 1992, followed by Beijing in 1995, Shanghai in 1996 and subsequently many other places. In 1997, 14 million workers and retirees were participating in similar schemes. As with the Combination System, different versions were tried out. There exists a Beijing, a Chengdu and a Shanghai model, differing in number and kind of beneficiaries, in percentages of contributions and limits of coverage as well as administrative responsibility. But the special trait in all was the limitation to certain kinds of illnesses and that individual accounts were not involved.

Based on experiences from these trial reforms, a national compulsory system of health care insurance was proposed with a State Council decision of December 1998. According to the decision during the year of 1999 a basic health care insurance system should be set up at district (*xingzheng qu*) or city (*shi*) level in all provinces with the participation of all work units – state, collective, foreign funded or private, as well as state organizations, public service units, social (i.e. non-state) and non-profit organizations and their employees. Provincial governments were free to include rural enterprises as well. In order to protect the economic vitality of the enterprises there were ceilings on the size of contributions. Work units should contribute no more than 6 per cent of total salary bill and individual workers' salary should be deducted with 2 per cent to be paid into the agencies. The relation between the two contributions and the combined rate could be raised gradually in line with economic development and advance in medical technology. The 2 per cent employees' part should go directly into the individual accounts while the work unit part was divided with 70 per cent going into a social pooling fund, paying for expenses in relation to hospitalization, and the remaining 30 per cent being put into the individual accounts, used to pay for medicine and visits to doctors. The employee gets a card where the movements on the individual account are recorded. The two parts, social pooling fund and individual savings, should be strictly separated and it is not permitted to transfer funds from one to the other. The individual account is personal property that can be paid out as a lump sum or inherited

Chart 6.2 Collection and distribution of health care benefits

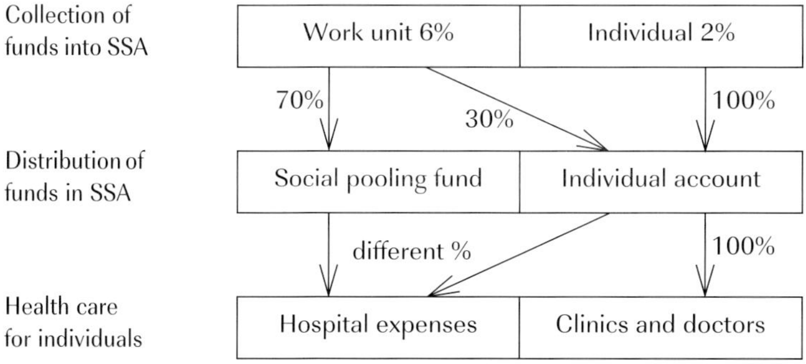

in case of death of the employee. Note that of all people covered by health care in urban China only a small minority (15 per cent) participated in this scheme as of 2000 (see Chart 6.1).

According to the version used in the two Jiangs' model, the social pooling fund is to be used in some special circumstances if the individual account is exhausted. Within the fund two levels are set. A lower level (*qifu biaozhun*) at 10 per cent of average local wage and an upper limit (*zuigao zhifu xian'e*) of 4 times average local wage. Expenses up to the lower limit are covered by the individual account or by the person him- or herself, expenses between the lower and the upper limit are mainly paid by the social pooling fund with a certain percentage of individual contribution, and above the upper limit expenses are paid again by the individual account/person or by commercial insurance, if the person has one. So the individual account or the person's own pocket has to pay for everything up to the lower limit, for the individual percentage between the two limits and for everything above the upper limit.

An example: with a local average monthly income of 800 yuan (i.e. 9,600 annually) the low level will be 960 yuan a year, while the upper level will be 38,400 yuan. The individual account of an average employee will be accumulating 32 yuan a month (2 per cent from the employee and almost 2 per cent from the employer) or 384 for one year. Prices of health services are not low, estimates stating that in 2000 one visit to a clinic on average cost 79 yuan and a stay in hospital almost 3,000 yuan (Zuo and Hu 2001: 103–104). In the new system health expenses can be a burden to workers, especially those with chronic diseases, and to retirees who normally have more health problems than younger people. As for some chronic ailments, specific costs may be covered by the social pooling funds depending on the local situation.

The purpose of the limits inbuilt in the social pooling funds is said to be to raise people's awareness of the cost of health, to link their expenses with their own economic choice within a basic level of coverage and, most importantly, to promote a concept of thrift and economy. The former system did not impose any restrictions on how many times a patient visited a doctor or how much medicine was prescribed. This weakness is made up for now by imposing a limit below which there is a personal gain by saving money. Furthermore, the aim is to relate health expenses to the overall capacity of social pooling funding and to prevent unnecessary expenses and purchase of excessively costly equipment.

Control of the cost of hospitalization is a widespread concern and the social security agencies have become responsible for selecting key institutions (hospitals and clinics) that have to be used when drawing on the health insurance savings.[19] Two measures have been introduced to regulate the relationship between the agencies and the health institutions: 'Payment according to type of illness' (*anbinzhong fufei*) and the 'System of a fixed pre-paid sum' (*zong'e yufuzhi*). The first principle entails that social insurance agencies and hospitals negotiate a price for a standard treatment for each type of illness. If the hospital can do it cheaper, it reaps a profit, if not, its profit will be reduced or it will sustain a loss. Under the system of a 'pre-paid sum', the social insurance agency, in collaboration with the health institutions, will decide on a certain amount of money to be paid annually for each person based on expenses for that person of the preceding year. The hospital or clinic will subsequently be responsible for the treatment of the insured person no matter what the real expenses are. By these two measures the responsibility for controlling expenses is placed in the hospital administration and not at the level of the work unit or the insurance agency.

According to an unpublished report from the Development Research Centre of the State Council, the reforms so far have had some effects, while many problems are still not solved. Difficult to measure, but certainly an achievement, is a public understanding and acceptance of the personal responsibility for good health and an awareness of the costs involved. Experiences have been collected on how to unify the formerly divided management of health

19. This arrangement sounds very reasonable, but personal information pointed to potential questionable results. The work unit in question had authorized a nearby hospital that was known to deliver very bad services and furthermore treated inmates from a jail in the vicinity. The latter responsibility did not exactly enhance its status, so most staff members would choose to spend their own money to be treated elsewhere. Consequently, they did not enjoy the benefit of their own health care insurance. In principle it is also clear that the selection process of the health institutions offers good grounds for bribery.

care and how to share the burden between more actors. Finally, it has been possible to lower the price of some expensive services though the core problem of getting expenses under control has not been successfully solved yet.

Pensions

The ageing of the population, manifest in China as elsewhere in the world, raised the burden of social protection immensely for the work units during the reform period. The dependency ratio, i.e. the proportion of retirees to the number of employees, increased from 1:6 in 1985 to 1:8 in 2000 (*ZTN* 2001: 35). Total amount of pensions paid by all ownership units rose from 15 billion yuan in 1985 to 273 billion in 2000, showing an annual increase rate of 23 per cent (*ZLTN* 2001: 481), to be compared with an annual GDP growth rate of 9.4 per cent (*ZTN* 2001: 23). In some places the proportion of pensions relative to total salary had risen from 3 per cent in the 1950s to over 20 per cent in the late 1980s (Wang Mengkui 2001: 5). And in the future the proportion of the elderly over 60 years old is projected to continue to rise from 10 per cent in 2000 to 24 per cent in 2050 (Lo and Cheng 1996: 179).

Reforms of the pension system began after scattered experiments in different places, as in Guangzhou, with a State Council decision in June 1991 promulgating a 'Social Fund System' (*shehui tongchou*) according to which employers and employees should contribute a certain percentage by discretion of the local government to funds jointly administered by labour bureaus and public finance bureaus (*ZRGLSBFQ* 1999: 361–362). But incentives were few because the system in reality meant that 'young' work units paid for 'old' ones that were unable to shoulder the social burden by themselves, so units with many young workers were unwilling to participate. Part of this problem was addressed by adding the element of individual accounts to the system after the decision to establish a 'socialist market economy' in 1993. The trials had created disagreements over how to proceed, so in a State Council circular of March 1995 work units were given two models to choose between, in which the size and role of the individual accounts differed (Ge Yanfeng 1997: 9).

The final decision from July 1997 urges localities to adopt a unified system built on the combination principle. Local government at all levels should incorporate pension schemes in their plans for economic and social development, including unemployment insurance and a minimum living standard scheme as well. Furthermore, they should encourage the establishment of supplementary insurance schemes at the work unit level and promote the development of commercial insurance companies. The contribution of the enterprise is to be not more than 20 per cent of total salary excluding the individual share, which is to begin with a minimum of 4 per cent of individual salary and grow to 8 per cent over the next 8 years, deducted by the work unit. Both shares will be transferred to the social security agencies established at the city level. The individual accounts shall contain 11 per cent of the individual salary. For new employees, i.e. those employed after the promulgation of the 1997 policy document, the individual monthly old-age allowance will consist of two parts: one share from the social pooling fund amounting to 20 per cent of local average salary and 1/120 of the content of the individual account. A calculation based on an average salary of 800 yuan a month and allocation to individual account of 11 per cent gives the result that 15 years seniority (which is the requirement to participate in the scheme) will provide

Chart 6.3 Collection and distribution of pensions

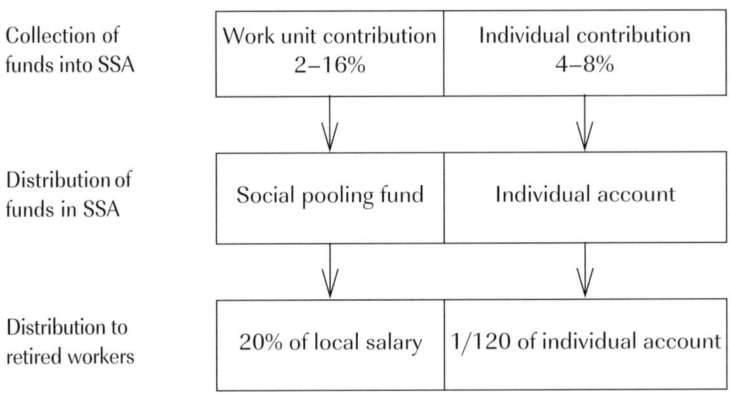

the retiree with 292 yuan a month, which is not much more than the minimum living standard for a place with that kind of salary. After 40 years of work, the pension subsidy will be 512 yuan a month. The two examples give replacement rates of 37 per cent for 15 working years and 64 per cent for 40 years of work.

Example:

Given average salary 800 yuan per month = 9,600 yuan per year, 15 (40) years seniority, individual account 11 per cent:

The content of individual account will be 15,840 (42,240), then allowance each month will be:

From fund, 20 per cent of 800 = 160 yuan

From individual account, 1/120 of 15,840 (42,240)132 (352) yuan

Total 292 (512) yuan

The individual account is personal property. The content will follow the worker when changing job and be paid to dependents in the case of death. Persons already retired at the time of enforcement of the decision will be cared for according to the former pension procedures. For the (in 1997) existing employees, transitory measures will be worked out by the MOLSS and other relevant departments. Persons who retire within less than 15 years after promulgation will not be covered according to the decision, but will be paid the lump sum of their individual account when retiring. It is explicitly stressed in the decision that there should be a sharp division between the social pooling funds and the individual accounts and it is not allowed to use the latter to make up for deficits in the former.

Administration

Final rules for the sound management and preservation of the funds were published in January 1999. These regulations stipulate social security agencies to be set up by the local government, which appoints staff, pays salary and monitors the administrative work, see Chart 6.4. The agencies are often physically placed in the city halls together with the staff of local government, but they are meant to be financially independent units belonging to the category of public service units (*shiye danwei*). From 1999 administrative costs are not to be covered by the contributions from employers and employees but should be part of the budget of local government. Thus, the contribution of the state is administration, including salary, plus the missing tax income as the social security savings are tax-free.

The social insurance agencies shall establish separate accounts in a state owned bank for the social pooling fund of each branch – health care, pension and unemployment – of social service, as well as open individual accounts for each individual participant. The agencies are accountable to the provincial government for preserving the value of the accumulated funds and they can impose fines on enterprises that do not transfer the contributions in due time. In some provinces the local tax bureaus have taken over the administration of the funds in order to combat mismanagement. In these cases the agencies are left with the task to collect the contributions and keep the contributors informed. The agencies are obliged to inform citizens about the content of their individual accounts at least once every year and the work units likewise have to publicize their contributions to the social insurance scheme 'at fixed intervals'. This administrative set-up is often described as 'socialized' welfare provision (*shehuihua fafang*).

Chart 6.4 Administration of social security funds

The funds can contain different branches, normally health, pension and unemployment, but sometimes also maternity and work injury

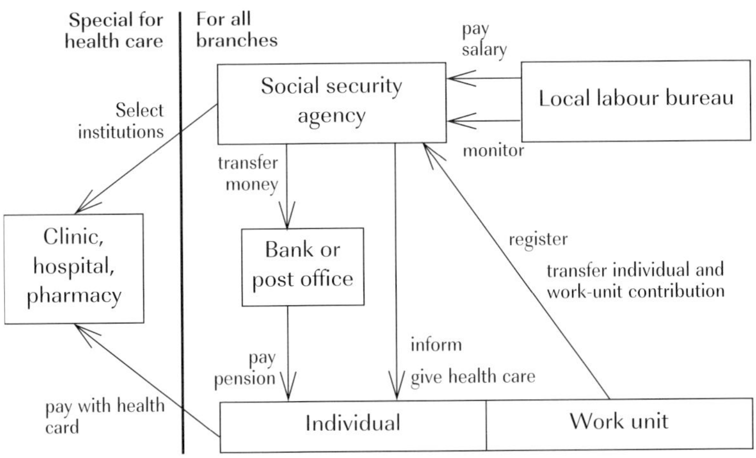

IMPLEMENTATION PROBLEMS

The feature immediately catching the eye is that coverage under the new systems still is restricted to urban people. Peasants continue to be left out, with no state guaranteed protection in case of illness or old age, as is explicitly stated in the core decision on establishment of a socialist market economy from 1993: 'Social security practices for urban and rural residents should be different' and concerning pensions 'The support of the aged in rural areas will be shouldered chiefly by their families and supplemented by community assistance' (*BR*, vol. 36, no. 47 1993: 23). The policy line of the central party apparatus is to continue the preferential treatment of urbanites, constituting only 36 per cent of the population according to the official figure from 2000 (*ZTN* 2001: 91).

Not only the rural/urban divide was upheld but also employment as a precondition for receiving social benefits. For all kinds of social protection the new systems were set up for people employed somewhere, not for persons outside the labour market. This narrow coverage is one of the most commonly heard criticisms of the reform policy and extension of the group of beneficiaries is constantly mentioned among the most important objectives of reform. During experimentation the scope of coverage varied between the different reform models, e.g. concerning health care with a relatively broad spectrum in the Shanghai 'Serious Illness Scheme', protecting not only formal state employees but also workers and staff in joint ventures, private businesses and some family enterprises, while the 'two Jiangs' model' only protected the same groups of people that were protected under the pre-reform systems, and Xiamen and other places had less coverage for 'non-formal' employees than for ordinary ones. In the final decision on management of funds, coverage differed a bit between the different areas: health care had the broadest coverage, with all kinds of work units compelled to participate, while for pensions and unemployment only productive enterprises were to be included.

Even for employees the level of protection become moderate compared to the level for the same group of people before the reform era. This contains some logic in light of the fact that the motivation for reform came exactly from the excessive, and constantly increasing, burden of social expenses. The level of social services for urban workers was simply too high before to allow for the desired economic growth; it had to be lowered or directed elsewhere and the urban citizens' expectations of government support also had to be gradually changed. Where the replacement rate of pensions before the reforms usually was 80 per cent or more, it will be under 60 per cent according to the new rules. Where health care earlier was free, it will now inevitably be a burden for many family economies, as calculations above have shown. So while the principle of occupational welfare is a clear continuation of the principles behind the former system, the coverage is now at a more meagre level. But the financial burden of the work units is still not negligible, as it amounts to at least 28 per cent of total salary – 6 for health care, 20 for pensions and 2 for unemployment insurance – only counting what they are compelled to save according to the official documents. The financial costs have not been much reduced then, but the schemes could help share risks among a wider group.

Some problems have been encountered and at least in theory solved along the way, such as problems with how to combine social pooling funds and individual accounts. In the beginning the separation between the two was not strictly enforced, with the result that expenses belonging to the social pooling funds were taken from the individual accounts. In the experiments in Zhenjiang and Zhujiang in 1996 mis-allocations resulted in 29 million yuan from the individual accounts being used to cover up for a deficit in the social pooling fund. A serious lack of legal and administrative resources underpinned the possibilities of misuse. The realization of the problems led to articles in the final decisions explicitly forbidding the mixing of the different accounts, demanding strict separation between the different social pooling funds and the social pooling funds and the individual accounts, respectively. But poor implementation is more often the problem than insufficient rules. The willingness of the enterprises to pay their contributions is sometimes limited, as will be seen in the local material, and a host of creative measures have been invented by provincial governments to force work units to comply with the rules (*Shehui baozhang zhidu*, no.2, 2001: 62).

Moreover, the individual accounts in themselves pose a problem and the concept is criticized from various angles. They are built on the Singaporean idea of a Provident Fund, with the aim of collecting funds for future risks and controlling expenses consisting only of individual accounts. The system in Singapore is compulsory and employers and employees pay the same proportion, each 20 per cent, into the fund that is used for pension, health care, housing, education and family allowances. As in China, this kind of social protection is thus confined to working people, but unemployment in Singapore is very low, which may make it a lesser problem than in China, where unemployment is predicted to soar in the coming years. Some of the Chinese criticism is prompted by the very principle of personal savings, lacking the redistributive element, connected to the idea of social justice still prevailing at least in some academic circles (He Jinglian 1997: 352). Not only is protection restricted to working people but the existing income disparities are retained as the size of the contribution is a percentage of personal salary, i.e. the work units pay more to the individual accounts of people with high income than to those with low income. Another comment is that in reality the Chinese version still follows a PAYG principle, because individual accounts are emptied to provide for the present expenses. Consequently, the problem of 'notional' or 'empty' accounts, meaning accounts where there is no real value behind the deposit, especially for pension insurance, is frequently mentioned and discussed.

The latter situation is also more a problem of enforcement than of regulation. To blame is not the idea of individual accounts as such, but the poor implementation of existing rules and regulations, which in this specific case is hard to avoid as long as sufficient measures have not been worked out on how to solve the transition problem of caring for the so-called 'middle persons' (*zhong ren*): those that have worked under the old low-income, high-protection system and are now ill or retired or soon to retire. They have no personal savings, their accumulated capital (created by their work contribution) is bound in public property. If the funds allocated to individual accounts cannot be used for the benefit payment of existing pensioners and the middle persons, the state owes them a debt that should be paid back. Attempts have been made to compensate them for some of the debt, as we saw in housing reform, but not enough has been done to secure them economically. E.g. in the current pension regulations the problem is addressed laconically with the words 'Pensions for persons retired before the enforcement of these regulations shall be paid according to the former state rules' (*ZRGLSBFQ* 1999: 388). But the work units do not have money to pay pensions anymore, as the preconditions for their doing so disappeared with the transition to a market economy, so the money is disbursed from the newly established funds.

Two different problems, namely a system for future generations and a solution to the problem of 'the middle persons', have been mixed together and this overlap is especially critical for the future of social security. The lack of separation of the two problems has created a situation where the insurance system in fact has become a PAYG system, contrary to the wishes and expectations of decisionmakers (Ge Yanfeng 1997: 10; Wang Mengkui 2001: 7). The size of the unfunded individual accounts has been estimated to be 24 billion USD by the end of 2000 (ADB 2001: 1).

A proposal for a solution has been put forward by a group of scholars from the State Council Development Research Centre involving to pay the debt back by selling off state assets. In their view the present government is legally bound by a promise of social security to industrial workers. A calculation of the needed amount of capital to cover pensions for the group of people already retired or soon to retire shows the 'debt' to amount to 20 per cent of GDP (in 1994 prices), which is said to be low compared to corresponding figures from Chile or Eastern Europe, where a transition from a PAYG system to a savings system also have taken place or is about to take place. In the same analysis it is pointed out how effectively managed social security funds can serve as an engine of economic growth, and thus in the long run help to develop the market economy (Wu Jinglian 1998: 293), a viewpoint that has been put forth concerning housing funds as well.

The problem of the 'middle persons' can immediately be seen as a transitory phenomenon, but a failure to solve it can have serious consequences for the viability of the future savings, system and the legacy of the past will thus shape the future protection in a negative way. Consequently, some scholars view this as a core problem in the area of social security. Not only will one generation, the people now in their 40s and 50s, suffer bad living conditions with derived hazards to their children, but the present accumulation of funds will also be affected, in turn jeopardizing the livelihood of future generations. The picture of the serious situation facing a potentially 'lost' generation appearing from the local investigation supports the concern and confirms there is reason to fear lasting effects by failing to adress the issue in the present generation.

INTERNATIONAL LAW

Social security is addressed in many conventions and instruments as a joint category involving different components, like health care, pensions and maternity benefits. The right to health has been singled out and has got its own articles in the core documents, and health rights are the subject of a separate General Comment from the Committee on Economic, Social and Cultural Rights. Old age benefits, on the contrary, are not addressed as a special category, but subsumed into the general term of social security or the right to an adequate standard of living.

The basic paragraphs on social security are article 25 of the UDHR, which promises everyone the right to 'security in the event of unemployment, sickness, disability, widowhood, old age or other lack of livelihood in circumstances beyond his control' and article 9 of the ICESCR, which as the shortest article in the whole Covenant, states that 'The States Parties to the present Covenant recognizes the right of everyone to social security, including social insurance'. As can be seen, both documents use a very short and general wording, which could be connected to the extensive regularization of the area by another UN organization, the International Labour Organization (ILO).

> The text of the Covenant, is . . . rather general on social security issues, which can be explained by well-developed ILO standards in this field, and the intention to continue with ILO standard setting and implementation. (Scheinin 2001: 214)

The principal document within the ILO system is Convention no. C102 *Social Security (Minimum Standards) Convention* from 1952, defining social security as consisting of nine 'branches':

1. Medical care
2. Sickness benefit
3. Unemployment benefit
4. Old age benefit
5. Employment injury benefit
6. Family benefit
7. Maternity benefit
8. Invalidity benefit
9. Survivor's benefit

The list is repeated in the reporting guidelines to the ICESCR article 9, confirming the strong links between the two instruments.

The heavy reliance on the ILO standards is interesting in light of the fact that emphasis by definition in this regime is on the protection of economically active persons. According to the most specific explanation of States obligations, they only have to protect employees and not even all of them, as appears from the basic stipulations of the C102 Convention:

- *Persons protected*: Not less than 50 per cent of prescribed (= as defined by law) classes of employees or of economically active persons or residents. In less developed countries the figure can be converted to not less than 50 per cent of employees in industrial work places with more than 20 workers.
- *Benefit*: Can be in the form of care or cash. For most branches the benefit is in the form of periodical payment.
- *Qualifying period*: Will most typically be employment or residence. The length of time required is specified for some branches with 'may be' (e.g. for pensions 30 years of employment), for others no limits are given.

So the social security obligations of member states according to the ILO are to secure *the persons protected* the provision of *benefits* at least to persons who have completed such *qualifying periods* as may be considered necessary. Even lesser demands are made on governments in developing countries, where the persons protected can be restricted to half of those working in enterprises employing more than 20 people and the country will still comply with the Convention.

Health rights have an independent status with much more elaborate standards and the area is not so closely connected to the ILO regime. The first explicit formulation of a right to health is found in the preamble to the first constitution of the World Health Organization from 1946 (Toebes 2001: 172), and sickness is included in article 25 of the UDHR from 1948, as shown above. Treaty provisions not only proclaim a right to health care services, but include various conditions for obtaining and preserving good health, like access to clean water and air, sanitation and safe working conditions.[20] The obligations of States Parties in relation to health rights in article 12 of ICESCR are more precise than what goes for social security.

> The States Parties to the present Covenant recognize the right of everyone to the enjoyment of the highest attainable standard of physical and mental health.

The steps that have to be included to realize this right are divided into four groups:

1. To reduce infant mortality and promote healthy development of the child.
2. To improve environmental hygiene.
3. To control contagious diseases.
4. To create a system of public health services.

These can be counted as the core rights that states should guarantee under any circumstances i.e. they should not only be subject to the 'progressive realisation' mentioned in article 2 of the

20. The last point would be included in point 1 of Chart 1.1 e.g. state supported sanitation or environmental hygiene systems are a form of indirect social protection.

ICESCR.[21] It is the last element, i.e. the obligation to create public health services, that concerns us in the following section.

A General Comment on article 12 from the Committee on Economic Social and Cultural Rights was published on 4 July 2000.[22] Its outset is that health protection is a cluster of rights closely related to other human rights, to economic/technological level, natural conditions (including man-made changes to these), cultural traditions and personal lifestyles. The interdependence of rights is clear, as the right to health contains both freedoms and entitlements. Freedom from being subject to torture, violence, unhealthy working conditions, etc. and entitlements to professional care, medicine and rest. As we have seen, in theory the interdependence goes for all rights but with some it is more clearly understood than with regard to others. On top of confirming that the right to health extends to both health care and underlying socio-economic factors affecting health, the General Comment interprets the right to further include the 'participation of the population in all health-related decision-making at the community, national and international level' (para. 11).

The clause about public participation is one of those that addresses the political system of a country and advocates standards of good governance. It is repeated in the part on implementation at the national level, where states are entrusted with a margin of discretion 'in assessing which measures are most suitable to meet its specific circumstances' (para. 53). This margin does not contain participation, as can be seen from a clear stand that 'Effective provision of health services can only be assured if people's participation is secured by States' (para. 54). At last the Comment demands of states that health services be available, accessible, acceptable and of good quality (para. 12), and it presumes that 'retrogressive measures taken in relation to the right to health are not permissible' (para. 32).

---

21. For a discussion of the concept of core rights, see Chapter 2. More core elements are added in the CESCR General Comment 14, viz. to ensure freedom from hunger and access to basic shelter and sanitation, as well as to provide public information concerning health problems and appropriate training for health personnel (para. 43).
22. UN doc. E/C.12/2000/4 (Eide et.al. 2001: 679–695).

To sum up, social security for people outside the labour market is rather meagrely addressed in the international instruments, while health rights are singled out and treated in a more extensive manner. Many national constitutions have incorporated the right to health, one of the earliest being Chile in 1925, followed by Holland, Hungary, Finland and many others (Toebes 2001: 173–74). Social security and health are also both mentioned in CEDAW, CRC and in the European and American regional instruments.

China has been a member of the ILO since the establishment of the organization in 1919, with a 'break' of 22 years between 1949, when Taiwan got the China seat in the UN, and 1971, when the People's Republic (re-)entered the United Nations. The restoration of the membership of the ILO was done unilaterally by the ILO Governing Body without asking whether the PRC was interested in resuming the relations and it took ten years before China became an active member (Kent 1999: 124). The PRC has ratified 20 ILO conventions, but not the C102 on social security, so the country is not bound by it, but it is obliged by the corresponding provisions in ICESCR, article 9, by virtue of its ratification of that Covenant in March 2001.

DISCUSSION: RIGHTS AND SOCIAL POLICY

It is a common assumption that social policy will be developed along with industrialization, i.e. the more industrialized a society is the more comprehensive social schemes will be set up (Lin Ka 1999: 15). Two Scandinavian scholars have studied the sequence with which the different branches of social services have been introduced in East and Southeast Asia and their introduction in relation to the economic development of the region, what they call 'developmental time', measured by proportion of the labour force in the non-agricultural sector at the time of introduction of social security schemes (Hort and Kuhnle 2000: 181). Their conclusion was that East and Southeast Asian countries introduced welfare schemes in approximately the same temporal order as has been typical in Western countries. Occupational injury would come first, then pension/health care insurance, then, but often very much later, maternity and family benefits. These findings are not confirmed when looking at China, which seems to constitute a special case. In China one may say it all started at the same time, namely with the establishment of the socio-economic programmes in the 1950s.

The dismantling of these and efforts to build new schemes from the middle of the 1980s began with pensions, followed by unemployment and health care insurance, while maternity benefits and occupational injury have been given much less attention. The different order for this 'second round' of introduction of social security programmes is probably due to the structure of the existing social protection: people are used to being covered in case of illness and old age, the two most expensive areas, so this guarantee cannot just be taken away without some kind of remedy. The government simply had to find alternative ways to protect these two vital needs.

Then how does China perform in relation to the international human rights obligations on social security and health? The General Comment 14 will be used, as it is the latest and most authoritative document. Its part II, articles 30 to 45, concerns States Parties Obligations, where the important clauses in the present context are:

- Retrogressive measures are not permissible, only if the State party can prove it has 'carefully considered all alternatives' (para. 32).
- The state has to adopt a national health policy ensuring equal access to available, accessable and acceptable health services and to regulate those provided by third parties (para. 35 and 36).

In the section on national implementation we have furthermore seen that even though every state has a margin of appreciation, non-discrimination and people's participation are unavoidable principles behind formulation of national policies and plans of action (para. 18).

For urban people the new state of affairs must without doubt be characterized as a retrogression in relation to the former abundant guarantees. The replacement rate of state pensions would be reduced to two-thirds of current level in a long transitional period or in the far future and the reimbursement of expenses on health is now to varying degrees to be paid out of the pocket of employees themselves. This retrogression, however, can be defended by pointing to the non-discrimination clause, as it is necessary to lower the guarantees to secure a larger part of the population. It can also be explained as an effort to bring government spending in line with the economic level of the society. The traditional system constituted in reality an overspending that was unequally divided and unaffordable for society as a whole. In a rights perspective it must be correct to lower the protection of a privileged group in other to be able to protect more people. But the problem is that too little has been done on extending effective social guarantees to larger groups, such as people in rural areas and people without working ability. The Chinese Government just recently ratified the ICESCR and therefore has not yet made any State Reports, but it could be a point the Committee would express concern about in its concluding observations after having read a future Chinese report. Likewise, and on the same grounds, the equal access to available, accessible and acceptable health services is a matter of concern. Even among the urban population, health care is considered a burden on the family economy and in the rural areas the concept of 'health poverty'[23] is an increasingly serious threat not only to the affected individuals but to social stability at large. Last but not least the request for public participation is not complied with. The beneficiaries or citizens receiving social services do not have any real representative forums to communicate their needs and complaints. They are virtually without a voice in the policy formulation phase and the complaint options are far from sufficiently known and used.

---

23. A phenomenon defined by Meng Qingguo and Hu Angang as the situation of 'being ill leading to poverty and vice versa' (Shi Guang and Li Weiping 2000: 2).

7 只能靠自己

The Right to Education: Basic Schooling

> *People say that if you go to primary school for five days in a week, you pay for the four of them. A big difference nowadays is all the fees that we have to pay for going to school. Before, the teacher had to help the children and give extra lessons, if somebody was behind the others. Now it all costs money; they tell you to buy some books, and sometimes do not even use them. I think something is wrong in this field.*

The annual report from the World Bank for 2000 lists lessons on successful development strategies from East Asia and Eastern Europe. The negative examples are from Eastern Europe and address a lack of legal framework, lack of competition and widespread corruption. The positive experiences are from Asia and two out of six bullet points concern education and knowledge. The East Asian economies are said to have invested heavily in education, thereby narrowing the knowledge gap with high-income countries (World Bank 2000: 17) and on this foundation to have been able to achieve high growth rates for decades without seriously raising income inequality (Tang Kwong-leung 2000: 149). The focus on education and knowledge is no accident. Education is commonly believed to be vital to economic and social development and thereby in turn to progress in human rights protection, and the link between human development and human rights is also the topic of 'Human Development Report' from 2000 stressing the common purpose and common motivation between the two movements.[1] While the link between human rights and human development concerns all types of rights,[2] social rights possess a special relevance for development because 'Securing the means of livelihood, whether through access to food and water or to shelter and clothing, remains sadly a salient priority of the majority of Third World populations' (Sano 2000: 750). In focus in this chapter is the basic level of education, viz. the right and duty of everyone to receive basic education free of charge, so the financing of basic schooling and the implementation of compulsory basic education for all in reform China will be discussed.

LOCAL IMPLEMENTATION

Education and schooling are mentioned in many of the interviews as the most important element in securing a better life in the future.[3] As mentioned before, money and good relations are ranked first as guarantors of social security. These goods are hard to come by if you are middle-aged and do not have them already. The most promising resource ordinary people have is their children and great efforts are put into providing them with more opportunities than their parents have had. Like one mother said: 'We old people

---

1. 'Human rights can add value to the agenda of development . . . The tradition of human rights brings legal tools and institutions – laws, the judiciary and the process of litigation – as means to secure freedoms and human development. Rights also lend moral legitimacy and the principle of social justice to the objectives of human development . . . .Human development, in turn, brings a dynamic long-term perspective to the fulfilment of rights. It directs attention to the socio-economic context in which rights can be realised – or threatened.' (UNDP 2000: 2)
2. The core of a human rights approach to development thus relates to personal integrity, equal opportunity, and livelihood security.' (Sano 2000: 751)
3. This view is expressed in many other contexts, e.g. from the Pearl River Delta in 1995: 'Regarding education as a fundamental force to drive society forward, many people are eager to spend more money on children's education' (Mok and Chan 1996: 249). Or from an article from Internal Reports (*Neibu wengao*) in 1996: 'Many parents have come to understand that compulsory education is not free education; compulsory education can only ensure that a child is able to go to school and study, but investment is both a requirement and a necessity if one is to choose a school with good conditions.' (Rosen 1997: 31)

are used to suffer, we can stand it. We just wish our children should not suffer the way we did'. Education becomes a means to escape the suffering of earlier generations as well as nurturing the hope of a better life for the parents in their old age. The strong wish that the kids will do well in school is echoed through the material, both from the north and the south, as are also the worries because education has become more and more expensive. The cost is mentioned by many families as a big burden on their economy.

> If the government cannot support our children in school, we have to do it ourselves, they have to get a good education, no matter how much we shall skimp and save. I tell the children, go and study, wherever you are able to get in, we will support you, do not speculate about where the money will come from. What we have, we will spend, what we do not have we will borrow, you can pay back later. If you miss the right time, you will not get another chance.

Before the reform period it did not matter very much whether one had graduated from junior or senior high and with what marks, to get a plain factory job. The kinds of jobs sought by the interviewed kinds of people were announced through local labour bureaus and grapevine and applicants were admitted after a short health examination. No test, no money, no certificates from school were needed. But now the enterprises, who are doing well, only want to employ people with at least a junior middle school degree. They are in fact mostly asking for senior middle school graduates. And as good jobs are in short demand, academic results become a highly priced commodity.

Introduction of fees into the school system disables weak families in more than one way. The schools charging less fees will also be of poor quality, as the good teachers seek the key schools with high status and abundant salaries. The school of the dyeworks in Xingtai (the dominant work unit in the Xingtai area) is said to be a 'bad school', with low quality and lax discipline. 'They only want our money' as the complaints go, though the school is rather cheap with its fee of 150 yuan per term. The grandchild of a cadre truanted a lot, but the teachers did not tell the parents, as they were afraid these would then move the child and the school would loose the money. When the parents found out and moved the boy anyway, the school charged them 300 yuan in spite of the fact that there was a regulation forbidding the charging of fees for school shifts, and the parents knew that.

Furthermore, the problem of an 'outsider' household registration, which is most often a problem for families with few resources e.g. farmers from nearby villages, enhances the inequality of opportunities. One example of the price difference is given by a couple with a daughter of 15 and a son of 10. The daughter got into a 'good' middle school because her father's sister was married to a man in the Tax Bureau who knew the head of the Education Bureau. Their household registration had just been moved to the East Gate District, where the school is located, but when the girl entered school the formalities surrounding the change in household registration were not completed yet, so they had to pay 200 yuan extra. But the father explains that if they had not 'known somebody' they would have had to pay 1,000 yuan more than others, because of the outside household registration. This school was not especially expensive, a permanent resident would have to pay 200 yuan into an education fund (*jiaoyu jijin*) upon entry; on this background 1,000 extra appears to be a lot. Another economic effect of an outside household registration is seen in work unit schools and kindergartens. In one case the price for a three year old in kindergarten is 50 yuan a month for the couple interviewed because the mother/wife inherited her father's job at the textile mill, while her friend from another work unit has to pay 150 yuan to have her child in the kindergarten of the mill. The textile worker is awfully worried about what to do when the child soon has to attend primary school, because she has heard it is very expensive, but she does not know anything about it and has not even tried to find out.

But how serious is the economic burden exactly? The official figures of the development in expenses on education are given as: in Xingtai 373 yuan for a family in 1992, is rising to 866 yuan in 1996.[4] In Guangzhou school fees given are 230 yuan in 1992 (Ikels 1996: 75), while the annual expense per family in 1997 is 1,190

4. The figures for the years 1984 to 1992 are zero (*Xingtai shi 1996: 379, 1997: 754*).

yuan (*Guangzhou shi* 1997: 346).[5] As the last figure is an aggregate figure, including night school and the universities (which are usually the most expensive part of education), it is difficult to ascertain the proportion for compulsory education.

In the two surveyed places great fantasy seemed also to be exhibited in imposing various fees. The interview answers from Xingtai and Guangzhou show great variety between the different institutions levying charges on schooling. In Xingtai the typical amount is 400 yuan for school fees for one year (200 for one term) and 50 yuan for books and miscellaneous fees (*za fei*), to be paid from the average monthly income per family of 700 yuan. In a hypothetical average case the annual expense on basic schooling would be 5 per cent of household income, viz. the proportion of 450 yuan to 8,400 yuan.[6] The miscellaneous fees are seldom specified but counted as one separate category, and many of the interviewed persons are not clear about what they actually cover.

> I am not sure, what it is used for. I haven't asked. Everybody pays, so how would it look, if we alone asked for an explanation? We do not want to stick out from the others. That could hurt our daughter.

Besides the miscellaneous fees, money for uniforms and money to build teachers' living quarters are mentioned. A kind of deposit is the 'pooling fee' (*jizi fei*) that is paid when starting in first grade and the money is returned upon leaving school. This is only mentioned in one case with no specifics attached. Parents complain and expresses doubt about whether all these fees are really reasonable, as e.g. the following two different household heads:

> Some years we have to buy uniforms twice (700 yuan each). If you do not buy the teacher gets unhappy, they have them on commission, so they earn money each time one is sold. You have to buy or your child will suffer and be treated badly. If we cannot afford it, we have to borrow money.

---

5. The two points of information are not directly comparable, as the first is Ikels's computation of 'school fees', while the second is the category 'education' in the Guangzhou Yearbook. Ikels's source is also official Guangzhou statistics.
6. The percentage of course has to be taken with caution. The income is subject to the biases mentioned in Chapter 1 and the expenses are highly varied between the different families.

> Last year the school built houses to the teachers, and they wanted money from the pupils. Soong Qingling foundation[7] paid half, and we paid the other half. We had to pay 200, and we could not protest. Society is no good.

Marks have also been commercialized. One family is able to buy additional marks, needed for entrance to a key middle school, for their eldest son. His performance in primary school is not sufficient, so through friends they organize the purchase of 11 marks for 3,600 yuan.[8] The family is so poor that they have a poverty card, which reduces their school expenses by half – but not the 'purchase of marks', of course. Regular pay just to enter this particular school is 4,000 yuan, and 1,700 yuan each term on top of that. Other key middle schools in Xingtai are said to be at the same level. A bitter remark came from a 75-year-old illiterate worker with two sons and three teenage grandchildren:

> It is not easy to get into school these days. If you do not pass the entrance exam (*kaoshi*) you have to buy . . . When the enterprises announce for workers they always ask for senior middle school people.

In Guangzhou the expenses are much higher than in Xingtai. A big majority of the interviewed families with school-age children in Guangzhou have expenses over 1,500 yuan a year for primary school and junior middle school,[9] but a great variety is also found here. School fees are to be paid by the average monthly family income of 1,300 yuan, giving the proportion as 10 per cent – 1,500 to 15,600 in annual income. Several families report of a 'support fee' (*zanzhu fei*) of 10,000 yuan, a one-time charge ostensibly recently decreed by the City Government. A fee of 3,000 yuan with the same

7. A private children's fund established by the wife of Sun Yatsen, China's first president after the 1911 Revolution overthrew the Qing dynasty. Song Qingling was an honoured non-communist in the Chinese leadership, without political power but great moral authority. She became a member of the CCP in the same month as she died – May 1981.
8. The transaction is formulated as repeated here. Based on other sources and general information, I believe it is just as appropriate to say that the entrance fee to the school is higher if the marks are low. So one does not buy a certificate with higher marks but just pays a higher price as an entry fee or whatever it is called. But the actual character of the 'trade in marks' is not clear. I am also unclear of whether it is an open or a hidden practice.
9. Ikels discusses the amazing amount of fees in Guangzhou and counts up to 24 different kinds of charges (Ikels 1996: 156).

name is even demanded for entrance into a kindergarten, according to one informant.

> I think it is not good. When I was going to school [mid 1980s], your marks counted, missing one or half a point would not do, at that time we relied on our capabilities. Now you can get in everywhere and study as soon as you have money. What I fear most is that my son will not get good enough marks next year. Then we will have to pay more to keep him in school.

The material of Charlotte Ikels, dated a couple of years earlier, states expenses in Guangzhou for elementary schools at 600 yuan, presumably for one term, that means twice a year (Ikels 1996: 156), besides diverse one-time expenses, like 'construction fees' (*jianshe fei*) or fees for 'school-selecting students', which can amount to several thousand yuan. Private schools are a rapidly growing industry in this area, they 'usually ask for a large sum of money as debentures from the parents, or else charge high school fees for courses' (Mok and Chan 1996: 252).[10] Private educational institutions are not mentioned in the Xingtai material, neither is support from the state except for a few cases where a poverty card can reduce the school fees. But in that case it will be support from local government, not central authorities.

REFORM PROCESS

The expropriation policy of the CCP after 1949 involved education and from 1956 all schools were public schools under the authority of the Ministry of Education (Mok 2001: 91). Teaching methods and content as well as institutional structure were for a large part imported from the Soviet Union and the Soviet influence is discernible even today. During certain periods of Maoist reign scholars in particular and academic activity in general were subject to political persecution, most dogmatically during the Anti-Rightist Movement in 1957 to 1958, and under the high tide of the Cultural

10. Precise amounts are not given, but an indication of the character of the cost is found in the quote 'tuition fees of these private schools are so expensive that they are beyond the reach of most ordinary people.' (Mok and Chan 1996: 253)

Revolution from 1966 to 1969 (Fairbank 1992). But economic reform quickly restored the respect for knowledge and the acceptance of schooling as an important means for social development.[11] The 'low quality' (*di suzhi*) of the population has since then become a public concern expressed ad nauseum in open societal forums. The human quality referred to concerns not only educational level of knowledge, but is also an expression of ideological, political and moral make-up of the person, and it is supposed to rise with development of civilisation (Bakken 2000: 57).[12]

As in the other areas, the educational reforms are meant to divide responsibility of financing between more actors and thereby to relieve the central state of a burden. Education, like housing and social security, is going to be 'socialized'. Local government will bear the lion's share of basic education but private donors, social organizations and parents are to become involved, too. The new channels of financing schooling, though, are not meant to totally dismantle state control and funding. During the reform period the expenditure on all kinds of education as percentage of GNP has risen from 2.3 per cent to 2.6 per cent and educational expenses as percentage of total government expenditure have risen from 7 per cent in 1979 to 19 per cent in 1998 (*Xin Zhongguo* . . . 1999: 13–14). So a provision in the Education Law from 1995 that the proportion of educational expenditure in GNP shall be gradually raised is ful-

11. 'We should affirm that, guided by the theories of Deng Xiaoping, society as a whole has, since 1978, completed a basic change in its cognition of the importance of education, a change that started with creating order out of chaos and then proceeded to shifts in key areas and finally to a strategic reestablishment of positions'. A vice-minister of education said in a report to the Party School of the Central Committee in 2000 (Rosen 2000: 8).

12. In an official analysis of socio-economic development during twenty years of reform *renkou suzhi* is one of six index numbers, the others being social structure, economic efficiency, life quality, social order and social stability. According to the investigation the human quality of the population has been improved by 4.1 per cent in the 26 years before the reform year, set to 1978, and with 4.9 per cent in the 21 years after; of these, 5.8 per cent during the 1990 decade. The human quality index is almost exclusively composed of educational indicators: 1. population growth, 2. the proportion of persons with educational level above junior middle school, 3. the proportion of university students, 4. the proportion of persons with a technical degree (*da zhong zhuan*), and 5. number of employed with vocational training (*you zhuanye jishu renyuan*) (Ru Xin et al. 2001: 367).

filled.[13] But the numbers do not reveal the structure of expenses that is which political level pays for which educational level. The composition appears in the following chart, showing clearly that basic schooling financially has been transferred to local government.

Middle school refers to a combination of junior and senior middle school (*chuzhong* and *gaozhong*), where the first category is part of the period of nine-year compulsory education. No statistics have been found on the development of the composition, i.e. how fast and in which sequences the state has succeeded in disengaging itself from economic involvement in the primary stages of education.

Concerning non-state actors and financing from civil society, private schools have mushroomed since the beginning of the 1990s and the industry grew rapidly, especially in the southeastern part of the country (Mok and Chan 1996: 242). The statistics show an increase in non-state financing of education from 19 billion yuan in 1990 to more than 90 billion yuan in 1998, divided between schools run by individuals or social organizations (25 per cent and 5 per cent for the two years, respectively); income from fund raising and donations (10–15 per cent); tuition fees (8 per cent and 40 per cent respectively) and 'other', which ironically accounted for the big-

Chart 7.1 Structure of educational expenses, 2000

	National expense	Centre	Local
University (*gaodeng*)	92,532	38,573 (41.7%)	53,959 (58.3%)
Middle school (*zhongxue*)	100,802	218 (0.2%)	100,584 (99.8%)
Primary school (*xiaoxue*)	100,232	45 (0.05%)	100,187 (99.95%)

Unit: million yuan (*ZJJTN* 2001: 4–9).

13. But not as much as the goal of the Education Law that the proportion in 2000 should have been raised to 4 per cent (Rosen 2000: 32).

gest single contribution among them all (40–50 per cent of the total) (*Xin Zhongguo* ... 1999: 14). A rough estimate is that total non-state actors financing has increased by almost a factor of five in the last ten years of reform and the increase is primarily made up of more tuition fees, fund-raising and 'other', while the proportion coming from private schools has declined though the absolute figures are kept at the same level. The numbers cover all levels of education. Concerning student enrollment in private and public schools, respectively, in 1999 2.4 per cent of the pupils in primary and middle schools (*xuexiao*), amounting to 4.5 million persons, were enrolled in schools run by individuals or social organizations (*minban xuexiao*) (Ru Xin et al. 2001: 124).[14]

Educational reform at basic school level has been focussed on popularizing nine-year compulsory education (*pujiu*). The dominant policy is called 'two basics' (*liang ji*) in educational work, meaning to universalize compulsory education and wipe out illiteracy among young adults. The policy was initiated from the adoption of the Compulsory Education Law in 1986 and has been carried out nationwide during the 1990s. In a forerunner to the law, the decision from the Party Central adopted a year before, the country was divided into three areas with different degrees of economic development, that should attain the goal of universal nine-year compulsory education at a different pace (*Jiaoyu fa quanshu* 1995: 66–72).[15] The responsibility for the campaign was imposed on provincial governments that often would delegate it downwards to counties and towns by a layered contract system, set down in the 1992 regulations where article 34 prescribes the establishment of a 'goal responsibility system' (*mubiao zeren zhi*), transferring individual responsibility for achievement of the goal onto the involved civil servants. According to the system, implementation of compulsory education should be the main content of assess-

14. For regulations of private schools see 'Regulations on Schools Run by Social Forces' (*Shehui liliang banxue tiaoli*) adopted by the SC, 1 October 1997 (*Jiaoyu fa jiqi peitao guiding* 2001: 64–73).
15. A Party 'decision' is not as legally binding as a regulation, and from the 1992 regulations referred to above it appears that the goal has moved a bit. According to the regulations, nine-year compulsory schooling would not be reached in the 20th century.

ment of proficiency (*zhengji kaohe*) and could thus determine the career prospects of individual staff members in the system.[16]

In the official statistics for 2000, the percentage of school-age children (6 years of age) enrolled in primary schools is 99.1 per cent (raised from 49.2 per cent in 1952) and the percentage of graduates of primary schools entering junior middle school is 94.9 per cent (*ZTN* 2001: 656). It is explicitly stated that the gender difference in primary schools has been narrowed – an indication that school attendance for girls is still a problem (Ru Xin et al. 2001: 121). In the same source the illiteracy rate is given as 4 per cent in urban and 8 per cent in rural areas (*ZTN* 2001: 97).[17] The 1985 plan of completing nine-year compulsory schooling has not quite proceeded according to schedule, though great strides forward have been taken. In 1999 the goal is said to have been reached for 80 per cent of the populated areas in the country (Ru Xin et al. 2001: 21), but in the same year a report from the Ministry of Education postponed the goal to be reached in the whole country to 2010 (China Daily, 12 December 1999: 1). The official statistics aside, serious problems appear to exist in financing of and attendance to basic schooling, as will be further explained below.

Public propaganda has underpinned the efforts to make social actors contribute to the school system by accentuating heroic examples of private entrepreneurs donating funds for school buildings in their village. Case stories from China Education News (*Zhongguo jiaoyu bao*) describe leaders or ordinary citizens taking personal responsibility for parts of construction of a school system in poor areas (Rosen 1997). The World Bank and funds from Hong Kong, Macao and Taiwan were matched by individual and corporate donations, even down to the township in one place, where each inhabitant donated ten catties of grain for the building of a school, together forming a multi-channelled system of sources for invest-

16. The principle is widely used in Chinese administrative practice; remember how the labour bureau tried to compel enterprises to pay salary and pensions in Xingtai (see Chapter 6.). Other examples could be the one-child policy that is somewhere conducted in the same way and that the method is reportedly used to compel localities to prevent Falungong demonstrators from going to Beijing to demonstrate.
17. The distribution is very uneven, from the top of 36 per cent in rural Tibet to the bottom of 2 per cent in urban Hebei.

ment in basic schooling. It is not uncommon to hear university professors or teachers, who do not belong to the most well-paid section of society, boast of having paid for buildings or for keeping poor children in school in their home town.[18] The story of Ole Bruun, referred to before, likewise tells about the efforts of local government in Chengdu to make private business people pay an 'education fee', though without great success (Bruun 1995: 198). And as a last example a teacher among the interviewed persons in Xingtai tells that every worker in the city had been deducted 10 yuan of their salary to invest in a middle school, with the argument that it was part of compulsory education.

The story of 'Project Hope' constitutes another example of non-state efforts participating in realizing the goal of nationwide nine-year education. The Communist Youth League, a mass organization formally unattached to the state apparatus, has since October 1989 raised 1.6 billion yuan for keeping poor rural children in school. The project has attracted wide publicity and is known by most Chinese. The foundation has been criticized for embezzlement and nicknamed 'Project Face' (Inside Mainland China, September 1999), and in 1999 it streamlined its procedures and changed its strategy from targeting all basic school dropouts to support only those who show promise to continue their education to post-graduate level. The fund will help establish direct contact between donors and brilliant students and in this way 'conform to international practice', as it is phrased (*SCMP*, 23 February 1999). The reason for the new approach is said to be that universalization of compulsory education is perceived as nearing its completion.

By the end of the 1990s the official stand of the political elite on education is that basic education has come a long way towards being made universal and the priority will switch to raising the quality of education, involving higher fees at all levels. In spite of a recognition that only six-year compulsory education is reached in 90 per cent of the country and nine-year is only reached for 65 per cent, vice-minister of education, Zhang Baoqing, states that 'we are now in a position to talk more about quality [than about quanti-

18. Personal information 1999–2001.

ty]'. In a rather detailed report to the Party School in January 1999 he does not mention school fees for compulsory education as a problem, on the contrary he states that

> The amount of school fees paid throughout the compulsory education stage must be increased along with the raise in citizens' standards of income and the level of acceptance of students and their families. (Rosen 2000: 35)

The acceptance called for implies that every citizen in the future has to accept that the biggest expense in the future will be first housing purchases, secondly sending children to college (after all non-basic education). He further predicts that the percentage of school fees for compulsory education might be raised from the current 20 per cent of costs up to 50 per cent of costs by the year 2010 (Rosen 2000: 16 and 35). However, the criticism of excessive school fees has not stopped completely. In the same month, vice-premier Li Lanqing criticized primary and secondary schools for levying a host of unjustified fees (*Zheng ming*, January 1999: 38), which problem will be discussed below.

INTERNATIONAL AND NATIONAL LAW

The right to education is formulated in a range of different human rights instruments and is special in that it pertains to all three generations of rights, and as one of few rights is generally accepted to involve both a right and a duty (Nowak 2001). Rooted in article 26 of the UDHR the right to education is most comprehensively laid down in article 13 of ICESCR, which is the longest provision in the Covenant, and the right is further interpreted in various declarations and conventions adopted especially throughout the 1990s.

Education in general serves two purposes: one is the more practical aim to impart skills to children and adults enabling them to make a living and the other is the more vague goal of developing human capacity to participate successfully in social life. Already in 1948 the aim of education was seen as not only the dissemination of knowledge and skills but also as having to be '. . . directed to the full development of the human personality . . .' (UDHR, article 26.2) and in 1966 the goal is formulated as nurturing human dignity i.e. the basic character of human life that has become the core concept in human rights thinking.

> The States Parties to the present Covenant recognize the right of everyone to education. They agree that education shall be directed to the full development of the human personality and the sense of its dignity, and shall strengthen the respect for human rights and fundamental freedoms. (ICESCR, article 13.1)

Furthermore, many scholars underline the importance of education in securing all other rights, both civil, social and collective or group rights. Freedom of information and the right to vote are hampered by lack of reading ability; enjoyment of the right to work hinges on intellectual and technical skills; participation in politics presupposes knowledge of society and economy . . .; the list of examples may be prolonged indefinitely, making the importance of education self-evident. The CESCR calls education an *empowerment right* in the sense that:

> Education is the primary vehicle by which economically and socially marginalised adults and children can lift themselves out of poverty and obtain the means to participate fully in their communities. (CESCR, General Comment no. 13, para. 1)

At the more practical level states are obliged to ensure that basic education is compulsory and free; secondary education is generally available and accessible to all; and higher education is 'equally accessible to all, on the basis of capacity . . .' (ICESCR, General Comment no. 13, para. 2.c). The special link between right and duty is bound in the concept of *compulsion*; parents and children are not free to choose not to receive schooling up to a minimum educational level laid down by the state. The bottom line of state obligations is thus to establish compulsory, free, primary schooling, and if sufficient resources are not available article 14 of the ICESCR demands that the state make a plan of action for ensuring free primary schooling '. . . within a reasonable number of years . . .'. Should problems still exist the state has to seek international cooperation and the international community in turn has an obligation to assist the country in obtaining the goal (CESCR, General Comment no. 11, para. 9). Primary schooling for free or a plan for realization of this goal are obligations of result, i.e. the state has to immediately and without delay fulfil these specific components of the right to education, not only respect or protect them. The second generation right and duty to *receive* education is the core of the right to education under international law, but many other aspects that will not be further treated here are involved in fulfilling the right to education: e.g. non-discriminatory and equal access to educational facilities; the liberty of parents to choose form and content of schooling; freedom to establish educational institutions; protection of pupils against inhuman disciplinary measures; and academic freedom (Nowak 2001).

The CESCR has adopted two General Comments on the right to education, one on each of the two articles 13 and 14 (Eide et al. 2001: 656–658 and 665–678).[19] Of relevance for our purpose are the following passages:

- The issue of 'free of charge' is interpreted as meaning that fees or direct costs imposed by government or any other party shall be eliminated progressively or their elimination shall as a minimum be included in a plan of action. But not only that: 'Indirect costs, such as compulsory levies on parents (sometimes portrayed as being voluntary, when in fact they are not), or the obligation to wear a relatively expensive school uniform, can also fall into the same category.' (CESCR, General Comment no. 11, para. 7)
- Four essential features are listed that education in all states shall exhibit: (a) availability, (b) accessibility, (c) acceptability and (d) adaptability.[20] Availability means that institutions and programmes shall be available in sufficient quality. Accessibility addresses the non-discrimination clause; it includes physical accessibility, like the simple demand that schools must not be too far away from home and it also repeats the claim that education has to be afford-

19. Both are from 1999. General Comment, no. 11 treats ICESCR article 14 on plans of action for primary education, and General Comment, no. 13 comments on ICESCR article 13 on the right to education.
20. The same analytical approach has been used in other texts of the Committee, as shown before. See for example the General Comment, no. 4 on the right to housing, para. 8, where the notions of availability, affordability and accessibility are also used.

able for all. Acceptability concerns good quality and cultural relevance and adaptability likewise points to cultural diversity, as it stipulates that education must be able to adapt to changing societies and 'to the needs of students within their diverse social and cultural settings'. These principles shall govern not only primary schools but also secondary and tertiary institutions of learning and they are of the utmost relevance for all developing countries, including China (CESCR, General Comment no. 13, para. 6).

In sum, to comply with international standards a state must ensure free and accessible education at the primary level to all irrespective of gender, nationality, religion, etc. Primary schooling is not defined in number of years, but is up to each state to determine. Most states stipulate seven to nine years[21] and a much shorter duration would probably attract comments from the CESCR. States Parties do not have to provide the institutions, they can be run by private actors and these can be costly, but the state shall see to it that citizens have the option to receive education without paying.

In the history of the PRC the right to education has been contained in all constitutions, but only in the last Constitution from 1982, article 46, is it supplemented with a duty:

> Citizens of the People's Republic of China have the duty as well as the right to receive education. The state promotes the all-round moral, intellectual and physical development of children and young people.

The value attached to education matches the classical Confucian notion that man is able to achieve virtue through education (Buhmann 2001: 212) and thus is backed by traditional thinking. Since the beginning of the reform period the area of education has been subject to legalization, as have so many other areas. Most important for our purpose is that the Compulsory Education Law (CEL) came in 1986 and the Education Law (EL) of the PRC went into effect from 1 September 1995. These two documents codify a system of nine-year compulsory education divided into primary school (*xiaoxue*) and junior middle school (*chuzhong*) for all citizens

21. A non-systematic search gave the lowest figure of 6 years in Burundi and up to 11 years in some US federal states.

regardless of ethnic group, race, sex, etc. (in the following the two stages combined will be called basic schooling). The central government shall decide on teaching methods and content while local authorities are entrusted with the responsibility for establishing basic institutions and they are called on to levy surtaxes (*jiaoyu shiye fei*) for the cause of funding compulsory education, amounting to 2 per cent of corporate tax.[22]

With the 1986 law the primary financial responsibility for basic education was decentralized to local authorities with the qualification that the state should subsidize those areas that were unable to introduce compulsory education for economic reasons and the central government would institute a system of grants to support school attendance of poor students (CEL, article 10). Local authorities were in the 1995 law specified as 'at or above the county level' (EL, article 15).

> As have been familiar during the reform period, improvements at the basic level are expected to depend most heavily on local government and support from society, whereas the top level of the system will be heavily funded by higher-level state organs and external sources. (Rosen 1997: 3)

Both laws stipulate that the central and local level shall raise the proportion of educational expenditure relative to GDP, in other words 'State appropriations for compulsory education shall increase at a faster rate than regular state revenues . . .' (CEL, article 12). They also both include a non-discrimination clause in accordance with the human rights obligations. The 1986 law, article 5, mentions sex, ethnicity and race, while discrimination on the basis of 'property situation' (*caichan qingkuang*) and religion is added to the list in the 1995 education law, article 9. Both laws also confer the responsibility of receiving education to parents or guardians. The 'support from society' referred to by Stanley Rosen means that apart from local government levying surtaxes, the 1986 law encourages 'enterprises, institutions and other segments of society to establish schools of the types prescribed by local people's govern-

---

22. The amount of taxes is set to 1 per cent in 1986 and to be doubled to 2 per cent in 1990. 'Additional interim provisions of the SC on levying education fees' (*Guowuyuan fabu zhengshou jiaoyufei fujia de zanxing guiding*) 28 April 1986 with amendments 7 June 1990 (*Jiaoyu fa quanshu* 1995: 952 and 958).

ments and in compliance with the basic requirements of the state' (CEL, article 9) and it supports 'individuals and all segments of society to make donations to help develop education' (CEL, article 12).[23]

Regulations for the Implementation of the CEL were promulgated by the SC in February 1992 (*GWYGB*, no. 10 1995: 373–383). There one again finds the distribution of responsibilities between the centre providing rules for content and curricula on the one hand and the local authorities providing the investment in school buildings, teaching facilities and enrollment of qualified teachers on the other hand. The provincial government is responsible for drawing up plans of action for implementation of nine-year compulsory education in its area by the end of the last century, at least as far as the first stage (*chudeng* meaning primary school) is concerned. In poor regions it is sufficient to institute universal basic schooling for five years. Special rules concerning household registration stipulate that if a child wants (or normally of course it would be the parents who want) to receive education in another place than it is registered the child has to get permission from the local government in the place of registration (para. 14). And most important for the present inquiry, the implementing school (*shishi xuexiao*) is allowed to levy 'various fees' (*zafei*) without further definition except that these must not be 'in a disorderly way' (*luan*) (para. 17).[24] The central government itself, however, will not impose fees (CEL, article 10).

Rules concerning the 'support from society' came in 1997, allowing and encouraging (*guli*) organizations and individuals to establish and run schools on a non-profit basis (*Jiaoyu fa jiqi peitao guiding* 2001: 64–73). On the level of compulsory education the private schools shall serve as a supplement to public schools, they are accountable to local government and supervised by the State Council under the same conditions as other schools. Further important laws in the field of education have been a Teachers Law

23. The decision to open the educational field to other investors than the state was first introduced in a policy paper from the CCP Central Committee, 'The Decision to Reform the Educational System' (Mok 2001: 92).

24. The expression is used for fees charged in violation of relevant government regulations.

(1993), a Vocational Education Law (1996) and a Higher Education Law (1998), but these are out of scope here and will not be further discussed.[25]

PROBLEMS

In the area of education the government is faced with the difficult task of cutting down on expenses and improving quality and output at the same time. The introduction of a 'socialist market economy' demands the former while the desired economic development requires the latter result. According to the source quoted above the balance between equality and efficiency is sought to be obtained by first popularizing basic education and then raising the quality. In theory a reasonable order but in reality the economic burden of basic schooling has successfully been transferred from the central to the local level and from there to an excessive degree further sent down to the economy of private households, with a result that could have been foreseen: the poor get poor schooling or no schooling at all. The two most important, and interconnected, problems are rising costs at the family level and high drop-out rates, especially in rural areas and especially among girls.

As money plays an increasingly important role, the educational distance between rich and poor segments of society increases. At the top end unhealthy practices like bribing your way into good schools appear, especially in the big cities.

> The increasing importance of the 'backdoor' in school enrollment can be seen in the acknowledgment that 50 per cent or more of the students in key schools in Beijing generally are admitted either because their parents have contributed a significant amount of money to the school, a memo has been written to the school by a high ranking official, or the parents have influential connections. (Rosen 1997: 4)

The phenomenon of the three types of students (*sansheng xianxiang*) concerns 'memo students, connections students, and banknotes students' (*tiaozi sheng, guanxi sheng, piaozi sheng*), posing an in-

25. They are all contained in a bilingual edition from Foreign Languages Press, 1999.

creasing problem as they occupy the best schools at the expense of children from families with fewer resources. The three types are also called 'school-selecting students' (*zexiao sheng*) and are pupils enrolled outside of the government targets. They include children who are not formally entitled to attend a certain school, either on account of a 'wrong' household registration (like a household registration in another place than where the good school they want is located) or parents not being employed in the 'right' place (e.g. not being employed in the work unit that runs the good school), but whose families are able to pay.[26] Formally this type of enrollment is limited to five students per class but especially attractive schools overshoot the limit because these students pay well.[27] The problem has been addressed in many directives from the State Education Commission but without avail (Rosen 1997: 30). From a rights perspective it is not a problem of school attendance as such, as it is possible to get into the schools without paying, but it has a discrimination bias as the use of money or political power to get good education disadvantages vulnerable groups or even just people with average income.

Another problem exacerbating inequality in school opportunities is the structure where compulsory education is divided into two stages based in two different institutions. Five years of primary schooling is taught in primary schools while four years of junior middle school are conducted in middle schools that combine the junior stage and three years of senior middle school. The institutional linking of the two middle school stages has led to establishment of entrance examinations to the schools, so in reality to go from primary to junior middle school the child has to pass an examination. Formally, compulsory education should not require examination and children should enroll in the school nearest to their place of residence – according to their household registration.

26. The high pay for the so-called 'school-selecting' students has been widely debated in the media. From the prestigious Haidian district in Beijing up to 50,000 yuan is reported as admission fee (*Liaowang*, no. 19, 1996: 34; *Qingnian bao*, 7 July 1995 and 21 September 1995: *Tansuo yu zhengming*, no. 6, 1995: 7; *Beijing shifan daxue xuebao*, no. 3, 1996: 55).

27. Mok mentions that 25 per cent of students in the fee-paying category have been allowed since 1993 (Mok 2001: 94).

That is reasonably simple for primary schools,[28] but the competition to get into good middle schools is fierce and the entrance examination therefore constitutes a real pressure on pupils and their families. So recommendations have been put forward to delink junior and senior middle school and establish a consecutive nine-year educational period in one institution (Rosen 1997: 59).[29]

At the bottom line of the social ladder drop-out rates have increased. The drop-out rate for primary school students is given as 0.9 per cent in 1999 (Ru Xin et al. 2001: 122); in a country the size of China[30] this amounts to around 1.8 million children. An important reason for dropping out is the imposition of high fees:

> Even though compulsory education is claimed to be free and poor families are exempted from a few yuan in entrance fees, the 100 yuan per term in primary school and more than 200 yuan in junior middle school added by all kinds of miscellaneous fees are difficult to accept for poor families in the mountainous border areas of Guangxi and other economically disadvantaged areas. (Ru Xin et al. 2001: 128)

The World Bank in 1999 financed an investigation of the drop-out problem in poor areas and found a striking discrepancy between the percentage of drop-outs given by the authorities and the picture emanating from interviews and field visits. The school authorities told the investigative unit that 7.3 per cent dropped out during primary school, while the figure emanating from the on-the-spot investigation was more than 18 per cent (Postiglione 2001: 50). The reasons for dropping out were not only economical but also, secondly, views of schooling being useless as children would not get very far anyway, especially girls would be unable to find good jobs, and thirdly, bad quality of teachers and teaching equipment was mentioned. But the problem predominantly hits backward rural areas and seems to be less serious in the cities.

The general problem of parents having to bear a great burden to pay their kids' tuition fees is confirmed from many different sources. Most convincingly, many originate at the official level,

---

28. Except for children of migrants, as is shown in the interviews.
29. As the famous Jingshan school in Beijing.
30. China had around 192 million children in primary school and junior middle school in 1999 (*ZTN* 2001: 649).

e.g. that the State Council in 1996 issued 'Proposal to Check the Indiscriminate Collection of Fees in Secondary and Primary Schools' (*GWYGB*, no. 15, 1996: 561–565)[31]; or that Li Lanqing in 1999 expressed concern over unjustified school fees (*Zheng ming*, January 1999: 38). At a national level an increase of 23 per cent in family expenses for education from 166 yuan in 1995 to 204 yuan in 1996 alone is stated in official statistics (*Zhongguo jiawu* 1997: 153). In 2000 over 60 per cent of residents of Beijing, Shanghai and Guangzhou surveyed by the National Bureau of Statistics declared that their economy was heavily affected by education expenses at the same time as they considered investment in education crucial for their future (China Daily, 15 April 2000: 1).

The 1996 proposal is sent from the General Office of the SC and signed by the State Education Commission, the State Planning Commission, the Ministry of Finance and a unit called the SC Office to Correct Malpractices in All Trades and Professions (*guowuyuan jiuzheng hangye buzheng zhi feng bangongshi*).[32] Local governments are encouraged to sign responsibility contracts with lower levels and establish a system of 'fee supervision cards'. Examples of malpractices mentioned are that some schools in the name of work-study programs request services or property from parents; others force or 'persuade' parents in the countryside to contribute to building schools; still others force pupils to participate in insurance schemes; or charge excessive fees for the 'school-selecting students' in the cities. It is stressed that it is legal to impose fees but the size of fees gives ground for concern. Fees have to be necessary; they must not be linked to admission qualifications and schools have to be non-profit organizations. At last, provinces are requested to report on the situation in their jurisdiction to the local party committee and the local people's government, as well as all the undersigned institutions at the central level.

---

31. The document is preceded by many other directives up through the 1990s trying to address the wide-spread abuse of the possibility to impose fees locally (*Jiaoyu fa quanshu* 1995: 950–964).
32. It appears from the document that provincial governments also will have such an office (*jiufengban*), which together with the Education Bureaus are responsible for establishing units that can institute the above mentioned responsibility system.

A further problem is that children of the rapidly increasing migrant population cannot enroll in schools on equal terms with permanent residents (Solinger 1995: 132); they can sometimes get access to city schools by paying more, as the stories above have told, but this is totally at the discretion of local authorities. The legal basis is found in the aforementioned SC regulations from 1992, saying that to be admitted into a school in another place than where one is registered one needs a stamped document from authorities in the home place. This rule seems not to be implemented severely if the local material is to be believed. The only problem in the families with an 'outsider' household registration mentioned is that the schools charge higher fees than for the children with a permanent residence permit.

CONCLUSION

With regard to basic education in China, school fees and low quality of education are a wide-spread complaint and an outcome of the devolution of authority to the local level. Concern about children and their future fate fills much in the minds of Chinese people and their education is a decisive element in perceived life quality. Much time and money is spent in an effort to secure offspring a job or a residence, and education is a reliable means so most of the connections and the inventiveness is used for this purpose. Asked about anxieties in the future, a common answer is that people fear their children will have difficulties finding employment. Education is considered to be the key point in opportunities in the labour market at this basic level, just as it is in academic analysis, cf. the World Bank report quoted in the beginning of this chapter.

But competition is severe and economic constraints disable certain groups in the quest for academic degrees. The school fees are legal within certain limits but the degree of imposition of them creates a situation, where basic schooling becomes a burden to the family economy in some places. In the course of reforms options and choices on basic schooling have been diversified to a great degree, but the ghost of inequality sticks its head out as money increasingly buys high quality schooling. The appearance of practices where money and power overrule academic qualifications in entering educational institutions amounts to discrimination of weak families,[33] and even charity organizations, engaged in poverty alleviation, have adopted a strategy of only supporting bright pupils from poor, rural areas and not caring for 'ordinary' school drop-outs.

Going back to the international obligations described above: States Parties must ensure that basic education is compulsory and free of charge on the basis of the principles of (a) availability, (b) accessibility, (c) acceptability and (d) adaptability. That is, not only shall basic schooling be gratis, it shall be of good quality, possible to get to physically and it shall be accepted by and adapted to the needs of students. The material presented in this chapter pertains especially to the 'free of charge' concept in General Comment, no. 11, and consequently to the question of affordability in General Comment no. 13. In this regard China can hardly be said to live up to its obligations, yet. The specific permission to impose fees in the various laws and regulations, e.g. in article 57 of the EL, is in itself problematic, seen in light of the text in the CESCR Comment that even indirect fees, like the obligation to wear a uniform, should be eliminated or at least the elimination of them should be included in a plan. To my knowledge the Chinese government does not intend to discontinue the practice of local fees on basic education, on the contrary there are signs that they will be increased, and it shall be interesting to see what recommendations the CESCR will give China on the matter in its response to China's first report under the ICESCR, due to be submitted in June 2002 but still pending in the hour of writing, April 2003.

As a consequence, problems exist around the issues of availability and accessability of basic education, especially for the rural poor, but also for poor urban households who can be in danger of ruining their economic basis to keep kids in school, with dire consequences for the future well-being of the whole family. We have

33. Cf. Statement adopted by CESCR confirming that poverty in itself is a human rights violation leading to discrimination ('Poverty and the International Covenant on Economic, Social and Cultural Rights:.10/05/2001. E/C.12/2001/10).

seen examples resembling this situation in the local material and in stories from the official paper, China Education News. By imposing fees that make access to schools more difficult, the problem of discrimination arises and discrimination is illegal according to article 9 of the EL quoted above, which even specifically mentions discrimination on grounds of 'property situation' as being unacceptable. Being able to buy fewer goods (here: education) because of lack of money is of course a general situation in all societies and not in itself a violation on the grounds of discrimination, but the argument one could put forward here is that basic education in reality is not affordable for some people and they do not in sufficient numbers get the stipends or other support they are entitled to according to the CEL.

By being a precondition for development, educational level also influences future social stratification. More children in the countryside miss school years and the children of the workers in Xingtai have few prospects of getting to senior high school. The present unequal access to good teaching can, if unaddressed, in the long run breed future inequalities in access to education, and thereby also to other areas of social rigths, like employment, housing and social security.

8 只能靠自己

Reactions and Perceptions

> *We have been going to complain (zhao ren). Then the City Government paid something for two months but that stopped again. We retired people then went together to the work unit. We do not want to go to the City Government again and disturb them, they are very busy.*

We know quite a lot about the general attitude of the Chinese population towards the reforms. It has been followed rather closely by Chinese observers. At the official level annual 'Social Blue-books' (*shehui lanpishu*) have been published since 1992 in a cooperation between the Chinese Academy of Social Sciences and scholars from important ministries and commissions (Ru Xin et al.). These contain results from research on social issues and from surveys on popular expectations and reactions to social and economic change. According to the findings social security and employment problems have attracted increasing attention as key points of concern with both cadres and workers in urban areas. Most recently the blue-book from 2000 shows negative expectations of housing, health care, employment and enterprise reform for more than one out of four respondents, with a significant increase from 1998 to 1999 (Ru Xin et al. 2000: 85). The questions were 'Do you think xx reform will be good or bad for you?' Worries were greatest concerning health care, with almost 40 per cent voicing the opinion that reform would be harmful to them. Earlier, Tang and Parish found that threats to social security are a major source of dissatisfaction for half of the respondents already around 1990 before work unit reform had seriously begun to hurt (Tang and Parish 2000: 108). Generally, contacts with Chinese citizens and visits to the country reveal a fast growing concern over problems related to welfare issues and social security.

In discussing winners and losers in the transition from plan to market in China and Eastern Europe, Szelenyi and Kostello conclude that:

> Workers who were employed in those sectors of the economy that were the most heavily subsidised by the redistributive mechanisms (e.g. the highly skilled workers in heavy industries) are certainly losers. (Szelenyi and Kostello 1996: 1094)

In the Chinese context the most subsidized layer were the industrial workers in state-owned, and to a lesser degree, collective enterprises. They got far more of their share of collective wealth, but they got it by way of decisions at the top of the political hierarchy, not by their own performance or resources. These are the people that form the basis of the present investigation and whose situation has been described in the former chapters. Some scholars find that the changed social structure creates a new value system wherein people 'begin to accept income disparity and social inequality' and feel proud by being able to move up and down the social ladder by their own efforts (Mok and Chan 1996: 256). This attitude might be found in some places but is not characteristic for the group under scrutiny here.

The social space of the respondents seems to be divided in three layers: closest is the family enriched with friends and neighbours, then comes the work unit presided over by local government and as a third layer the concept of 'society' (*shehui*) has been introduced for the rest. One can be compelled to go to 'society' to get a flat or look for a job. Or a poor mother with a disabled child feels that 'society' ought to know about her situation and do something about it. The laid off who take to peddling in the streets go to 'society' to sell their goods. The local people use the word for an apparently unknown and somewhat disturbing world 'outside' where they are used to operate. 'Society' can be the marketplace, but it can also be the authorities or the media, and it has a slightly negative connotation. In academic discussions the same idea appears, albeit in a more technical shape: commercialization, e.g. of housing, is named 'making societal' (*shehuihua*) and transferring pension insurance to local government is called 'extend to society' (*shehui fafang*), the former corresponding to our 'commercialization' and the latter matching our 'centralization'. But in the public debate 'society' is decisively a positive term. *Shehuihua* is the road ahead for the Chinese nation.

This chapter will proceed from the social environment perceived by the people from Xingtai and Guangzhou and trace their reactions and worries against the background of the debate on dependency as a systematic consequence of socialist systems and the development of a new social contract under economic reform. The chosen angles are how local people perceive and relate to leaders and rules, which in turn affect how they handle conflicts and design strategies. Do the interviewed people express the same 'feelings of hopelessness, powerlessness and passive strategies of protest . . .' (Tang and Parish 2000: 5) as their East European fellow sufferers experienced under socialism and the planned economy? Do the coping strategies of the families give an idea of the prospects for the future relationship between them and the state, i.e. the structure of the new social contract?

RELATIONSHIP WITH THE WORK UNIT

When the father in the Yao case – mentioned in Chapter 4, where only one of eight children and children-in-law has an income from their work unit – says at the beginning of the interview that all the children 'go to work' (*shangban*), even though only one of them actually goes to the work-site every day and earns an income, it is not the impression that he is trying to cover their miserable situation by lying, but rather that he perceives their continued affiliation with the work unit as being that they 'have a job'. A strong perception of attachment to the work unit is found in all answers concerning the issues but the feelings surrounding it are ambivalent. On the bright side many people regard the affiliation with the work unit as a kind of security. Several of the Guangzhou interviewees have a general feeling that they themselves and the work unit together will find a way out, if they are in trouble, but in both the studied places some also worry that the work units depend on state policies, and the state is in trouble.

> No matter what, the life guarantee rests with the work unit. If the state is fine, the work unit will prosper; if the state has troubles, the work unit will suffer. Isn't that true? If the work unit does not pay salary, where shall we go? We can only go trading in the streets but everybody does that. Who will buy?

One important aspect – apart from the social benefits, which are often not forthcoming – of keeping relation with a work unit is that it keeps the personal dossier (*dang'an*). The keeping of the file is regarded as a kind of safety, which might look illusory seen from the outside, but is reality for the respondents. The hope is still alive that the enterprise will recover from economic difficulties and be able to care for its employees, an expectation so strong that even people with little or no income are willing to pay to keep their place on the unit roster.

One worker quit his job in 1992 but wanted to keep his dossier in the work unit, for which he paid 80 yuan a month for two years. After that he stopped paying, but is still 'in' according to a system called 'two not caring' (*liangge bu zhao*), i.e. neither part pays anything to the other. Another interviewee tells:

> To be laid off is in reality to be unemployed. The unit does not pay you anything. Furthermore, if you are not of retirement age and not qualified for internal retirement, but want to do business outside, you have to pay 50 yuan a month to the factory. If the unit will let you be laid off, you don't have to pay them and they don't pay you or care about you in any way.

Another motivating factor is that if the relationship with the work unit is severed the personal file will have to be deposited with the neighbourhood committee or the job information centre, which for some people amounts to a public humiliation. Similar stories are heard from other places, e.g. as David Wank tells from interviews with businessmen in Xiamen

> Many took unpaid leaves of absence, paying the equivalent of a third to a half of their public wages for a period of three to five years to maintain their seniority and benefits in their public units. (Wank 1999: 119)

People wanting to take a job in the free market can also be forced to pay a one-time or a monthly fee either to get away from the unit altogether or to work elsewhere but leave their dossier with the unit, as is the case with one family in Guangzhou. The thinking behind this is that the unit had paid for their training and was entitled to reimbursement (Ikels 1996: 192), so the continuation or discontinuation of the relationship is not always a matter of free choice for the employee.

In both places an SOE – and among them local government units like water supply or electricity bureaus are highly ranked – is still the top priority among job seekers or the parents of youngsters waiting for employment. In spite of the new employment opportunities many people still look to the state sector as the ultimate guarantor of social security, even though units are unable to fulfill their social obligations to employees because of exposure to market competition. Most people have not lost confidence that in the long run work unit employment is the best position. So it is seen as a privilege, not obtainable by ordinary people anymore. It was no problem ten or twenty years ago, but newcomers to the labour market cannot easily get into a good work unit. In spite of the fact that work units are constantly proven to be unreliable masters, the traditional idea of the state/employer as the ultimate provider (father) still lingers in people's minds:

> The government line is good, but the individual factory can spoil it. No matter if it is a big or a small factory, it is like a family. If the mother and father are in harmony, the children will listen. But if the two quarrel and split up, the children will make trouble or not be able to study hard. If the leadership of the factory is incompetent and bureaucratic, and the economic results are bad, the losers will be the workers, just like in a bad family, the losers are the children. If the workers have enough to eat, the social environment will be good.[1]

Here we see very clearly the idea of the work unit as the parent of the worker, illustrating the paternalistic employment structure as

1. The same observation seems to have been done on political participation in Beijing, see book review by Kevin J. O'Brien: 'The survey showed that regime-challenging actions are rare and that protest activities are usually individualized and directed against work-unit leaders rather than the political system itself'. From a review of Tianjian Shi (1997) *Political Participation in Beijing*. Cambridge: Harvard University Press in *The China Journal*, no. 41 1999: 159–169. See also Fei-ling Wang, '. . . under Mao, the whole country was organized as a giant family' (Wang 1998: 17).

discussed, for instance, by Anita Chan in her comparison of the organization-oriented and the market-oriented management model, between which two poles the Chinese work unit reform moves (A. Chan 1997).

But as a parent-child relationship can be a mixture of dependency and mistrust, so can the feelings for the work unit sometimes be full of contradictions. On the dark side there is a great deal of suspicion regarding the intentions and reliability of unit leadership. In several instances workers are angry that the enterprise ostensibly has money to spend even though pensions and salary are not paid. One unit had built a big new warehouse, where it earned money by letting space to outsiders, while its leaders said they could not afford to pay the pensions or only paid them irregularly. A common remark is that the enterprises have grabbed the money of the people.

> My work unit has robbed me over the last few years. They owe me more than 10,000 yuan in missing wages. My husband is a Party member and still they treat us like that! But the leaders policy is all good; it is just the lower levels which do not implement the policy in the right way. We have been complaining to the work unit, but we do not want to go on to the City Government.[2]

The suspicion also hits a sensitive problem in all post-socialist economies, like the sale of state assets.[3] Among the answers we find doubts surrounding the sale of enterprises, like the following statement from a retired worker at an aluminium factory:

> Today they [the leadership] sell this machine, tomorrow they will sell that, they will soon have sold the whole enterprise. Workers love the machines like peasants love the land but soon it will all be gone. They say they sell it to pay our salary, but who knows where the money will end?

Implied is worry that the problematic economy may be misappropriation of funds or outright fraud rather than bad management or bad market conditions, as is often the official explanation. Deng Xiaoping's so-called 'cat-theory' – 'It does not matter if the cat is

2. This impression is supported by other sources, e.g. by an article on labour unrest in *FEER* 25 February 1999: 47, '. . . much of the [workers'] anger is directed at company bosses and local officials, whom workers often accuse of siphoning off profits and bankrupting enterprises'.
3. For an overview of the problem of selling state assets at a national level, see Russell Smyth 2000.

black or white, as long as it catches mice' – has been re-phrased as: 'It does not matter what colour the mouse has, as long as it does not get caught', heard in an interview from Guangzhou.

Another bad example comes from the Yao family, referred to above. On top of their other troubles, they probably lost more than 20,000 yuan (which is not a typical situation, though), when the tile factory where the husband of the first daughter worked had to close down. It was a state-owned enterprise with more than 1,000 employees. The factory had run a savings bank where the family had deposited its savings. The bank promised very high interest and the factory leadership had orally stated that the activity had the permission of the City Government, but it turned out that they had no written evidence to prove this. After the bankruptcy the local government denied any knowledge about the savings bank and all its accounts were frozen for the formalities around the closure. At the time of the interview the workers had sent people to the factory director to ask for information, but they did not get any. The situation seemed likely to cause social unrest, but the attitude of the interviewed person (the father-in-law of the tile factory worker) was very pessimistic and yielding. There was nothing to do, in his opinion; nobody would listen to them. But he obviously did not mind telling about the incident and complaining loudly, which in some way can be viewed as a more passive form of protest than actively doing something to change the situation.

Some also mistrust the new arrangements for social security, arguing against the compulsory deduction of their salary. They feel the work unit forces the scheme on them and express doubt as to what will happen to the money that is put aside. Will they get their share back ever or will it disappear like the money from the sale of machines or the rent for buildings they know are going into the enterprise, at the same time as the management claims there is no money? As with the comment on 'work unit robbery' above, most anger and resentment is generally directed against enterprise leaders, while respect is often expressed concerning the plight of the state. The family in Case F 15 XT declines to accept a poverty card on the grounds that so many people in the neighbourhood are needy, so there will not be help available for all of them. They step aside to let other more needy families benefit, as the City Government is 'short of money'. The step-back can reflect a socially responsible attitude but the act can also be influenced by the humiliation connected to receiving social assistance.

So neither local nor central government are bearing the brunt of the criticism. The claims on state support have been given up in a somewhat fatalistic mood, as a leader in the Sheepmarket Street Office saw it:

> In the beginning the laid off people looked to the Government and the Trade Union for help but they do not do that any more, and when they do go they get no help. The City Government can only give preferential treatment to those setting up their own businesses. Early and late they flood the streets with their stands. The government can grant them a small place in the street and exempt them from taxes. That is all.

Demands relating to government responsibility are stable prices and law and order. A common remark is also that the state should do something for the unemployed and the weak groups in society, but often followed by a doubt about the economic might of the central state apparatus. It is almost as though some people pity the government, 'The problem is that the government does not have the capacity to support all these people' or 'There are too many unemployed, the state cannot possibly take care of them' or 'What can they [the government] do? So many places do not pay salary, how can they help?'

Similar results are obtained in urban public opinion surveys from 1999 and earlier conducted by Wenfang Tang. The conclusion is that dissatisfaction with both the pace and content of market reform is coupled with widespread support for the political system and growing nationalistic sentiments. The data 'raised the somewhat provocative possibility that the leadership was doing a good job at deepening economic reforms while successfully silencing public dissatisfaction' (Tang Wenfang 2001: 905). The most disaffected were exactly the kind of people we deal with here, manual workers, retirees and unemployed.

Voices critical of government are few, though existing. A cadre at the harbour administration in Guangzhou is very outspoken in his attacks on government policy.

> The government should be ultimately responsible for people's living conditions, lower the interest level, complete the legal system. Destroy the rich and powerful elite. It can be done but it becomes more difficult each day.

Still others find the duty of the government is mainly to curb the greater instability and rising crime rates caused by the reforms. Especially the people in Guangzhou are worried about prostitution, drug abuse and a general decline in social norms and moral values. This corresponds to the statistically documented higher incidence of social problems in the area. Migrants are easy scapegoats in the eyes of the permanent residents. As we have seen, the ratio between the two groups in Haizhu district is very uneven, with one permanent resident for nearly ten migrants, so obviously the people 'from outside', as they are called, fill in a lot in the physical and mental landscape of the suburb. Not only crimes, but also filthy streets, abusive behaviour, swearing and disrespect for the elderly are blamed on them. In Xingtai crime and bad moral is also thought to be connected with bigger cities. There they say it is very dangerous to go to Shijiazhuang because the city is full of hustlers and petty thieves.

ATTITUDE TO RULES

A common answer to how they think the state ought to act in relation to basic needs, like work and housing, is that people need public rules they can count on. The lack of transparency, which is also criticised in the public debate, is heard here from the ordinary people. Lack of participation opportunities and of information is often pointed out as the most frustrating experience during the reform era. A big problem is that people do not know what is going on. Why do they not get their wages or pensions and when will the situation get better?

> Why do they not pay salary, they do not tell us anything about that. Is it bad economic results; are the leadership to go? It doesn't help just to change leaders. The party secretary of the province came to

> a big meeting at the factory, and the director got dismissed, but it did not help. The director is not showing up anymore, but nobody knows if he really is fired or not. The workers don't know when they will get paid. They have been to the city hall but the government cannot pay. The state cannot just pay one time after another.

So a shared nuisance is *ignorance* or *misinformation* about own possibilities. As has been shown in the preceding chapters, there certainly are rules but they are sometimes not implemented and people are not sufficiently informed about them, so they do not see them as guarantees they can count on. Most people do not know or know very little about their formally guaranteed rights, like health care insurance or free schooling. But they ostensibly do not care about them, either. One attitude is that rules are not that important, 'they are not useful to ordinary people'. Laws and regulations are not viewed as the basis for rights claims, but as something distant you can read about in the papers or hear about on TV. The information does not affect expectations or alleviate worries about when to get the next salary or how to pay the medical bill.

As an example many people are sure that when you are laid off, the work unit does not have to care about you in any way, which is simply not true, as explained in Chapter 6. Few know anything about alternative ways of securing your old age or health care expenses, and much mistrust is connected to other ways of insuring oneself, especially in Guangzhou.

> I have not thought of buying an insurance. In the first place I do not believe in it, secondly I am young and healthy and have just not reached that stage, yet. We do not believe in the commercial insurance companies. So many things can happen before one needs the money one has invested.

The knowledge different people have often does not fit together, even if they are in the same work unit. One person says internal retirement is 5 per cent deducted from an ordinary pension, another in the same unit that the arrangement is without rules for remuneration, so the unit does not have to pay a fixed subsidy. A widespread understanding is that welfare services such as pensions and health care depend on the income of the work unit, and this is true in practice, but exactly an arrangement that the reform measures are meant to change, which is clear from the trials conducted in the two cities. But the people do not seem to be aware that efforts are undertaken to solve these kinds of problems.

HANDLING OF CONFLICTS

There is only little indication in this material of people trying to organize and protest in a more systematic manner, as has been heard from other places in China. In a well-known case in Yibin, Sichuan province in April 1997, a demonstration of more than 4,000 people blocked the streets for two hours and 200 policemen were on the streets. The demonstrators were protesting against their factory for failing to pay them pensions (*China News Digest*, 12 April 1997). Many similar incidents have been reported, involving sit-ins, taking of hostages, imposing of curfews and other forms of repression especially in Sichuan, but also in Jiangsu, Shanghai, Fujian and Guangzhou (Potter 2001: 97). The protests seem to have escalated during the autumn of 1998 and have reportedly caused the government to postpone enterprise reforms to prevent local level unrest (*SCMP*, 18 and 20 January 1999).

Measures taken by the authorities reveal a growing nervousness about reactions to worsening social and economic conditions. Instructions from the central government are reported to list laid off workers as the third-most likely group to pose challenges to the administration, after groups claiming autonomy for Xinjiang and Tibet (China Rights Forum, 1997–1998). The site of the Guangzhou Party Congress in May 1998 was heavily policed for fear of social unrest, and in the same month a circular from the Central Committee of the CCP asked Party Propaganda Departments to control media reporting of employment problems more tightly. The presentation of petitions in the traditional way have ostensibly been used and is in some cases tolerated by the police (China Aktuell, 1998: 490). Apart from clamping down on demonstrations the authorities are often reported to try to buy people out. Most recently in March 2002 oil miners demonstrated in Daqing, Heilongjiang because the local authorities that were their employers wanted to buy them off with a lump sum of money and in return discard their social responsibilities. The demonstrations gathered more than 20,000 people for several weeks in a row and were even reported in the People's Daily (*Renmin Ribao,* 15 March 2002). Problems on this scale are not reported from Xingtai or Guangzhou.

From one factory in Xingtai, though, we hear a story about workers actually uniting because of delayed salary. They go to the leadership who says they have no money, then they go to the city hall where the mayor tells them to go back to the enterprise leaders, who tells them that the more they complain, the less likely they are to get any money at all. And that silences them, but there had obviously been an attempt to organize in order to defend their rights. Retired workers with wage arrears have also been reported to go to the factory leadership together and ask for the missing payments. There has been shouting and arguing, but not more violent actions like the ones heard of from other places.

The validity of the threat that public protesting will be punished is not proved in one story where the interviewed person is a foreman, so he feels he cannot participate when laid off workers 'make trouble' (*naoshi*), but he describes an incident where it appears that creating disturbances pays, as the 'trouble-makers' are rewarded on expense of the docile ones:

> I told the boss to inform people instead of just telling them to go home. If they are not properly informed about the situation, how can we avoid that they create a disturbance? The workers understand that we are short of money, tell them and explain why! But he would not listen and just told people to go home and not come back the next day. More than 30 people gathered in front of the factory, and said to the boss: 'If you stay, we stay; if you go, we go; if you take your car, we will take your car, too'. Then he promised to pay them salary, because they made a noise, and they went home. So now they get money, while I do not. I asked to retire early because I did not agree to what he did. But the head of the accountants office adviced me to wait a couple of months, because if I just retired the unit would not care about me anymore. So I plan to stay until retirement age to be able to get my pension.

The events took place in May 1997. The interviewed person was 51 years old at the time, so he will have to wait four years to reach the formal pension age limit, and it can be doubted whether the work unit will exist at that time in its present form.

The trade union and the party committee at the relevant level seem strangely invisible in cases like the above mentioned. If you ask if the trade union cannot interfere, the answer is they are of no use in this kind of situations. Only the 'leadership' takes decisions and releases information. The workers representative meeting (*zhidaihui*) is said to have more power than the trade union. It is an organ comprised of both workers and cadres. Where it works, it gathers once or twice a year and discusses problems about production, wages, benefits, etc. One worker tells that in his unit these meetings are run in a really democratic manner, where issues are debated again and again until agreement is reached. This is not a typical picture, though. The trade unions and workers' committees are most often mentioned together as of no value in conflict resolution. Likewise nobody seems to think that party organs or party members are the right places to air their grievances. The focal points are the leadership of the work unit first and the city government second. Other studies support the understanding that the party and the trade union are not visible as a support in people's daily lives (A. Chan 1997: 101).

Also invisible are the mediation and arbitration systems set up under the Ministry of Labour and Social Security. No work unit mediation or government arbitration committee is mentioned in spite of the many irregularities occurring. Not even the Neighbourhood Committee or Street Office seem to be aware that a labour dispute system has existed since 1987 and has been developed and codified in the Labour Law of 1994. Or if they know about it, they either think it does not apply to cases of missing pensions or they believe it not worth trying.

STRATEGIES

It appears that reacting to socio-economic changes in urban China under reform is a creative process, as there are no strictly enforced rules or generally accepted procedures to follow. A lot of energy is spent on bureaucratic matters. Two types of strategies are the most common: the wait-and-see attitude and the taking-matters-into-your-own-hands attitude. The first type is mostly seen with all the pensioners. When they feel wronged, they do not believe in their own ability to change the situation, so they tend to wait patiently, and hope their money will turn up one day. It is seen as reasonable that old people get another treatment than the young ones. For the retired, things should go on in the old way with the state taking responsibility for basic livelihood, while the young can better be asked to take care of themselves by finding suitable employment. Some elderly people place great hope on their children and expect that these will take care of them if they become ill or frail in old age, while others specifically point out that they do not want to depend on their children, usually because the children have enough problems without having to care for their old ones.

Younger people tend to invent alternative plans to cope with upcoming problems, often based on the use of personal connections (*guanxi*) and mobilizing individual resources. One younger worker states with great certainty that without money and connections nothing can be achieved at all, a feeling confirmed by a majority of the interviewees. Connections are 'pulled' (*la*) by giving gifts – often money – by visiting people and by offering them help or explaining one's situation. Actually, everybody talks about gifts; the ones they have given, or will not give, or the ones they have to give in the future; even the ones they did not had to give.[4] Take for example the woman of 37 who has got sick leave by way of a doctor's declaration and good relations. Her husband says:

> You have to have good connections to get sick leave, even if you are mortally ill. I had to do a lot of visiting and talking and shouting to get it. We went to Beijing and to Shijiazhuang, we sent gifts, we went to the leadership of the factory and to the hospitals. I said that if they did not give in, I would go to their homes and bother them.

If you try to get another job or create an activity to secure a new source of income, you may run into other problems. The work unit can prohibit or prevent you from doing certain things. A man in Xingtai tells that his wife wanted to give up her position in a state-owned unit and become self-employed. They moved to the city from Anhui, and she paid 1,500 yuan as a deposit to get a job. She

4. On gifts and favors in Chinese social relations, see further Mayfair Yang 1995.

considered it to be a permanent position and was willing to pay for this security, and she was told that she would get the money back if she wanted to leave. She was never allowed to begin to work, however, as they did not have any work for her to do. So she decided to quit and start a small business. But the unit would not pay the deposit back, the manager saying – again – they did not have the money. Her husband, however, had a good job in the Water Conservancy Bureau of the Municipal Government. He talked to the leadership of the women's work unit, and promised them trouble with the water supply of the factory if they did not refund the family the 1,500 yuan, with the result that the deposit was paid back. Another family has had the same problem, and they also 'managed' to get the money back by using the influence of some friend or a friend of a friend. There is a clear gender bias in the example; it is the husband who complains on behalf of his wife. Now he is the one who has the job enabling them to threaten the employer, but it is no accident that he is the one with the good job and he acts in a very 'creative' way. The women questioned tend to be less inclined to act in unconventional ways than men and they are often in a worse position than their husbands vis-a-vis their work unit. Men tend also to act on behalf of and decide for their wives and daughters. The mother in Case F 4 XT would like to send her son to the Procuratorate instead of going there herself, but refrains from doing so on account of his temper. In other cases husbands dare not let their wives or daughters travel alone to Shijiazhuang, the provincial capital, even though they have to go there to buy goods to sell on the streets. If they have work themselves they persuade some male relative or neighbour to go with the women. Care and control is probably mixed in such efforts and the subject is not further explored in the questioning as it is not one of the central topics.

Another reaction can be just to do by yourself what needs to be done, like the grandfather in Case F 2 XT whose youngest grandchild, together with five others, needed books to pass the middle school examen. The other children in the class had books but the school ran out of copies and did nothing to get more. The man ran around everywhere and succeeded, through friends and colleagues, to obtain a number of the school books which he donated to the school. He ostensibly spent a lot of time in the process and was very proud of his deed. He was a little angry with the school but it seemed unimportant to him to blame the matter on anyone in particular. He was satisfied in getting books to his own grandson and even donate more books to other needy children.

According to most answers in the present study people in Xingtai and Guangzhou are concentrating on their own situation and how to make ends meet, rather than deliberating collective actions. Their primary concern is not to protest or criticize policy, but to find a way out for themselves and their families. Their stories and replies are filled with fatalistic remarks like 'we must go ahead (*wangqian zou*)' or 'one step at a time (*zou yibu shuo yibu*)'. Even though complaining about objectively very unreasonable treatment, when discussing a more systematic joint reaction, the interviewee stubbornly insists that it is no use to appeal to the authorities, it only makes things worse. There seems to be a strong constraint on claiming one's rights at the appropriate level. This is often not because they do not know who ought to be responsible, but out of very low expectations in relation to public authorities. And in all problematic cases treated, solutions have been found so far by relying on family and friends; no one reports directly on starvation or failures to get vital medical treatment because of lack of funds. The social network is effective in these places and great hope and expectation are put on family members. The problem seems to be insecurity about the future; a feeling that one can still manage, but for how long?

GENERAL ASSESSMENTS

In spite of the increasing insecurity described above, an overall evaluation is most often positive. Very few raise the demand that the state ought to provide jobs, housing and free medical care to the citizens, as it did before the reforms started. There still seems to be widespread support for the reform programme in spite of all the problems with implementation. People claim life is better now than before the reforms.[5] After describing their hardships they generally express a sentiment of improvement both in terms of relaxed social life, but also in economy. Their situation may be less secure, prices are higher, morality is declining, but they certainly have more to eat and better clothes than before, and, as mentioned above, many express a fair degree of trust in the government.

A typical overall evaluation of the new times from a Guangzhou docker sounds like this:

> You ask about the most important changes in the last 20 years. Briefly I can say the economy has improved and the social morality has deteriorated. On night shifts in factories the workers will sing Karaoke until the early morning. The security of person and property is in danger. Many bicycles are stolen, I lost seven or eight bicycles myself. The economy of my unit is not good and the salary is low. The quality of the law personnel is too bad. In our neighbourhood a factory is running all night and making noise and polluting. We have complained several times and when the police came at last, they were very inefficient. After they left, it started immediately again. The fees for education are far too high. Work units should help employees to cover expenses on schooling of the children. Ordinary families cannot bear the burden. But anyway, life is better now than before, when it was difficult even to move around freely.

In Xingtai the most conspicuous threats are not social morality but instability in the payment of wages and pensions, and never ending negotiations about bills from hospitals and doctors. The worry about morality exists, though, like that of the 43-year-old father of two who rhetorically asks: 'Do you think that order and conscience come automatically if you have money? Not necessarily!' The difference between the two places conform to their different economic and political position. The northern community is poorer and more 'backwards', making the threat of poverty a real danger, while people

5. As a comparison it is interesting to see Ssuzsa Ferge's reference to a survey of East Europeans where a majority still (in the middle of the 1990s) think the new system is better than the previous one, but the trend is growing disappointment with, among other things, the loss of social security and the withdrawal of the state. 'The attraction of the velvet revolutions is apparently fading in the light of the new experiences' (Ferge 1997: 37). But here it must be remembered that Central and Eastern Europe, unlike China, suffered from negative economic growth and huge unemployment rates as a cause of political and economic transition.

in the more prosperous and 'modern' area in the south worry more about declining law and order and the spread of moral vices and a corrupt mentality.

In both areas the reforms have clearly caused a greater uncertainty in relation to the economic and social conditions in the future, coupled with more freedom and reward for individual activity. Social and economic relations are not stable anymore. Lifelong employment in a work unit still exists but is marred with fears of being laid off and failing fulfilment of obligations from the side of the work unit. The prospect of leaving the traditional labour allocation system for some kind of self-employment is the new option. This does not dissolve the uncertainty, but gives a much more diversified range of choices and the possibility of becoming well-off. From a human rights perspective this can even be seen as progress, following the definition of the UNDP from 1990:

> Human development is a process of enlarging people's choices. In principle these choices can be infinite and change over time. But at all levels of development, the three essential ones are for people to lead a long and healthy life, to acquire knowledge and have access to resources needed for a decent standard of living. (UNDP 1990: 10)

The report in this way connected human rights and development concerns by a definition of development as encompassing all the core rights codified in the international texts. The link between rights and development was further elaborated in the 2000 report, where it was stated that 'Human freedom is the common purpose and common motivation of human rights and human development' (UNDP 2000: 2). Thus, in the eyes of an important UN actor, freedom and individual choice opportunities loom large and almost overshadow the need for security and care. In this light the new priority in China of more freedom and less social security fits very well with the global agenda.

CONCLUDING REMARKS

In the beginning of this chapter 'hopelessness, powerlessness and passive strategies of protest' are quoted as inborn traits in the mind of people living under socialism. The reactions of the Chinese surveyed here is similar but also different. Hopelessness is surely there but mingled with optimism; powerlessness on the other hand permeates most of the stories while passive strategies of protest are sometimes changed into protesting by taking the matter into one's own hands, concerning minor practical matters at least.

The greater latitude of choice is not unconditionally appreciated in the two researched places. The choices available are not sufficient and many people are disinclined to disassociate themselves from the former safe havens. Great confusion reigns over which institution or level is responsible for what and where to go and claim one's rights. Generally we meet a tendency to wait and see, not to go out and organize for change, but finding unsatisfactory individual solutions to what are really common problems, and what is also perceived as common problems by the persons involved. This attitude does not prevail all over China these years, where we see both spontaneous protests, like the labour disputes mentioned above, and more systematic long-term organizing, at least among some groups e.g. women activists (Hsiung et al. 2001).

There are two obvious reasons why stories of active protests and complaints are not told on the scale that some of the difficulties could have justified. One pragmatic understanding of the low level of organized protesting is that it is dangerous. It is not at all free to air one's grievances in the public space. One risks being registered and subsequently suffering harassment from the authorities individually, but sanctions might affect one's relatives as well. Another, more culturally based, explanation is that a tradition for organizing outside formal channels has been lost through three decades of socialist authoritarian rule, and may never have been especially strong in China anyway. Here the dependency mentioned in the introduction fits the pattern of reactions voiced by the interviewees, where it will be argued that the dependent mentality is maybe a 'systematic consequence' of a socialist system, but exacerbated by certain traits of a traditional Chinese authoritarian culture. So the two reasons for a relatively low level of social unrest – the immediate risk and a dependent mentality acquired through years of socialist rule – are not in contradiction but supplement each other and work in the same direction.

However, opposing forces are at play. The dependency concept would normally be understood as being in direct opposition to a rights-based approach. Docile subjects do not claim rights. But this reasoning does not entirely cover the attitudes and vocabulary in the Chinese public forums and private conversations. A rights terminology is used more and more often. In the words of a close observer of the civil society scene in China for the last decades: 'There is in fact a thriving rights discourse in China, which is also rapidly becoming a litigous society' (Young 2001/2002: 7). Newspaper articles in local papers – not intended for a foreign audience – may speak of the 'rights' of laid off workers, or that women's 'rights' have been violated in this or that situation. Gradually the word is becoming part of the new vocabulary, like *'xiagang'* (laid off from the work unit) or *'huobi fenfang'* (commercial housing). A special problem exists when 'rights' become '*human* rights', a concept still highly politicized and sensitive, somehow placed in another category than all other kinds of rights.

The rights vocabulary is not often used in the interviews, but it appears that people have a clear sense of what kind of treatment they are entitled to. They do not feel the state ought to provide them with jobs, free housing, free health care, etc., but they think that they should get their salary on time, that things ought to go by the rules and that weak and vulnerable groups should be protected – by local community or by government. Most of the interviewed people in both localities do not know the rules precisely and do not care. They do not count on a judiciary to protect them against abuses, but they express a clear understanding of their entitlement to a certain minimum living standard. China is clearly still not a society ruled by law, but instead of law a widespread feeling of the state's moral duties exists, in reality corresponding to the state obligations contained in the international human rights regime.

The Chinese citizens have also got new options and a new social space in the form of the idea of a 'society' that might be frightening but is anyway there and can be used by families and individuals for obtaining goods and services necessary for social protection. These possibilities did not exist before. One Chinese scholar stressed that in pre-reform China the government had to provide social security because people did not have any freedom to act economically (Zhu Ling 2000). The provision was not based on humanistic concerns but was an inborn part of the basic economic structure. As this structure – some call it a contract – is dismantled, the free space is offered to people as a compensation for the loss in security and people accept the new deal – though not always willingly – until now at least. But it might be argued that it will take more than one generation to enable Chinese citizens to fully utilise the possibilities of the new distribution of powers and freedoms, and the people in this study and their offspring are maybe not the best equipped to do that.

9

只能靠自己

Consequences of Economic Reform for Social Rights Protection

> *The aim of monitoring is to discern changes that can be related to specific laws, policies and interventions. The rationale is simple: there is no 'perfect' state of human rights that can be attained once and for all.* (Tomasevski 2001: 542)

TRANSFORMATIVE PRINCIPLES

To analyse the state of social rights protection in the Chinese reform process the content of new policies as well as the method used to carry these out will be discussed in this chapter. By content is meant the fact that the transition process in China consists of a movement from one economic system to another, and by method that it has been conducted as a gradual course where two fundamentally different systems overlap and exist side by side for a period of several decades and it has been necessary to design transformative mechanisms to carry out the change. The content and the method have affected and keep affecting rights protection in a dynamic interaction where strong and weak points intermingle and can be sorted out, but there is no single point in time when a final evaluation can be made, as stated in the quote beginning this chapter on the aim of monitoring human rights protection. So the approach will be to identify the actual and potential consequences of reform for protection of the rights treated in the preceding chapters.

Content: from administrative to monetary resource allocation

The content of the transition, as discussed before, basically implies the intention to change the mode of allocation of economic and social resources from administrative allocation to allocation by market forces, and consequently a change from state accumulation to individual (non-state) accumulation of material and social capital. Following the logic of transfer of economic decision-making power from state to 'society', the government in the process loses capacity to redistribute and reallocate resources from wealthy regions, institutions and individuals to needy ones. This loss of control is exactly the very aim of the whole venture. Thus, the decentralization of economic power to the market has eroded the capability of the state to uphold social safety by direct interference. The latitude of government has narrowed, impairing the possibilities of central government to fund social welfare policies. And as governments constitute the focal point of rights protection, loss of state control is an essential factor to keep in mind.

Wang Shaoguang and Hu Angang have dealt extensively with the decline in state capacity since the beginning of the reforms and they claim that China has a low ratio of government income to Gross Domestic Product (GDP) even seen from a global perspective (Wang and Hu 2001: 46 and 50). The proportion fell from 26 per cent in 1980 to 15 per cent in 2000 (*ZTN* 2001: 246).[1] The ratio of GDP to government income is a measure of how big a part of a society's economic activity is under government control. But even though the part controlled by the central state has shrank considerably the percentage going to social development has doubled. The structure of government spending changed during two decades of reform with a cut by one-third on economic construction, almost a doubling of expenses for 'social, cultural and educational development', a cut on defence expenses by two-thirds, and a threefold rise in expenditure on government administration. So with a relatively smaller income the government shoulders a relatively larger share of social responsibility than before. The structure of

---

1. The corresponding figures for selected developed countries for 1985 are between 33 % for Japan and 65 % for Sweden (Wang and Hu 2001: 35).

Chart 9.1 Government expenditure by category of expenses

	Economic Construction	Social Development	National Defence	Government Administration
1980	715 (60%)	199 (17%)	194 (16%)	76 (7%)
2000	5748 (41%)	4385 (31%)	1208 (9%)	2768 (20%)

Unit: 100 mill yuan (per cent of government income) (*ZTN* 2001: 252)

government expenses has changed in favour of social expenses, expressing a political willingness to make up for losses incurred in the transformative process. That government income has declined relatively is not only a consequence of decentralization to non-state economic units but can also be attributed to transfer of power from central to local state level. The distribution of expenditure between the central and the local governments have changed from 54 per cent and 46 per cent, respectively, in 1980 to 35 per cent and 65 per cent in 2000 (*ZTN* 2001: 258). Policies have been introduced to regain central control over part of the economy. As part of the renewed drive to establish a socialist market economy in 1993 a comprehensive tax reform was adopted to generate more revenue for the central government. Six new categories of taxes were introduced, among them value-added tax, enterprise income tax and individual income tax (Cheung 1997: 514), but implementation was not effective, and the percentage of revenue in relation to production continued to fall, as we saw above.

Method: gradualism

The Chinese way of reforming has become famous for its incremental character (Woo 1999: 117) in contrast to the more abrupt parallel economic and political changes in the former Soviet Bloc. Incrementalism has necessitated the creation of the transformative mechanisms meant to facilitate the process and mitigate the hardships encountered by the involved institutions and individuals. Concerning the topic of this study we have seen different variants of these mechanisms like the re-employment campaigns, the practice of laying off, the subsidized sale of housing, the Hope Project etc. These mechanisms have become tools of reform, and because the new institutional set-ups and distribution forms are partly created to ease the pain of transition they preserve elements of the former power structures that in turn affect the framework within which new institutions can be thought out. The degree and duration of the influence of earlier structures have been the subject of academic scrutiny and debate since the consequences of reform began to take shape. Many scholars have pointed to the problem that the former structure 'invades' or distorts implementation of new policies and/or that the way the reforms are constructed in itself blocks their successful implementation (Francis 1996: 858; Lo and Cheng 1996: 51; A. Chan 1997: 107; Gu 2001a: 148). Reform measures trip themselves up, so to speak.

An academic debate on winners and losers in the transition from plan to market has taken place during the last half of the 1990s between primarily American, Chinese and East European scholars under the name of the 'Market Transition Debate'.[2] One viewpoint in the debate was that in the course of economic transition a new entrepreneurial class will emerge enriching itself on the opportunities of the market (Nee 1989), while another was that the former elite of administrative bureaucrats will take their share of the profits (Bian and Logan 1996), i.e. that the former power-holders will keep their elite status and just uphold it by other means than before. The former standpoint goes under the name of a 'market transition model', viz. the idea that market distribution will prevail over and be detrimental to the former political power structure, while the second is referred to as 'the power persistence hypothesis', meaning that the former political elite will occupy a leading position in the new social balance of power. An excellent expression and discussion of the power persistence idea is found in David Wanks' study of private businesses in Xiamen in the beginning of the 1990s, with the thesis that the state is not retreating, instead its power is commodified and the boundaries between state and so-

2. See *American Sociological Review*, vol. 61, 1996: 739–758; vol. 62, 1997: 339–385 and *American Journal of Sociology*, vol. 101, no. 4, 1996: 908–1096; vol. 105, no. 4, 2000: 1175–1195.

ciety are riddled with new patterns of alliances (Wank 1999: 9–10). Subsequently, other scholars question the bipolar distinction between administrative and monetary distribution, painting a more diversified picture adding new actors like intellectuals (Tang and Parish 2000: 13). The concept of 'power persistence' in the transition process can be applied to the area of social security reform, where vested interests in crucial ways affect the result of new economic and institutional measures.

As the objective of this chapter is to trace how the reform features just outlined have affected the re-structuring of social policies that constitute the legal and institutional frame-work for social rights protection, the two basic parameters are on the one hand the distribution of obligations between state, market and family and especially the new role of the state, and on the other hand the influence of former structures will be used to address the issue of pro- or retrogression important in the human rights regime. Thus state control and power persistence will be used to discuss the reforms' effect on social policies that in turn affect protection of social rights for the group of people discussed in this study, i.e. urban workers affiliated with state- or collectively owned enterprises.

Implications for social policy

From state to family care. The new social policies are first of all characterized by the continued existence of layers of social distinctions, firstly between urban and rural residents, secondly between urban workers and urban non-employed citizens, and thirdly between different kinds of employees. At each layer different social guarantees are granted. The reforms are, thus, rooted in a complex hierarchy, inherited from the Mao period, and the grading of citizens seems not to be dissolved by the new economic mechanisms. The unequal access to social services is formed on the basis of an unequal relation to the labour market in accordance with the pre-reform set-up. In theory the basic criteria for public support have not changed, though the system has been enlarged with new possibilities, e.g. unemployment subsidies and minimum living standards. On the basis of the former distinctions new rules and regulations have been established with the aim of standardising and unifying social protection within each group, most comprehensively for public employees, less so for private employees and non-employed urbanites, and very little for the peasants.

But in practice the foci of social responsibility in all groups are slowly reverting to a pre-revolutionary position based on family care. During the Communist reign or the 'Mao-period', 1949–1979, responsibility for social protection gradually moved from the family to the state. The government systematically tried to weaken the role of family loyalties and transform them into loyalty to the party-state. A variety of means were at play, not least the destruction of the economic foundations of clan rule by deprivation of private property and by institutionalization of strong state interference in all aspects of private life. In the cities, work units – in the countryside rural collectives in different guises – replaced the family as the main caretaker (Whyte 1997: 2). Consequently, social welfare for urban people during that period came mostly to be guaranteed from one single source, i.e. the work unit, but in the course of reform the different welfare services have been diversified and spread out to the main actors – local state, market and family[3] – in the way that employment and housing have mainly gone to the marketplace, where expenses are born by the family economy, while expenses on education in reality are divided between the local government and the families, and health care and pensions have become the joint responsibility of employers and employees. The reforms reversed the direction of three decades of socialism and, as has been shown, in reality a substantial part of the burden has been lifted back onto the shoulders of the family.

Efforts to care for people outside the labour market have been made e.g. in designing the system of minimum living standards, by granting 'poverty cards' and by other measures, an important one being that the legal obligation of grown-up children to support

3. As explained in the introduction no distinction will be made between family and individual here because there is still a solid interaction and interdependency between family members in Chinese society. On the same grounds the move to family care will be included under the concept of 'individualization'.

ageing parents has been preserved in the Constitution. With the weakening of work unit protection article 49 in the 1982 Constitution becomes crucial in the movement towards family care with the provision: 'Parents have the duty to rear and educate their minor children, and children who have come of age have the duty to support and assist their parents.' The provision is not new but it is a new phenomenon that it is used in the court system where old people claim their rights to support from children and often win (Michelson 1998: 88; Xu Yuebin 2001: 314).

The interviews likewise give a clear picture of persisting strong family ties and a high degree of family support regarding important areas such as work, schooling and housing. Parents have a very clear picture of what they want for their children, they have a fairly strong influence on the priorities and behaviour of them and they are prepared to sacrifice much of their own comfort to help them. Likewise, grown-up children report to care materially and emotionally for their parents, though co-residence in three generations is not the most common form of housing arrangement; 33 per cent in Xingtai and only 14 per cent in Guangzhou live with married children. But not living together does not sever ties of daily contact and common decision-making on vital issues. Adult children always know exactly who takes care of their parents to what degree and they will usually be involved themselves, even in cases where a parent live in another province. Several cases of grandchildren living only with their grandparents for some practical reason are recorded in Xingtai without the informers ostensibly regarding it as something special.

These results accord with other studies confirming that Confucian familism so far is surviving modernization and 'sentiments of filial obligation remain robustly intact' (Whyte 1997: 31). It seems that both the material structures and the psychological disposition of family solidarity have been hibernating over the years of collectivism and have been revived in this time of crisis (Ikels 1990: 381). Family support seems not only to constitute an emotional attachment but also an economic and material necessity in order to cope with the imbalances created by the ongoing transformation of the social structure where e.g. revived clan organizations try to grab political influence (*Shehui gongzuo yanjiu*, no. 4 1995). The special sort of Chinese social support build up around the family and the close community has been sought and found in several empirical studies. Angelina Yuen-Tsang, in an investigation of social networks of working mothers in Beijing, describes how work unit support is replaced by support from families and neighbours and how families work out joint strategies, trying to get the best of two worlds: 'Madam Yu said it was their strategy to have one person working within the Government and one working in the private sector . . .' (Yuen-Tsang 1997: 129). The Beijing City Government out of social concerns adopted a rule that two persons in one family should not be laid off at the same time, thereby acknowledging that a family has to be counted as one economic unit that support all its members.

However, the dependence of the family can be foreseen to run into problems as effects of modernization might make the family less capable of providing basic social security in the future than it is now (Yuen-Tsang 1997:120). The change in family patterns normally found in modernization processes has made its entry. Individual family members have become more mobile and can be separated from the family for long periods of time. Co-residence of three generations is on the decline, at least in the cities, and is replaced by the nuclear family. Import of new ideas and lifestyles from abroad divides the generations intellectually and emotionally and adds to the need for a social safety net outside the family. Whether these trends will weaken the revived family solidarity and further individualize social protection remains to be seen, but it must be accepted that the two tendencies are opposing each other.

The family support network is supplemented by and intermingled with support from the whole web of connections known by its Chinese name, *guanxi*, wherein the family is a crucial element.

> Guanxi networks can be constructed on the basis of friendship, common school ties, and many other grounds, but in general one's family is the most secure and readily available basis for building ties with outsiders. (Whyte 1997: 24)

Comments from a docker in Guangzhou confirm that good connections are created outside of the workplace. Asked about whether he had any good connections in his work unit, he replied, 'No, I know them all through work'. To 'have a background' (*you beijing*) is also heard for 'pulling connections' (*la guanxi*). The personalized exchange of gifts, services and obligations has existed all through the Mao period and seems not to have been weakened by the market economy (M. Yang 1994). On the contrary, a new element have been added making the system more complicated, mirrored in the repeated comments from the interviews that

> . . . now one has to have both money and good connections to obtain anything. Money alone is not enough, one also has to know somebody to get a job with an income or a decent residence or whatever one needs.

The 'individualization of welfare' in formation throughout the world (Ferge 1997) is in the Chinese version giving social duties back to the family and non-formal networks, granting protection through a combination of social ties and money.

State capacity. When rights protection is 'individualized' it is because the former provider or protector has lost control or deliberately has shed its obligations or a mixture of the two factors, as has been the case in China. At the same time as we have seen a drastic rise in relative expenses on social development and government administration (Chart 9.1.) we have also seen that only a meagre social protection of urbanites has been instituted and other sources show that a safety net for farmers is non-existent (Wu Jinglian 1998: 229; Xu Yuebin 2001), hinting that the loss of state control by far outweighs the effect of a larger proportion used for social issues and administration. The weakening of central state control over economic resources, both in the course of time and geography, interferes with the aim of social policy reform, which is exactly the opposite, viz. to broaden and standardize a nationwide system (Li Jingwen 2000). The transfer of economic power to local government and to non-state productive units impedes the prospects for success in building unified systems valid for all regions, which the state expresses the intention to do. Wang Shaoguang and Hu Angang put forward suggestions to enhance both the government's capacity to extract society's resources through taxation or other means and to increase the ability to make use of fiscal capacities through a system of revenue sharing. Thus a recommendation from the two highly profiled Chinese academics points to a strengthening of central power, but on other grounds than the former centrally planned economy.

> During the transition to market economy, enhancing the state's financial extractive capacity and giving play to the leadership role of the central government are extremely urgent tasks that must be fulfilled. These tasks are fully integrated with the formation and establishment of a socialist market-economic system, and involve systematic innovation. It is only through forming and establishing a governmental system, a fiscal system, a currency system, and other systems such as a supervisory mechanism that are fully in accord with the market economic orientation, that we can hope to fulfill these tasks. (Wang and Hu 2001: 157)

An enhancement of what they call 'financial extractive capacity' could also provide the foundations for broadening of social security schemes that still are reserved for people that have managed to get a job, as we have seen. It also has to be noted, though, that apart from forcing work units and workers to save, the state retains influence by establishing and monitoring social security funds which in due time might amass fortunes. Using its legislative power the government can influence the operation of the funds and in other ways support the establishment of social guarantees, as will be discussed below.

So what the government lacks in economic control – in social policy terms, input to direct welfare provision – it could make up for in political control, giving the means a state has to regulate and monitor social services provided by other actors. Political and administrative control, however, seems also to have been on the decline, as can be recognized in the difficulties in implementing laws and regulations illustrated throughout this study. 'The state is simply not capable of delivering even the limited rights it accords its citizens' (Young 2001/2002: 8). The use of political and administrative measures instead of economic power is exactly the goal that the reform efforts are directed towards, but the goals are somehow hampered by the means.

Power persistence. The obstacles to using central political and legal control lie with the incremental reform principle, as the transformative mechanisms continue to ascribe a significant role to the work unit in spite of the aim to free the units from their social burdens. According to the most recent regulations, introduced in the preceding chapters, social insurance funds have to be extracted at the work unit level, preserving the unit control over economic resources of the employee and probably also supporting the psychological feeling of dependence on unit leadership that is the legacy from the former system. The units are responsible for transferring both their own share and the individual share to a local government body and if they fail to do this the benefit of the employee will be affected. Thus while the administration and distribution of the funds are lifted to a higher bureaucratic level the primary source of accumulation and the transfer of resources are kept at the level of the former power-holder. This does not mean that the units in principle bear the responsibility alone. To the degree one can speak of legal liability, the units are obliged to contribute to the funds and the social security agencies – i.e. local government – are obliged to distribute them. So as the regulations are constructed the responsibility lies with the agencies or ultimately with local governments, which are also reported from many places to have intervened and compensated citizens for losses or omissions caused by unit leadership.

But from the interviews it is clear that people *think* work units are the place to claim their entitlements. The local government is contacted only after approaches to work units have failed. It is also clear that local authorities send people back to the units, or when they take action, they try to influence and persuade unit leadership to act, so they also behave as if the ultimate responsibility for social security still rests with the units and not with themselves, which should be the case according to the regulations. And many work units are trapped in the sense that they are unable to fulfill the obligations they have to contribute to the social security funds because of difficulties adapting to the new market situation. This is clearly seen in the Xingtai example, and also from many other places are debts and failure to live up to obligations reported (Hu Xiaoyi 2001; *Zhongguo laodong baozhang bao*, 12 May 2000; *Beijing qingnian bao*, 16 November 2000). And in spite of reductions in their social burdens the work units are still unequally equipped in the economic competition; e.g. units with many retired workers will reap less, maybe no profit.

The result of the change in social policies thus at this stage is on the one hand a tendency to return to a family care that on the outside is disguised as continued state care through the former provider, the work unit. On the other hand the services that nevertheless are being delivered are unequally distributed in a non-systematic and non-transparent fashion. The two factors in turn affect the prospects of social rights protection for the group of people in question. Furthermore, a non-change is essential and must never be ignored, viz. the continued narrow coverage where all new policies, however badly implemented, only cover urban employees.

Implications for social rights protection

Premises: rights protection and politics. In principle there is no human rights problem with the changed mode of resource allocation in China – from plan to market economy – as the human rights regime does not demand the adoption of any specific political or economic system to guarantee rights protection. The ultimate value of the human rights discourse is insisting on a bottom line of human life conditions that are unacceptable. What happens above the bottom line and how these conditions are prevented is a concern mostly in so far as it threatens or tends towards transcending this line. The thinking behind the formation of the system has been to circumvent political differences separating states and focus on the way a government treats its citizens in relation to basic conditions of livelihood. A crude example: human rights documents do not mention difference in income as a variable. A country can have very rich and very poor people, but the difference in life conditions is not addressed as long as they are not rooted in specific traits covered by the discrimination clauses, like sex, gender, religion, ethnicity, etc. Likewise, redistributive measures are not seen as an absolutely necessary precondition for protection of social rights. In reality, though, it is difficult to imagine the establishment of a social safety net without some measure of redistribution between rich and poor, but in the CESCR General Comment on the nature of States Parties obligations the formulation is as follows.

> The Committee notes that the undertaking 'to take steps . . . by all appropriate means including particularly the adoption of legislative measures'[4] neither requires nor precludes any particular form of government or economic system being used as the vehicle for the steps in question, provided only that it is democratic and that all human rights are thereby respected. Thus, in terms of political and economic systems the Covenant is neutral and its principles cannot accurately be described as being predicated exclusively upon the need for, or the desirability of a socialist or a capitalist system, or a mixed, centrally planned, or *laisser-faire* economy, or upon any other particular approach . . . (General Comment, no. 3, para. 8)

The word 'democratic' might seem to contradict the message but it is in the context linked to the 'steps' undertaken to achieve the realisations of the rights of the Covenant. It is thus not a demand for a parliamentary democracy with free elections but must be understood as a requirement of public participation in designing specific policies. Effective participation is integrated as a precondition in many human rights documents, notably concerning the right to education, the rights of the child and the right to development (Eide 2001: 249 and 358) but the demand does not expand to the choice of government or political system.

Anyway, even though the word 'democratization' may be misplaced in a Chinese context, the power relations between the people and the state have no doubt been changed radically as a consequence of the reforms (Mok and Chan 1996; Tang and Parish 2000). Protection of private life is far greater than under Mao and the social space within which people can move ideologically, economically and socially is much wider than before – a clear improvement in protection of civil rights. The formal and institutional expression of this changed relationship has for some part been described in the preceding chapters. Admittedly it is still weakly ingrained in social practice but the potential is there.

State obligations: will and capacity. The 'neutrality' of the international norms vis-a-vis political or economic systems does not

4. Quote from the ICESCR, article 2(1). See full text of the article in Chapter 2.

ease the task of evaluating the status of rights protection in any single society. On the one hand is the text of the Covenants, on the other the intentions, acts and capacities of states, and it is no simple task to translate one into the other, especially as few states have directly incorporated the different rights categories into domestic policies. The universal character of the human rights system prescribes that the same rights can be protected in many different ways, but how to measure and monitor if the very many different ways live up to the international standard? First of all it needs to be repeated that what has to be measured is state performance, as states are the ultimate duty holders in the regime. Any evaluation has to proceed from some fixed yardstick and two obvious possibilities here are either to compare states with each other or to compare the same country over time. New trends favour the latter approach and focus on progression or retrogression within a country instead of across borders: '. . . the need to analyse *trends* should take precedence over the widespread usage of cross-national comparisons and the ranking of countries' (Nowak 2001: 257). The approach is also commensurate with the principle of 'progressive realisation' of the ICESCR, article 2, which is normally regarded as one of the fundamental principles of social rights protection.

When measuring the pro- or retrogression in state performance in a developing country it is furthermore stressed as important to distinguish between the *will* and the *capacity* of a given government, linked to the formulation in article 2 on '. . . to the maximum of its available resources'. Especially concerning social rights it is crucial to acknowledge the difference between the two factors (Tomasevski 2001: 532). Still, the undertaking is no simple one, as willingness is not easy to measure and capacity is a flexible object of political priorities; furthermore, will and capacity are closely interlinked so it can be difficult to distinguish one from the other. Nevertheless, the endeavour will be made to discuss the performance of the Chinese government in relation to protection of social rights from a time perspective and with a view to willingness and capacity.

Concerning willingness the efforts to regularize and institutionalize social security are amply documented in the previous chapters. Serious efforts to solve social problems are being done in political as well as academic circles. But the sheer size of the task and the problems with implementation have also been documented. The distinction between obligations of result and obligations of conduct can be used here (see Chapter 2). Obligations of conduct concerning institutionalization of social policies have been fulfilled to a certain degree but obligations of result relating to enforcement of the regulations and reaching specific targets are unfulfilled. Seen from the position of ordinary urban workers, many of them have less basic security than they had before the reforms, but they also have unused possibilities of getting more than they actually possess. Concerning capacity, the problem with dwindling state control over resources has already been discussed sufficiently above; it leads to lacking protection for the majority of the population and low subsidies to a minority. It can be discussed whether the existing government funds could be used more effectively or additional funds could be raised, which problem has already been touched upon by domestic reformers, for example in proposals for turning state assets into sources for social funds (see Chapter 6).

'Legalization': from provider to regulator. Generally the role of the state in China has changed, as we have seen, from being basically provider to being more regulator of social services, in human rights terminology equalling a change from fulfilling to respecting and protecting social rights in accordance with the principles and the objectives behind the rebuilding of the party-state. Regulating, respecting and protecting rights are activities based in law and a 'legalization' of Chinese society clearly forms an integral part of the changes also in the area of welfare provision. It comes in a variety of shapes, from tax exemptions for private charity and 'forced donations' to hard law documents.

The concept of charity has been revived, underpinned by pre-revolutionary tradition and influence from the US. In imperial times the elite had a duty to support community activities like schools, temples, infrastructure, etc. The activities were taken up by foreign churches in the 19th and 20th centuries, but missionary activities were prohibited after 1949 and welfare responsibility was transferred to the Ministry of Civil Affairs (Wong 1998: 50). The moral obligation of rich people is now accepted again and strongly propagandized in state media and public institutions by urging people to donate money and goods to the poor, and by assigning different institutions the responsibility to support specific poverty areas. The Ministry of Foreign Affairs has the duty to raise funds for two selected counties in Yunnan; employees in state units are compelled to donate a small amount of money in emergency cases;[5] private companies are asked to contribute to local community building. Charity is called 'the third form of distribution' (*di sanci fenpei*) after state and community welfare provision. In 1986 a lottery system to raise money for social welfare was approved by the State Council; the lottery is driven on market conditions and taxes on the activity are used for social support through MOCA (*Zhongguo shehui bao*, 11 October 1997: 1). In 1995 the China Charity Foundation (CCF) was established as a social organization by permission from the National People's Congress. The chairman of the board of CCF was former minister of civil affairs, Cui Naifu (*Zhongguo shehui gongzuo*, 1996, no. 9). The organization takes inspiration from a US charity fund called 'United Way' and it raise funds by approaching private companies and individuals. It possesses a special transparency as it publishes annual reports with accounts audited (Young and Woo 2000: 24). Its profit is given a tax reduction of 30 per cent.[6] Within MOCA special offices are authorised to raise money from domestic and international donors for specific welfare projects[7], and localities have a helping-the-poor fund (*bangzhu pingkun jijin*) appointed by the local government. It imposes duties on private companies that are neither voluntary nor fixed, but can be negotiated annually.

These are all examples of welfare activities that are not provided by the state but where the government builds and supports a bridge between private capital and needy groups of the population; in an indirect way a redistributive function is performed.[8] In

5. Personal communications, March 1999.
6. Interview Yang Tuan, November 1997.
7. Interview Tu Lijuan, November 2001, China Social Workers Association.
8. Philantrophy is customarily frowned upon in a human rights context, but in the Chinese form, where it has a tax-like character and is encouraged and supported financially by the state, one should maybe revise the judgment a bit, at least deem that it is better than nothing. Ferge does not share the view, she views charity as governed by the new welfare agenda, as the last resort in a society where the search for security by collective means has fallen into disrepute (Ferge 1997: 26).

part the efforts have been interpreted as a way for the state to compensate for the widespread tax evasion that authorities find hard to cope with, but private business managers do not easily give in to the pressure, as the story from Ole Bruun (Bruun 1995: 198) and another from Charlotte Ikels show:

> Because of this assumption (that tax evasion is rampant ht) about entrepreneurs and their high incomes they are pressured to contribute to community projects, thus sharing their wealth. Consequently, many de facto private businesses mask their identity by registering as cooperatives or collectives. (Ikels 1996: 182)

As a more direct form of regulation laws have been passed where complaints over administrative errors can be addressed to the specialized chambers for administrative adjudication in the People's Courts. The local city halls have offices receiving phone calls and visits from the man in the street. Legal aid units exist in the aegis of the Ministry of Justice and at the universities. Disputes over fulfilment of social security obligations within work units can be mediated in the work units first, then arbitrated at the level of local government and if the result is not satisfactory or an arbitration award is not executed, it can be brought before a People's Court. Mediation is an internal procedure, also taking place in the residential setting. It is free but not legally binding. Arbitration, on the other hand, is legally binding and there is an arbitration fee. So, there *are* legal remedies for violations of social rights, but they are not used as much as they could be, and many people hardly know they exist.[9] Stanley Lubman has made an excellent analysis of the whole legalization process in his book 'Bird in a Cage' (Lubman 1999).

Crucial is that the Party still has the ultimate power within which the legal system operates. The PRC Constitution clearly codifies 'the leadership of the Chinese Communist party'. The term 'socialist law' is repeated in numerous documents, most recently in the preamble to the Legislation Law from March 2000, and Party supremacy is in countless other ways firmly ingrained in legal

9. See Chapter 1.

institutions and administrative culture (Potter 2001: 19–20; Peerenboom 2001: 284). Other obstacles to effective legal redress can be behavioural patterns and level of information as illustrated in the local material. The tradition of relying on individualized connections has invaded the legal arena from the economic and social sphere. One young man in Guangzhou went to jail for hitting a man who had cheated his father in a deal. His explanation was quite plain:

> There was a fight between the two of us and later he sued me for assault. I knew some friend of a friend in the court and he intervened on my behalf. But the power of the one he [the person he fought with] knew was bigger, though he did not belong to the 'real power group' (*shiquan pai*). So I was convicted to three years in prison. My contact, on the other hand, was an administrator. He had 'real power', so he got me out after two and a half years.

In another example the father of an interviewed person got a new wife after the death of the mother and a conflict evolved over the ownership of the house, which was inhabited by his children. They thought they had inherited it, but now he demanded to get it back. The dispute was taken to court and the family won with support from the Street Office. The interviewed person commented, 'It is like that today, when you go to court you need to have good connections'.[10] The Legal Daily carries many similar stories involving interference with law enforcement from the concerned parties. Even violent attacks on judicial officials is mentioned by the Supreme People's Court in 2002 as a serious problem (Chen Jianfu 2002: 7).

A mixture of psychological disposition, information failures and lack of resources can be suggested as causes for people not to use the mediation, arbitration and legal channels available to them. The methods used in complaining are personalized and informal. Workers tend to find to the leaders they know in the work unit or the city hall and ask for what they think they have a claim to. *Zhao ren*, to seek people, is used as a general expression for the process of complaining or networking to obtain goods or services. The way that was used before and worked is still used, but it does not work

10. For government response to the problem of corruption in courts, see Peerenboom 2001: 303.

so good anymore, ironically in part because open rules now exist and they are sometimes effective. The jump from personal communication and negotiation to formal/legal actions is difficult everywhere in the world, so much more so in a system where the legal channel had been closed for more than a generation and probably never was part of societal practice anyway. Apart from barriers of psychology and culture, a genuine lack of knowledge and trust plays a part. Many have not been informed about what they can do, and some of those that have the knowledge do not believe the system will be useful for 'ordinary people' like themselves. Similar findings appear in other studies, as when Pitman B. Potter concludes about the Administrative Litigation Law:

> Ten years of practice under the Administrative Litigation Law suggest that protection against administrative abuses through effective judicial review remains an elusive goal. In part this is due to the intent and limited reach of the statute, but popular confidence in the law's effectiveness is limited – a study published in 1998 suggested that less than 20 per cent of potential claimants would be willing to file actions under the Administrative Litigation Law. (Potter 2001: 25)

Anyway, some people even in Hebei use the legal options. A household head in Xingtai tells about her home village where the leadership sold all the land without compensation to anyone, so the farmers had to find work elsewhere. The party secretary and other leaders had set up some enterprises – a medicine factory, a hospital, a restaurant – but they did not distribute profit to the villagers, who subsequently filed a law suit against their leaders. A working group from the county came to investigate the case, and that was the situation at the time of the interview.

Many factors are necessary for effective access to justice, among them laws and regulations; enforcement of legal decisions; information; economic resources; and trust. Of these, written laws are not the most pressing problem in the Chinese system at this stage. The failure of adopting a social security law is lamented by some scholars (Yang and Liu 2001)[11] while others are more doubtful, claiming that no law is better than a badly prepared law and ex-

11. Interview Yu Qiulin, Renmin Daxue, October 1997.

periences have to be collected before a good law can be made.[12] But the other factors are more or less critical for correcting wrongs in relation to social security. Generally implementation of court judgments is a huge problem subject to intensive efforts, like political campaigns conducted under the Supreme People's Court and the Central Committee of the CCP (Chen Jianfu 2002: 5).[13] Information on where to go when one's rights are violated is seriously lacking and so are economic means and trust for parts of the population. To sum up, the move from provider to regulator is not in itself problematic in a human rights context, as many countries have a system where the government does not provide much social service but guarantees – legally and through other means – that other actors will fulfill the task. But access to mediation, redress and the legal system at large is difficult and these systems lack enforcement capacity, amounting to a problem in rights protection.

Persistence of principles. However, the change in the function of the state apparatus has not included a shift in the principles underlying social welfare. As a logical consequence of the continued essential role of labour in welfare protection a contributory principle still prevails over a universalist approach. One could also say a duty approach is still stronger than a rights approach. This is in line with former policies and also with the systems in many other countries in the world, where people who work or have worked are in a much better social position than people who have not made contributions to society in the form of wage labour.

The survival of the 'duty' principle is related to the gradualism principle in the way that the government have not been willing (or able) to confront the problem of depriving urban workers of their advanced status. Naturally, civil servants and workers and staff in publicly owned industries have fought to preserve their privileges in relation to other social groups. They constitute the best educated people in the country and their positions have been closest to the political elite. Their welfare has been cut; even in the field of labour related social protection we have seen that a lifetime of work

---

12. Interview Ge Yanfeng and Li Lulu, April 2001.
13. 1999 was declared an 'Enforcement Year (*zhixing nian*)' by the Supreme Court.

does not guarantee basic social welfare, like pension and health care, but their advantage over peasants in relation to enjoyment of public services has not been basically challenged.

The group is highly heterogenous, though, including ministers, enterprise managers, school teachers and unskilled workers. Whoever – the former political elite or a new entrepreneurial class – has benefited the most from the new market opportunities, middle-aged un-skilled urban workers belong to those that have benefited the least, relatively speaking, i.e. in relation to their former status as the pampered avant-garde of the socialist revolution. Following the principle of measuring in time, their loss becomes relatively more serious as their status and social security have deteriorated considerably to a situation where the most unfortunate of them are at the risk of social exclusion. Whether the government has chosen the gradualist approach not to estrange its former supporters or the priority of urban workers is an accidental result of the continuation in leadership at large; the result is that former boundaries have not been broken down, and the continuation of a contributory principle has continued and exacerbated inequality.

CONVERGENCE WITH GLOBAL TRENDS

There is no doubt that the Chinese reforms in their course have increased income inequalities (Bian and Logan 1996: 739; Wang and Hu 2001: 135) and not only preserved the distinction between urban and rural citizens but also created and exacerbated inequality within the two groups.[14] When market mechanisms carve out a bigger part of distribution of social resources, inequality will rise, collective solutions to life problems will be replaced by individual solutions and social security will be threatened. The extent of 'decommodification' has been used to characterize different welfare regimes, pointing to the idea that the more workers have access to state funded social services the less vulnerable they are when con-

14. China was not a perfectly equal society before, either, as concluded by a Chinese scholar, 'In fact, distribution as such was neither equal nor efficient, and even ran counter to the original intentions of its designers' (Zhu Ling 2000: 85). But in global terms the inequalities before reforms were relatively small.

fronting the vicissitudes of life; and the other way round, the more they depend on the market the more unequally they will be protected (Philion 1998: 519). The reasoning goes partly for China where we exactly see that the transition towards market economy increases income inequalities, but ironically decreases inequality in protection of social rights, as the benefits of those favoured before decline and their protection becomes more equal with other groups in society.

Topping the agenda on social policy in the rich countries today is the question concerning the impact of globalization on social equity, and how to defend welfare policies against the spread of neo-liberal economic principles. The term 'individualization of the social' has been used to describe a whole new welfare paradigm, whereby:

> The state – as already implied – is shedding its former load. It is diminishing its responsibilities for legislating on social rights and for the enforcement of these rights. (Ferge 1997: 27)

The Hungarian sociologist Zsuzsa Ferge perceives the dominant institutions and operating principles of the new paradigm as being that the market is rapidly gaining ground at the expense of the two others pillars dominating a democratically organised nation – state and civil society. Relations between people are becoming more and more based on economic value, means testing replaces collective arrangements, leaving the individual to fight alone vis a vis the state for his or her own interests, and people withdraw from political activity that is left to technocrats (Ferge 1997). Ferge shares with other scholars and international agencies the following two assumptions:

- Globalization has increased inequality, vulnerability and social exclusion within nations and between nations.
- International economic liberalization has weakened state capacity and made it more difficult to pursue socially responsible policies nationally (UNRISD 2000).

The increased vulnerability and dwindling state capacity we have seen emerging as results of the Chinese reforms fit remarkably well with the global picture presented here.

The impact of globalization affects rich and poor countries differently. In the North most systems are in one way or another changing and conforming to global trends of privatization and commercialization of welfare. Scandinavian scholars see convergence within Europe as a dominant trend, '. . . all European countries will move towards more dualistic, socially segmented or class-structurated social security systems . . .' (Kuhnle 1995: 20). In the East (the former Soviet Bloc), Ferge finds an 'Overzealous alignment to the new expectations'; the governments in Central and Eastern Europe are more than willing to follow the advice of the IMF and the World Bank to cut back on social expenditure (Ferge 1997: 32). In the South public funding of social services is cut back or not raised, and new systems are established with a view more to economic efficiency than to social justice, as we see in East and Southeast Asia. We even see tendencies to glorify the withdrawal of the state in the new combination of a 'positive Orientalism' and a 'negative Occidentalism'[15] – discussed by Gordon White and Roger Goodman.

> Unlike Western Orientalism in its contemporary phase – a largely positive complimentary phenomenon – this breed of Eastern 'negative Occidentalism' portrays the West in highly negative terms, as a model to be avoided at all costs. (Goodmanet al. 1998: 5)

Commentators in the West praise the East Asian model, while Easterners are increasingly proud of their economic and social achievements which some attribute to an Oriental superiority. The viewpoint is expressed by one influential Chinese social policy scholar, who claims that Western European systems constitute a mechanism whereby the present generations leave future ones in heavy debt and therefore can be viewed as a totally irresponsible and unsustainable arrangement (Yang Tuan et al. 1996: 2).

Globalization is seen as favouring the adoption of selective contribution based schemes and impede universalist rights based welfare policies.[16] However, adverse trends are also being pointed out,

15. They are referring to the concept of Orientalism as phrased by Edward Said, who points to the mythological role of the Orient in Western thinking, primarily in the colonial period (Said 1995).
16. This analysis is contested by Gøsta Esping-Andersen, pointing to technological and structural change within nations as responsible for changed welfare options (Esping-Andersen 1999: 101–103).

suggesting a new sense of global responsibility in the international donor organizations and questioning some of the assumptions listed above, at least as far as poor countries are concerned (Deacon 2000: 1; Moore 2000: 22). UN agencies like the United Nations Research Institute for Social Development clearly favour a rights approach with universal coverage, even for developing countries (UNRISD 2000). This is not the place to argue for one or the other position, but enough to state that the conditions for social protection are undoubtedly undergoing great changes for all countries as a consequence of the rapidly shrinking distances on the entire globe.

The Chinese are in a commodification process in which we find traits resembling many other parts of the world. At the same time as distribution is continued by informal – and not economical – mechanisms, as mentioned above, we see an extreme 'monetization' of assets, like seniority where each year of work equals a certain subsidy in housing; academic accomplishments can be bought when bad school marks can be made up for with money; employment in a work unit is charged a 'deposit fee' or whatever it is called; measuring comes also in non-monetary form when a one-child certificate is equivalent to two urban household registrations and a university degree is equivalent to cadre position in allocating housing. The direct effect of globalization on social and economic policies is probably less severe in China than in many other places because of the huge size of the country. China successfully survived the Asian crisis in 1997 without depreciating its Renminbi and has kept clear of serious inflation for the last decade, so economically the country is not overly vulnerable. But she will not avoid being influenced by the closer ties to the world economy following admission to the WTO, which in itself puts high demands on the design of a new social policy.

Finally, widening the perspective, it is worth also keeping in mind that China is entering the capitalist world market *and* the human rights regime at a time when protection of economic, social and cultural rights are challenged by general trends in economic and political systems worldwide, as pointed out above. The current globalization, built on growth maximising strategies that create increased mobility, rapid technological change and growing social exclusion, threaten the establishment and perpetuation of systems of collective responsibility. An increasing individualization of social rights could be the outcome (Robertson 1994: 702), from the failure to build social security systems in the transitional market economies to the dismantling of existing welfare regimes in Europe. In tune with the spirit of the times, China experiences a parallel development, an 'internal globalization', characterized by a rapidly increased mobility and growth of an informal sector causing wider disparities in living standards. And the global power transfer from national to international level without sufficient transfer of responsibility is in China mirrored in an adverse trend, a transfer from central to local political level, but with similar results, seen from a human rights perspective.

只能靠自己

Afterword

The question of the uniqueness of Chinese culture has been a recurring theme in modern sinology. Are Chinese culture and politics fundamentally different from other systems and do they need to be treated with tailor-made methods and approaches, or is the Chinese civilization one among others – fundamentally similar (Nathan 1997: 136–151; Fairbank 1986: 39–45)? During each of the introductions in Chapter 3 the Chinese relation to the outside world is suggested and shall be summarized here as the claim that China is somehow related to many other cultural traditions, geographical/economic areas and political doctrines, but is a unique mix of those, and the country has numerous and complex interfaces with the rest of the world. It resembles its East Asian neighbours in cultural point of departure, expressed in the autocratic state structure, but differs from them with regard to economic system in contemporary history, and is now converging towards them economically with the liberalization of the planned economy. Until recently it resembled the other socialist states in its adherence to full employment and state provision of social security, on which latter point the socialist systems approached the European social democracies. In another direction China is still a developing country with a huge problem of alleviating poverty and social exclusion, and it shares the budget constraints and weak state capacity of other poor countries. At the same time China wants to be internationally recognized as a super-power commensurate with its size and potential resources.

In a historical perspective the present transformation of Chinese society is of short duration. The process was formally initiated in late1978 but the real social changes and new social policies began to take shape around 1992–1993 when the economic reforms in earnest began to touch basic societal structures like financial systems, ownership rights and social guarantees, leading to a crisis in actual social protection. The results from local studies show a slow penetration of new mechanisms and policies from the top down, right from the State Council to the families in Xingtai and the suburbs of Guangzhou. And they show very limited information the other way, from the 'man in the street' back to the decision-making bodies. People have not had many possibilities to formulate complaints or just needs in an effective way, and those they have, they do not know how to use. This lack of mutuality will be one of the great challenges in the process to come.

PROGRESS AND PROBLEMS

Basic *progress* in protection of economic and social rights during the reform process have been:

- Enactment of laws (on labour, women, marriage, inheritance, compulsory education, etc.)
- Establishment of a diversified system (legal and administrative) for complaints and remedies
- Increased protection of privacy (residence, correspondence)
- Adoption of insurance schemes in urban areas
- Establishment of minimum living standards
- International cooperation
- Support of private charity
- Liberation of control of movement

Basic *problems* with protection of economic and social rights under the present Chinese regime are:

- Continued division of the population into status groups
- Narrow coverage, especially for the rural population
- Unequal access to publicly financed social services
- Weak enforcement of existing regulations
- Fragile channels of popular participation
- Poor knowledge of complaints mechanisms and legal remedies

- State endorsed fees in primary schools, adding pressure on family economy
- Restrictions on freedom of movement, both in law and practice

The immediate results of the changes in the reform era for the Chinese population are more freedom of choice and movement for the individual citizen, but less stable protection of the right to work, health care, housing, education, etc. A general view of the reform of social policies shows a movement towards a system of social protection that continues to be based on labour contribution and continues to benefit the urban population most.

Appendix 1 只能靠自己

Interview from Xingtai, November 1997

F 33 XT

A. Let's talk about basics. Your family first. How many people are there in your family?

B. Only the three of us, me, my husband and our child.

A. Where does your husband work?

B. My husband doesn't have a job. He comes from a county under Xingtai municipality and his household registration is in the countryside. He is a farmer.

A. Where is he now?

B. He is with me here, but he is not registered. We now live at my parents' place.

A. What does he do?

B. He opened a medical clinic in a small rented room. He is a doctor, but it doesn't work very well.

A. What is his speciality?

B. All sorts.

A. Did he learn it by himself?

B. He uses qigong to treat the patients. And if one has a headache or a slight fever, he can prescribe some Western medicine, that's all.

A. Where is it?

B. Quite close in the Renmin Juchang (People's Theatre). Before he worked in Nanhe [30 km southeast of Xingtai], that was not good either. It was too far away from home. We couldn't find him if anything happened at home. Later he moved back here and a friend found the room for us. It is facing the street. He works there alone. My work unit doesn't pay salary, so our only income is what he can earn.

A. How much is that?

B. Not much. Just a little more than 200 yuan a month.

A. How much is the room?

B. We paid 100 yuan for it. All the neighbours try to help us find some work.

A. Does he need any licences?

B. He has a licence.

A. When did he get it? Did he get it in Xingtai or did he have one before?

B He had one before.

A. So he is experienced.

B. He has been doing this for many years.

A. Did he treat people in the countryside?

B. No, he didn't. He only worked as a farmer.

A. Where does he come from? Was it only after he left the countryside that he started treating people?

B. After he had left the village one of our friends suggested that he could treat patients, that he should open a clinic.

A. When did he leave?

B. Less than 10 years ago. In 1990 some of his relatives brought him here to find something, and they found him a job as a doorman. But he didn't do it for very long.

A. When did he start to work as a doctor and to treat people?

B. You cannot really set a fixed time when he started to work as a doctor. A friend got him the job as a doorman and in between he worked on the farm at home during the busy harvest time. We know many people here and one day one of them said that a doctor was needed in the neighbourhood, and asked my husband if he would not open a clinic because he has experience. So he tried to start one using his own methods.

A. How old is he?

B. 34. One year older than me.

A. He had graduated from junior middle school at that time?

B. No, from senior middle school. He studied by himself and his parents wanted their children to study so they did not ask him to do farm work. And they said: 'When you have earned some money, don't think of supporting the family, just use it to buy what you need.'

A. Did he learn medicine by himself.

B. Yes, but it is also family wisdom passed down from his ancestors. They have known this method for many generations.

A. So you can live on it?

B. No, it doesn't work now. Some people believe in it, some not. He also sometimes works on the farm.

A. How much can he earn a day?

B. Not a lot. Maybe five yuan per day, only 150 yuan a month. My factory also has problems so I stay at home (*xie*)[1].

A. Do you have a daughter?

B. A son.

A. How old?

B. Six years old.

A. Has he just started going to school?

B. Yes.[2] That's no good either. Sometimes he asks for this, and sometimes he asks for that, so I have to ask him if it cannot wait till another day.

A. How much have you paid until now?

---

1. The word *xie*, to have a rest or to stop working, is the most often used word in Xingtai describing the situation where people stay at home with or without the formal status of being laid off.
2. It later turns out that the child is in pre-school class and will begin grade one the following year.

B. More than 200 yuan.

A. What was the 200 yuan for?

B. Tuition fee, insurance fee and a fee for books and exercise books. We have already spent more than 30 yuan for books and exercise books.

A. How about the tuition fee?

B. We have paid 130 yuan.

A. How about the insurance?

B. Insurance 20 yuan. And you need to buy this one today, and another one tomorrow, they ask for money all the time.

A. Is the school close to your home?

B. Just over there. We only have this one child, if we had had more, we would really be in trouble.

A. Where did you work before?

B. At the station for recycling used material. This was my first job. I started in 1987, the economy of the station is not good.

A. Have you also graduated from senior middle school?

B. No, from junior middle school. After leaving school I had nothing to do but cooking and taking care of the home while my parents went to work.

A. Did you stay with your parents at that time?

B. Yes, my mother lived here before 1987. When it was my turn to begin to work,[3] my parents moved away. My mother and I work in the same work unit, but after my mother retired they have not paid salary and I just stay at home, it is even worse than not having a job.

A. How about your father?

B. He's in a transport company. He has retired, but it is also no good.

A. Does he get his pension?

---

3. It is probably an instance of 'inheriting a parent's job' (*dingti*) as she later tells that she was employed as a 'relative'.

B. He gets 300 yuan a month. But as my mother does not get paid, it is like a snowball in hell. And my mother has high blood pressure so she has to take medicine. She should get a pension, but her work unit can't pay her. My parents ask for the salary every day and they are told 'in just a few days'. My mother is quite old, but anyway she goes there every day to ask if they have money and they say 'no', they could pay neither January nor February.

A. How many months are they in arrears with the pension?

B. I don't know. My mother has been there twice to ask. She also cannot get the money back she spent for buying medicine.

A. How much has she spent, do you think?

B. Almost as much as one month's salary.

A. Hasn't she even got one fen back?

B. No.

A. Have you paid the medicine for her? How many sisters and brothers do you have?

B. We are three all together, and my older sister is better off economically, so she usually pays if my parents have trouble. My younger brother is not all right.

A. Have your parents moved away?

B. Yes, they have.

A. Do they have a house?

B. Yes, it is an apartment which was built a few years ago by my father's work unit.

A. With pooled funds?

B. Yes. After finishing the building with pooled funds whoever wanted to move in should pay. In the past the work unit would pay. Now you have to buy it yourself even though you have already payed when pooling the funds.

A. What did you do at the recycling station you joined in 1987?

B. I was a gate-keeper until I got married. Later I had a child.

A. Didn't you go back after your maternity leave?

B. I only earned 200 yuan a month when I worked there.

A. Which kind of work unit is it?

B. It is a collectively owned trading cooperative under administration of the municipality (*shi gongxiaoshe*).

A. Were you employed on a contract?

B. No, there were no contracts. I got the status of a relative (*jiashugong*). Quite a lot of us were employed under that category.

A. Didn't you try to find another job later?

B. No. My health is not very good, I have a cough and fever. My health is not good. Everything is wrong with my body. Someone introduced a new job to me, but I couldn't do it.

A. Haven't you worked during all that time?

B. My health is not good. I can't bear it. I started to work at four o'clock, and I got a fever at six o'clock, and I almost collapsed in the workshop. Someone had to take me back by bike. So I stay at home to rest. What can I do? But my work unit was very considerate. They didn't ask me to do heavy work. I only had to open the gate if a truck came along. I was allowed to go home to eat. But my mother still has to look after me – when I go to work, when I rest, eat and drink. If she has cooked some delicious food, she says to me: 'Come and eat'. If I don't come, she will come with the food by bike. She will also buy bread and a piece of cake for the child.

A. When did you get married?

B. In 1990.

A. So you worked there for three years?

B. Yes. I gave birth in 1991. After that I stayed at home.

A. How much did you earn during the years you worked?

B. Around 200 yuan a month, at most 240 yuan.

A. Including medical costs?

B. No. They did not care about medicine or other medical costs.

A. You said your status was that of a 'relative', so you did not have a position as a formal employee (*zhengshi gong*), did you?

B. They said that they would change my position, but they didn't because they could not get the permission.

A. Was there no recruitment quota (*zhibiao*)?[4]

B. No, there wasn't. There were many informal workers. There were only about ten of them who were within the recruitment quota. There were only a few positions within the recruitment quota, to whom should they give the chance?

A. So you didn't go back to work after 1990, did you?

B. No, I didn't.

A. How can you live then? Since you went back home, you haven't earned any money, is that right?

B. It is like this: I don't get a salary, so my mother gives me some money. But I also have to pay for medicine. And I did not work hard to find another job. I have to find out how to get a job now, I cannot just stay home here to rest. The child is big, and he has to go to school. We can't only rely on my mother. She also needs to buy medicine, and my father only gets his 300 yuan a month in pension. That's just enough for food, nothing else.

A. Can your husband earn some money as a temporary worker? Hasn't he done any temporary work these years?

B. No.

A. He had his last job in 1990 as a temporary worker (*linshigong*). Hasn't he been looking for something to do after that?

B. No. He was just a doorman. That was not an easy job, either. Now the work units don't do well. They have to pay more if they hire a temporary worker.[5] The less workers they have, the less they need to pay.

---

4. A work unit will get permission to recruit a certain number of people from the local government.
5. Temporary workers get higher salaries because they are not given social security and other subsidies. Other information points to the opposite effect; a woman tells that her husband's work unit is only recruiting temporary workers because the responsibility is less heavy.

A. Your husband hasn't earned anything during all those years, has he?

B. No. How could we be so bad off if we had had any income?

A. So it is fine now that he can earn 200–300 yuan by opening a clinic near the People's Theatre?

B. There are a few patients. But how can he refuse to treat workers and peasants that have economic problems and come from far away in the countryside, because they have heard that he is a good doctor? He has to treat them for free. Some of them were introduced by friends.

A. How could you live then since 1990? What was your source of income? Did you live on your parents?

B. My mother gave us some money. But it was not enough, because we had to pay a rent of more than 100 yuan and we had to spend some on the child, too.

A. How much did you need every month? And how much money did you spend?

B. How could we spend money we did not have? We spent less than 100 yuan a month.

A. 100 yuan for the three of you?

B. Less than 100 yuan.

A. How did you spend the money?

B. What can we buy? We cannot afford anything. We buy a pile of white radishes every day for one yuan to stirfry and eat them.

A. Then you bought some cereals?

B. One sack of wheat is enough for us to eat for a month. On the first of July I got a card (*tekunzheng*) from the work unit which stated that I have economic difficulties and can have subsidy for non-staple food and can buy cereals at stable prices (*pingjia*).[6] It is cheaper than market prices.

A. What about meat?

---

6. A stable price (*pingjia*) just means the price is subsidised.

B. I hardly eat meat at all. His father does not eat it either.

A. How about the child?

B. We used to buy a little meat – 250 gram to make some dumplings – and we fried some eggs.

A. It was just the time when the child was growing up.

B. Yes. We should give him some even though we didn't eat it ourselves.

A. So you had to count on help from your parents?

B. Yes. My mother said always to leave some for the child. She often came here by bike to give the boy a few sausages.

A. But the economic situation of your parents is also difficult and they can't get their pension subsidy.

B. Yes, but I pressed my work unit hard and asked them just to pay for a couple of months. So now I have been paid some money covering until July or August. The salary problem is basically solved. And they started to refund medicine expenses, but only with 120 yuan for a whole year. How could that be enough?

A. Do you receive 10 yuan a month for medicine expenses?

B. There is a rule which says 10 yuan a month for medicine expense can be refunded, but they won't reimburse us until the end of the year. If they have the money they will give it to us; if they don't have money, we could just as well forget about it.

A. Have they reimbursed your medicine expense this year?

B. No, we should wait until the end of December.

A. So they paid your salary up until August?

B. Yes, but we did not get a wage increase like they do in many other work units.[7]

A. Who gave you the card which says you are in difficulty?

B. It was the work unit. The work unit has reported our situation to the trade union in the city and they agreed to give it. There are more than ten workers in the work unit who need help.

---

7. I. e. an increase they are entitled to according to the local regulations.

A. Are you still counted as an employee of your unit?

B. Yes. I haven't been transferred.

A. Then what is your position now? What is the relationship between you and the work unit?

B. Laid off (*xiagang*).

A. Is it 'stop of salary, continuation of employment' (*tingxin liuzhi*)?

B. I guess not. I am still employed. If there is a census the work unit will report me as one of its staff.[8]

A. If you were not counted as a member of the staff, you could not get the poverty card. Is that right?

B. If nobody had intervened I would not have got it. But my mother went to my unit and asked them to give me something to do. She said that otherwise we could not make ends meet, and the child also needed food to eat. Where should the money come from?[9]

A. Did the child stay with the grandparents?

B. My mother's health is not good, she has high blood pressure; and my father is not well, either. He has trouble with his heart.

A. You say you have not felt very well these years. How about medicine?

B. I have tried to ignore it. What can I do?

A. Do you take medicine?

B. If I cannot stand it any more, I will take some. If there is some medicine in my husband's clinic I will take some. If there is no medicine in the clinic I will not take any. It is very expensive to buy good medicine; 2 or 3 yuan can buy you nothing, the cough medicine I need costs 16 yuan!

A. Don't you want to find another job?

B. I do, but what kind of job can I find? I can do nothing.

---

8. They would also do that if she was counted as a *tingxin liuzhi*.
9. Remember the mother is a retiree of the same work unit and has worked there before.

A. But what will happen if you do not find a job?

B. I think of starting to sell vegetables. The Xingtai newspaper also says that selling toilet paper might help. We can get it on commission and if you can sell some you can earn some money and they will take the rest back. There are some people who do it. You cannot earn much, but it is better than nothing. It can lighten the burden. My parents are quite old and they are not very well. They try to save as much as they can, and they have to look after us, too. Still, they live in their own flat and have to pay for that, too.

A. What about this flat where you live?

B. My father's work unit allocated it to him when he was transferred to civilian work from the army. The roof leaks every summer. When it rains I have to use 8, 9 or 10 bowls to catch the water.

A. How big is the flat?

B. Two bedrooms.

A. How many square metres?

B. More than 20 square metres.

A. Have you stayed with your parents here after you got married and had the child?

B. No, I stayed with them after I got out of school until 1987, then they moved out from here and I later got married in 1990.

A. Did they not have to return the flat after they moved out?

B. Yes, the work unit wanted to get the flat back, and they used as an argument that my father got a flat built with funds pooled by the workers at the transport company, like I told you before. But I just stayed here and nobody came and demanded to move in because the flat is not so good.

A. What would you have done if somebody had wanted to move in?

B. I would have tried to find another solution.

A. Where can you find a flat?

B. I would go where the flats are.

A. Do you need to pay rent for this flat?

B. No. They come to ask for it, but they will not repair the roof, so I will not pay rent. They say that the house will be torn down to build another building here. The situation was also reported to the army.[10] The two buildings around here will be knocked down to build new buildings instead. We can still stay here this year. But I do not know where we shall go when they begin to knock the houses down.

A. Do you need to pay for the water and electricity?

B. Someone gave us a meter. We pay by the meter.

A. How much does it cost per month?

B. 20 yuan altogether.

A. Why is it so expensive?

B. The meter does not work properly. In the factory there is a main meter and all the families have a subsidiary meter, but people play tricks with them so they do not move and then our meter will count all the water used by the six families living here. But the water is not the worst expense for us; the pay for electricity is another matter. The flat belongs to my parents (*wo ma de fangzi*),[11] so we do not need to pay rent. Otherwise we would have great difficulties in the months when we do not have any income.

A. How could you live in the months when he did not earn anything?

B. His mother also helped us by giving us some flour, 15 or 20 kilos a month. We would buy a litre of oil and use very little when we cooked. It worked when the child was small, but not when he started to go to school. He wants to have something to eat. He does not have what the others have. He asks for things when my

10. Because the army owns the building. The father got it after having been demobilized.

11. 'Belongs' in the sense that they got it allocated from a work unit. It is clear from the text that the parents did not buy the flat. She tends to use the word 'mother' when talking about her parents. It appears elsewhere that the flat is allocated by the father's unit.

mother comes, so my mother buys something for him. My mother has saved some money by not buying medicine for herself, just to buy some food for him.

A. I think you should find something to do.

B. I think so, too. But what can I do?

A. You feel that there is nothing you can do?

B. What should it be?

A. The main problem is that your health is not good.

B. When the winter comes I fall ill; it is fine when the weather is warm but not when it gets cold. Once I went to the hospital to get a tooth pulled out. Picking a number and getting registered alone cost me more than 20 yuan and on top comes examination and medicine. No money, no treatment. So I told myself to forget it and that the tooth would stop aching when I got back home.

A. Didn't you pay for it?

B. I took the papers with me and did not pay. I can buy a sack of flour for 35 yuan. Why should I pay 35 yuan to get a tooth drawn out? If I save as much as possible I will use the 35 yuan to buy some vegetables and some flour. I can get a lot for 35 yuan.

A. Can you live on your husband's income now and just maintain life?

B. How can we?

A. You say you only spend 100 yuan a month.

B. Less than 100 yuan. But we also have to pay the rent for the clinic.

A. Then you will have nothing left?

B. How could we? All the things we have are from my sister, for example shoes and clothes. I have not bought that kind of thing myself, neither before nor after I got married. I earned some money before I got married, but I had to buy medicine instead of clothes.

A. Do you have two sisters?

B. No, I have one.

A. Where does she work?

B. Xingtai Grain Depot.

A. How is her work unit?

B. It is good.

A. How much can she earn?

B. I have no idea.

A. Anyway, you think it is fine.

B. Sometimes when she gets her salary, she comes to visit my mother and gives my mother 100 or 200 yuan to buy some food. If she has some she will take care of my parents, and she tries not to buy much food herself. When I do not have any money, she will buy meat for me and cook dumplings and a few dishes for me and give me some money.

A. Then what are you going to do? You must try to find a solution.

B. What should I do?

A. Do you know if there is a minimum limit for the living standard in Xingtai?

B. I have not heard about that.

A. Now the City Government is planning to set a minimum limit for the living standard. You can inquire about it. Every work unit and Neighbourhood Committee is recording it. The minimum limit is 120 yuan on average per person.

B. Now the work units are more inclined to pay salary to people who go to work (*shangban*) than to people who do not go to work.

A. Maybe they are in the process now of calculating whether they can guarantee 120 yuan a month, it is not much but it can be enough.

B. 120 yuan must be for two months.

A. For you it is, you are thrifty.

B. I could manage until Spring Festival with 120 yuan. The work unit gave consideration to my mother's health, and my mother asked them to give me something to do, even if they just pay me 100 yuan. But the staff and workers cannot get paid, either, and they stay at home. And if there is one more worker, they need to pay more. Some of the work units give the staff and workers 80 yuan and some even give a 100 yuan a month as a subsidy [BLS].

A. And you get nothing?

B. Nothing. Not to mention buying medicine. The child is quite weak. He is short of nutrition. We buy some nutriments for his sake. He coughs, too. His health is not good.

A. How is he doing in school?

B. On the weekend his father gives him exercises and tells him how to write. His father can rest during the weekend.

A. What do you do at home?

B. I send our son to school and pick him up. I cook and feed the child since he does not eat properly.

A. You are feeding such a big boy?

B. He will be six years old this October. For example if my mother comes Sunday afternoon, and if he says he cannot eat the food, my mother will buy something for him.

A. I think you are still young.

B. I can do a light job, not a hard one. I have heard that you can earn around 10 yuan a day selling vegetables. Maybe not 10 yuan, 5 yuan or even 3 yuan is also all right, so I can earn 90 yuan a month.

A. Why don't you do it? Or what about setting up a public telephone?

B. Public telephones are everywhere in the street now.

A. Haven't you found a way? You should think about it, you cannot live like this forever.

B. Yes. The Spring Festival is coming, and it is now the end of October.

A. What do you want to do in the future.

B. I want to go back to work if I can.

A. Go back to the old work unit?

B. Yes, but I cannot do it now.

A. Isn't it because it is not possible? Think about something else. Your husband should think more about it. He left school after senior middle school, and he is in the working age.

B. We are both no good (*buxing*).

A. Talking about your husband I came to think about his household registration. Is there a quota for the number of people that can be changed from being a peasant to not being a peasant (*nongzhuanfei*)?

B. There was a quota this year and we missed it. It was already used when we heard there was a quota in Western Gate District.

A. You did not know?

B. It was too late when we heard about it. They have their rules.

A. Nobody had told you about it?

B. There was a big red notice on the wall. And I told my husband to write it down and go back to get it done. But he forgot it. It does not mean so much if you have the permanent urban registration. There is a quota every year, but it is not so useful now.

A. You cannot find anything to do, so he should do something. He is a man, he should be the one supporting the family.

B. The adults can scrimp and save. We can go without eating or drinking for one day, but the child cannot do that. He wants this today and that tomorrow. He will have to start school next year on the first of September and we should make a contribution.

A. You should make a contribution?

B. They have built a new teaching building. He is not in the first grade yet, but he will be next year when they will move to the new building. So we should make a contribution for the moving.

A. Have they said so?

B. Yes, it is normal in the school now. All should pay 200 yuan per person, plus tuition. Let alone other things.

A. Who paid the 200 yuan for the child to go to pre-school class?

B. We have saved up for it. Next year in September he will start primary school and we shall pay for it, otherwise he cannot go there. You have to pay. It is not like our patients who have no money, we treat them and give them some medicine so they can go back and get better. We say they can pay next year. It is not like that with the school.

A. What equipment does your husband have in his clinic?

B. There is no equipment, just a big table. Nothing else.

A. Isn't there a bed?

B. The bed belongs to the owner of the house. There is some Western medicine which is on wholesale.

A. It doesn't work if he never earns any money, only 200 yuan a month!

B. 200 a month, they pay more if their ailment is difficult to treat. We examine them all. If they have money, they pay; otherwise they don't. Sometimes it is just a kind of service, it is free for people in need.

A. You are also a person in need.

B. But he is a doctor. He treats those who come to ask for treatment even if they do not have money. Forget the money. It is just like that.

A. Has he been a doctor for more than one year in the area of the People's Theatre?

B. Just started.

A. For how long did he work as a doctor in Nanhe?

B. Two or three years.

A. Was it also a friend who helped him find a place?

B. Yes. He could not earn much then, either.

A. How much could he earn then?

B. Not much. He handed the money he earned to the hospital. It was a hospital, which had built the house and opened the clinic. He handed all his income over to the hospital and the money was divided.

A. How much could he earn then?

B. Not much. Except for the sum he handed to the hospital and the fee for the electricity and the heat, there was just a little more than 300 yuan left. And at home he should take care of the old parents.

A. Does he still need to look after the old people now?

B. Yes. His parents are not well, either.

A. He doesn't earn as much here as he could in Nanhe, or is it almost the same?

B. Yes. In Nanhe he had to eat in restaurants. Now he can eat at home. Maybe the food is not so good, mostly rice, noodles or corn soup, but it is warm.

A. How do you keep yourselves warm during winter? Do you buy coal yourselves?

B. Yes, we do! 325 pounds for 135 yuan. If you have the poverty card, one ton for 80 yuan.

A. Is it enough to buy 325 pounds?

B. No, it is not, but we can only buy 325 pounds in all on our card by using three tickets (*piao*). We have six tickets a year. From July to December we can buy 750 pounds.[12] We use it carefully. When it is almost burned, we close the stove door after having added just three pieces of coal. And after the cooking we cover the fire and close the stove door immediately.

A. Is 750 pounds enough?

B. We only have 750 pounds for a half year.

A. How do you keep warm during winter?

---

12. Probably a miscalculation. It should be 650 pounds.

B. We have used more than half of the 750 pounds we bought in July. We move the fire inside during the winter, but it is cold anyway. We cannot just use an extra piece. After cooking, boiling water and washing we lower the fire. If it is too bad, we buy some more coal at a high price nearby. It is very expensive, you have to count it. I will wait and see if we get tickets next year.

A. Maybe you can get the minimum living standard?

B. From the work unit?

A. From the Neighbourhood Committee.

B. Should the Neighbourhood Committee inform us?

A. I think the Neighbourhood Committee knows your situation. They have already reported it for you.

B. I know. I can only stay at home and do nothing.

A. Has the Neighbourhood Committee not tried to help you find something to do?

B. They have asked, but the child should go to school, my health is not good. If I walk too much I run out of breath. What I can do is to sit down and do something light. So the Neighbourhood Commitee said they would try to find this kind of job for me.

A. Do you have any plans for the future?

B. Find something to do to earn some money so I can buy a flat. The flat here is going to be knocked down next year.

A. So it is a big affair to buy a flat?

B. Yes, it is.

A. Do you have a specific idea?

B. The problem is we are short of money. Selling medicine at the clinic is good – medicine for having loose bowels and running a fever. If we can invest in medicine to sell, it will be good. It is a good business to open a medicine shop.

A. Do you want to open a medicine shop?

B. Yes, but we do not have the money. You can earn fortunes by opening a medicine shop, there are no price limits on medicine.[13] Even if you have paid a high price for it, you can sell it at a slightly higher price than they do in the big medicine shop, it doesn't matter. We are happy to earn just 5 fen, 3 fen or 2 fen. One has to save money little by little. You cannot become rich overnight, right? You have to save little by little. When we have saved enough money, we can talk about what we should do next year. It is October already and Spring Festival is in January next year. There are less than 100 days until Spring Festival, we are still only talking, it doesn't help. He can see a patient, if there is a patient; he has a stethoscope, he can measure blood pressure, he can give an injection and he can give an infusion. If you have a fever or headache, he can give you an injection; the children are afraid of injections so he can give them some medicine instead, and they will be all right.

A. Is it good that the Neighbourhood Committee has opened a clinic which sells medicine, too, so the residents come here to see a doctor?

B. That is not this Neighbourhood Committee. There is one here, and there is another one in front.

A. Do you have any ideas now?

B. Yes. I suggested that we could rent two glass counters in the People's Department Store. Now many staff and workers do not earn much money and many people are having a hard time looking after themselves. You have to rely on yourself now. What can we do? It would be fine to do that. I can sit there and sell medicine and he can see patients if there are any.

A. What do you think the government should do for you?

B. What do I demand? They should get me a job, so I can live.

A. What if they cannot?

B. Then they cannot. It is not only me who needs to get rid of this problem. There are many other people who need to solve this. They should live, too. We all have to think about ourselves first.

---

13. The high prices on medicine are one of the bigger problems in the health care system, see Chapter 6.

A. It seems to me that you do not want to depend on the government, is that true?

B. There is a limit to how much you can rely on yourself. If one cannot go back to work one needs to find a way.

A. There is the minimum living standard and you had better ask for it. I know they are doing this thing now, otherwise there are more and more people who won't be able to cope.

B. Yes, they cannot cope. As for me, I have tried my best. Last year at the Moon Festival – it is a tradition to go home to one's family at the time of the Moon Festival – on August 15 I went back to my mother, and I brought two watermelons and a box of moon cakes that a patient had given to my husband. I had my child with me and my mother opened the box to let him have a moon cake. But she said: why did you take them with you? The child hasn't eaten them yet. It is a present for you two adults. You should keep them and eat them yourselves. I said that I was ashamed I could not buy anything. So I had taken the present, and I didn't ask for money, either. We went there at noon-time and my mother asked us to have lunch. After the lunch the child was tired, so he slept there for a while, so we did not come back until six o'clock. When we came back, we found out that our TV was stolen. My mother and some patients bought it and gave it to us. It was good to have when my husband was in Nanhe. The story is that the patients trusted us and felt well treated. Some had pains in their legs, some had pains in their waist, some suffered paralysis, some suffered hemiplegia. Those who came and got treatment by my husband became better. They knew we were warmhearted people. After last Spring Festival they collected money for us, more than 1,000 yuan in all. And in May we bought the TV set with the money the patients had given us, some of our own money and 200–300 yuan which we borrowed from my mother. And now it was stolen. Someone broke in.

A. You lost your TV set?

B. Yes. I had locked the door when I left. I do not go out very often. But we have to visit our parents at festivals; they are not supposed to come and visit us. We have to visit them and buy them things. They are not supposed to buy things for us.

A. Don't you live in a courtyard?

B. In a compound occupied by many households. We live just near the gate in the first house when you enter the courtyard and all sorts of people live there.

A. But they would be able to see if somebody carried your TV set out through the gate?

B. The thief took the door off its hinges. He didn't unlock it. After noon a neighbour had come to see me and she saw that the door was open, the curtains were pulled and it was dark inside.

A. You had just left then.

B. Yes. I left at 11 o'clock, and people came back for lunch at 12 o'clock. They were all at home. There was nobody in the courtyard. And it was a Sunday, too. The neighbour called me, but I wasn't there. When I came back, they all said: Hurry up, your door is open. Go and see if you have lost anything There were a few people standing there watching. In the room there was medicine and other things on the floor. The neighbours thought that the door had been taken off its hinges because we had had a quarrel. When I came back at six o'clock it was just a mess at home. The TV had gone. Our neighbours gave us a few clues, one remembered having seen some young persons. He asked them who they were looking for and they gave a name he did not know. He told them to go and look at another place but they stayed around for a while asking who lived in our house. He said that we were at my parents place and would not come back before evening. They stayed for a while watching the door. Then they went away. The neighbour said he had been in the courtyard the whole afternoon, but they must have got in somehow from the other direction. I always have problems; to loose a TV we have only had for a couple of months! He [the husband] told me not to worry, we could buy another one when we have saved more money. I said why should we bother to think about a new one, we do not even have money enough to eat properly!

A. You should think about what to do. Open a medicine shop or else you will have more problems.

B. The child is getting older, it's a problem!

A. You will have to spend more and more money when he has started school?

B. Indeed! The tuition fee is expensive. People with a peasant registration should pay more, so it is good the registration status follows the mother. But still it is 200 yuan tuition and 400 yuan for different funds. We only have one child and can't have any more. One is already quite expensive. He is still a young boy.

A. I think that when your work situation is like this, you can't do anything about it. You would have even more trouble if you had one child more.

B. We will not be allowed to have another, even if we wanted to.

(Translated by Guo Lixia)

Appendix 2

只能靠自己

Selections from the Interviews, Arranged by Topic

EMPLOYMENT

F 15 XT

My husband was recruited from the countryside to work in a coal pit in 1957. Foremen from the mine came directly to the villages and recruited people. It was not necessary to know anybody. They just made a health check. He got reallocated from the pit because of lung problems. It was easy. One went to the City Labour Bureau and got a new allocation. At that time people were moving around a lot, one had one's household registration papers (*hukouben*) oneself and could move around and get a job. One had to take a job where they were applying for people. The local Labour Bureau was in charge, they wrote an introduction letter and one went to the unit oneself. In 1962 my husband was sent back to his old home, a county in Xingtai district, which was under a government policy called sending-down-to-the-countryside (*xiafang*).[1] Everybody had to go. The household registration documents were sent back to the village. At that time he had a work-related illness – he had broken his arm and it healed in an odd way. He was actually crippled, so he could not do manual labour. He got trained as a teacher,

1. *Xiafang* is not exactly the correct word here. The reason for Mr Liu to be sent back to his rural hometown was the national downsizing policy that was initiated in 1961 after China experienced three years of disasters, and the targets were factory workers who were recruited during 1958, 1959 or 1960, either from rural areas or from the city.

which work he did for the next 18 years. They got work points;[2] one point was 2 mao [10 mao equal 1 yuan].

In 1980 he succeeded in being transferred to Xingtai city and got a job in the Grinding Wheel Factory. He asked for the transfer himself, because he had heard in the village that there was a new policy of sending people back to town and the criteria would suit his case. He ran around from 1977 – 3 or 4 years – from the factory to the county to the city to the district to the province. Every level should verify that he could go back to the city. In his village there were some people from a 'Xingtai Policy Office' (*Xingtai luoshi zhengce bangongshi*). That unit was the most important one. Because he knew a person from the village who worked for the office, he got to know about the new regulations. At that time it was not so important about good relations, either you could obtain something or you could not on the basis of the real situation. At the factory he worked for 300 yuan a month until last year [1996], when his department was shut down. The young ones got moved and those over 55 years old were sent home without any pay. Now he wants to get his money, but it is difficult, no matter how many people he has tried to contact. The retirees just don't get their money. We need 300 yuan a month to buy food and get along, but we only have 50 yuan at the moment.

I followed my husband to the village in 1962 and back to the city again. In the village I did farm work for the collective and earned work points. I also took care of our private plot. Back in the city I took care of my old parents. They were in their 80s and lived with us. And I had difficulties finding a job. Now I would like to have something to do and to earn some money, but I do not have good connections or any capital to buy goods for trading.

Our oldest son got into a department store in 1990 because of an advertisement he saw on TV. He registered just by himself and passed a test. The second son got a temporary job at a police station through a fellow villager. He paid some 1,000 yuan for a driver's license, then he went to a place where private companies apply for workers. But nobody wanted to employ him as a driver because of

2. In the countryside income was distributed as work points, the value of which depended on the total income of the village in the given year.

his young age. They thought he did not have enough experience. Before that he also had a temporary assignment he got through some people he knows, and his wife likewise works in a village textile factory thanks to the help of some friends. Our daughter has problems with her eyesight and therefore has difficulties finding a job, so we tried through connections. It is not the children's acquaintances, it is our acquaintances, but they are not very close. Now we need to pull strings for even the smallest things. If the factory needs people and asks for more personnel, one needs good connections. The mother of a schoolmate of my daughter helped her get a job. The health examination was very casual because it was a family connection, so she got the job in spite of her bad eyesight.

F 35 XT

We both began working in 1980, my wife got a job in the City Garment Factory no. 2, a collective enterprise, and I got one in the Textile Mill, an SOE. We got jobs by testing (*kaoshi*) that year. The system was that a person applied to the Labour Bureau to work in a certain unit; we got the information on which units lacked workers through the Street Office. We chose where we wanted to go ourselves by looking at the efficiency of the factory and the type of work. After registering with the Labour Bureau we participated in a kind of examination, especially designed to get into the factory we wanted to work in. If the examination results were good enough we got allocated (*fenpei*) to the job. The units on the other hand reported to the Labour Bureau on their need for workers.

I got a university degree – by attending the electricity university from 1982 to 1986 – paid by the work unit; the trade union was active in getting that opportunity for me. But the Textile Mill started to lose money and I was helped by a relative to change jobs in 1993. The manager was not happy about it of course as they paid my education. The unit still owes me a deposit (*fengxian yajin*) of 200 yuan. I was told I would be paid back if there was money, otherwise not. But the agreement says you have the right to get the money back if you leave. When I left in 1993 the factory had not paid salary for four months and I have not got my money back until this day. In the last years the textile workers made demonstrations and therefore the factory was sold to the city. But my new unit, a machinery plant, also had problems so I am now at home, while my personal file is with the unit. I changed jobs to get better conditions, but the director of the factory I was transferred to resigned and the new one gave me a position below my qualifications and negative assessments every year. I had to haul goods, which I could not endure. So in the end my education was put to no good use. I am not fired, I retired early due to illness (*bingtui*) which gave 90 per cent of my former salary – 200 yuan – but that stopped after six months. For the last ten months I have not received any subsidies; I am laid off. I do not have very good connections, I only know people through my work. I do not have the right background (*beijing*). I have tried a little trading but I am not good at it. I have gone to the Job Introduction Centre (*zhiye jieshao suo*) of the city, this autumn they also opened a Re-employment Project (*xiagang zhigong zai jiuye xiangmu*). I went there but they did not really have anything to offer.

F 40 XT

I graduated from lower middle school in 1988 and had several temporary jobs while waiting for a more permanent assignment. A father of one of my classmates got me a two-month job at a foreign trade company, where I earned 20 yuan a month; after that a friend got me into a hostel, where I also worked for some months with a very small pay. I got my first real job in 1989 at the Metallurgy Factory, where I started as a temporary worker 'within the plan', which means as soon as there is an empty position and you behave well you will be offered to become a contract worker. I got the information that they were looking for people through the 'Xingtai Evening News' and I just went by myself to register at the factory. At that time it was not so difficult to get a job, one did not have to exploit any connections and the demands were easy to live up to. One had to be a waiting-for-job-youth, over 18 years old, and have completed lower middle school. I had to pass a test of my writing ability and health condition and after that three months of probation, which is a kind of examination time. During these first three months I got 60 yuan a month, which was later raised to 100 yuan.

In 1993 I became a contract worker and I now have a salary of 300 yuan but no bonus as the factory has no good economy, it cannot sell its products. The economic results began to decline in the last half of 1995. Now we do not even get our ordinary salary each month. We do not get paid for half of the time on average. For the missing salary they give us a 'salary card' (*gongzi ka*), which is a kind of proof that they owe us the money. If somebody has a very good reason and argues with the management he or she might be able to get some of the money by showing the card, but it takes a lot of effort. The management does not explain when we can get our money, they just say that they are short of cash, and they have to owe us the money for some time. Last year the electricity was shut down, because there was no money to pay the bill. We all complain and voice our opinions, but nothing else. In the Workers Representative Meetings there are very few ordinary workers, it is mostly foremen. There is a meeting once a year but they are of no use in this situation. Anyway I go to work every day, five days a week, eight hours a day. It is difficult to find another way to earn money and I will wait until our child gets older before I go out more in the world. I could try to do some business but there are too many small vendors in the streets and too few buyers in this town so even if it is an easy option it is not very profitable.

My wife has worked at the Radio Factory no. 2 since 1993 where she got the job because her father had worked at this unit, and it followed the policy of 'specially caring for children of employees'.[3] But the factory has stopped production since last New Year, so she has not got any salary for six months. Before she got 256 yuan a month.

My father opened his own small business in 1993 in a stall he contracted from the Knitting Factory where he used to work. He is still too young to retire and he keeps his seniority and his position at the unit but he does not get any salary or social security coverage from them. On the contrary, he has to pay 750 yuan each

3. The *dingti* policy was officially abolished in 1986, see Glossary.

month as a contract fee. He is dealing in non-staple food on a wholesale basis. It was profitable for the first two years but since then it has begun to go down. He had to borrow 10,000 yuan from the bank, so a lot of the profit goes to repay the loan and interest. It is not easy to borrow money from a bank, it is best to know somebody there or you can borrow in the name of somebody else. One also sometimes has to turn to private loans but they are usually more expensive.

My mother is retired from the Dying Works, one of the core enterprises in our area which is doing allright economically. Almost all families living here have some connection to this place. She has been a regular worker there and gets a pension of 500 yuan a month.

My sister has served at the People's Market since she left school in 1990 when she became a contract worker there. She also found the job announcement in the paper. But the market closed down in 1995 so she does not get salary any more but she keeps her seniority and the market keeps her personal file, even though the unit is just an empty name since all the counters have been leased out. She has been allowed by her work unit to go and find another job but it is difficult to find another place to serve customers, which is the only profession she knows. It is possible to get into the New Asia Market, but there one has to pay 10,000 yuan as a deposit to run a stall. So at the moment she works at a counter contracted by her boyfriend. She gets paid only if she sells something. She gets no help from the authorities; the problem is that we do not know where to go; is it the work unit or higher levels? When I ask other people they also do not know. But we cannot rely on the unit anymore, that is for sure.

J 17 GZ

I got my job in a collective enterprise when I returned after being an educated youth in the countryside. I got 700 yuan a month, my basic salary was 400.[4] But last year – 1996 – I 'retired' (*tuiyang*),[5]

4. The income of Chinese families is divided into basic salary (*gongzi*) and various subsidies and bonuses. Often the basic salary is the lowest part of the income.
5. A kind of being laid off (*xiagang*).

so I can help my husband who is a farmer and take care of our land. He also farms the land of some other people so in all we have 3 mu.[6] He earns around 10,000 yuan a year, then he got 7,000 last year in dividend (*fenhong*)[7] from the village and we let some rooms out for 12,000 yuan a year. I only get 381 yuan a month in basic subsidy from my work unit so I depend on my husband for a living. I could not manage on my own for that amount of money. I have not tried to find another job because I can help my husband on the land. I am old[8] and have no education; so it is very difficult to find a job.

J 1 GZ

We all come from Henan province, I was born there and so were our children. I served in the army for three years and after that I got allocated a job by the state in 1979. I was not demobilized before I had a job; that was a guarantee from the state. The Channel Bureau in Guangzhou [an SOE] needed to hire new workers (*zhaogong*) and we were more than ten persons that got in there. I have been there ever since but I have been moved to other positions within the Bureau twice according to the needs of the unit. We just have to follow the needs of the leadership. I plan to stay with the unit until I retire.

Now our total income is around 2,000 yuan a month; my basic salary is 332 yuan; my wife's is more than 600 yuan and then there is the bonus. Preferential treatment from the work unit, like promotion, housing allocation, salary rise, training, going abroad, etc., all depends on your contributions to the work unit and your capabilities.

F 21 XT

Both I and my husband are affiliated with the Light Industrial Bureau. We were schoolmates and got allocated a job at the same time

6. One mu is 666 square metres.
7. Is is not uncommon for the villages around Guangzhou to run productive enterprises, often by investing the money the village received as compensation for farmland being nationalized to industry. Villagers get shares in village enterprises and receive dividends once a year.
8. The interviewed woman is 46 years old and that is considered too old to start anything new. Even women in their mid-thirties can call themselves too 'old' to begin a new job.

in 1968. I could choose a factory among the many the Bureau had under its jurisdiction. I choose one which had good economic results. I was asked to work as an accountant there even though I had never done that kind of work before. Now I am retired and take care of my grandchild. We get our retirement pension in time because my department is relatively successful. In 1981 a new bonus system was introduced called salary according to results (*xiaoyi gongzi*) so each section now gets different results and pay differently.

My son got allocated a job within the same system as ours in 1988, my husband helped him into the Trade School of the Bureau, it only cost 100 yuan to enter. He chose it himself and we supported him. My daughter-in-law got a job in a commercial centre by paying 10,000 yuan in deposit. To get a good job today you may have to pay several times 10,000. My daughter wants to go to the university but we cannot afford it, so she has given it up for the time being. She now works in a beauty parlour and can earn 500–600 yuan a month. I wish we had an education insurance (*jiaoyu baoxian*) for her. State insurance companies do that now, if one pays 100 yuan a year until the child is 17 years old one does not have to pay university fees. We consider buying it for our grandson.

F 8 XT

I work in the City Hair Dresser Office of the local government. We manage all the public hair dressers in the city. My salary is 280 yuan all together, 204 is basic salary, then food and bicycle and some other subsidies amount to a total of 66 yuan. In 1979 I got my uncle's job (*jieban*) in the public baths and stayed there for ten years. My uncle retired at the age of 70. I had had several temporary jobs since I finished school in 1972. I only got 29 yuan a month at that time but I wanted a regular job and not a temporary one. I left around 1989 and then I got my present job at the Hair Dresser Office through an old secretary at the public baths who got transferred to that place and took me with him because he found me reliable. Working in a factory as a temporary worker in the middle of the 1970s yielded no welfare benefits but a good salary. Later I got a regular job with lower salary but all medical expenses paid. Then I only would get 5 yuan every month for medicine but now the performance of the factory is no good, so even this is not possible any more.

J 16 GZ

I have lived together with my mother and one of my sisters all my life. My father died when I was three years old. We are farmers, my mother works on our land. I worked in a private furniture company for four years. I saw an advertisement in the papers and got the job. My total income was 800 yuan, of which 500 was basic salary. As I worked in a private business I had no social welfare. But I was not satisfied with the management so I quit the job and now I am unemployed and live on my savings and help from my family. But I get dividend from our village. My mother also gets some. In 1997 I got 6,000 yuan. I look at advertisements in the papers and have friends to help me find a new job. From 1981 to 1994 I worked in a village-run garment workshop, but I resigned and then got the job in the furniture company.

I have not found a new job yet because my educational level is too low. When I was a child we did not have the money for me to continue my schooling. I quit in the middle of primary school. My two sisters quit in lower middle school. This wouldn't have happened today when the economy is better. Lack of schooling is a serious disadvantage now, because educational level means more and more. It is very difficult to get a job without a degree. This and one's own capabilities are much more important now than before.

F 4 XT

We are both retired, I from the Printing Press and my husband from a state owned department store. I began to work at the Press in 1966 and did the same job until I retired in 1987. The Press openly advertised for employees at that time and it was easy to get the job. I just went there by myself. At first I got 50 yuan a month. Now I just stay at home and do housework. My work unit is losing money, so I do not always get my pension in time. Last April they paid the salary of 1995, and in May this year they paid what they owed for 1996. I should have 280 yuan a month but it is never possible to know how much I will get. I retired early so I got a meagre pension. My husband should have 270 yuan a month but for example last month he only got 200. For the last year he has been pulling the cart for our daughter-in-law who sells sesame soup in the streets. She makes it herself at home and they can earn 10 yuan on a good day.

Our first son is in a paper factory which is also running at a loss. His salary is usually 350 yuan. It was easy for him to get the job back in 1979, I think it was. Our second son served in the army for 17 years and returned in 1995. He was a cadre. After he was demobilized the army was responsible for getting him a civilian job but it took nine months before they found him a job in a county farm. They pushed him from one unit to another and dragged things out and he also had to pay 4,000 yuan to get in there. He did not try to find any occupation by himself. The army only had to provide a job for him, not for his wife. She was with him in the army for three years as a relative. Before she followed her husband she worked in a cotton mill, now she works in her father's clinic part-time. He is a doctor in Chinese medicine, and he is so friendly that he treats poor people for free so they do not earn very much. They live three people on 500 yuan a month. Our third son has a job in a pesticide factory run by the City Government, he got it by reacting to information from the Labour Bureau in 1986. But he has now been 'on holiday' for half a year and lives on the salary of his wife. She is working in a dying shop in South China and sends 400 yuan back home every month. He is just staying at home and does not try to find anything to do. The child is choosy; he thinks he cannot find anything 'appropriate'. I tell him, go and find something to do. You have to earn some money. Should your wife make all the money? He comes to me and we discuss what he can do. His father will lend him a cart so he can sell things in the street. As he does not earn money he and the child come to eat at our place every day

F 23 XT

I got my first job through allocation from the production team.[9] At that time I was also a women's cadre. From 1960 my three kids and

---

9. A production team was the lowest administrative level of a people's commune.

I lived together with my mother-in-law, because my husband was in a military school in Nanjing, where he could not bring family. In 1960 we only ate leaves and bark. In Shijiazhuang I worked in the Street Office for no money. I do the same work in Xingtai now. From 1967 I had the responsibility for four neighbourhood committees with 3,000 people. I did not want to do the job. At that time it was easy to find a good job in Xingtai, there were many good factories, and I was only 30 years old. But the party leadership told me to work in the Neighbourhood Committee for 8 yuan a month. They said I would be taken care of. But they cheated me.

HOUSING

F 15 XT

When we lived in the village before 1980 the brigade[10] took care of housing by giving us building materials with which we built a house with three rooms. After returning to the city we lived in a house my parents got allocated just after 1949 because they were poor farmers. We still live there and now we only pay 30 yuan a month for electricity and water, there is no rent. My husband's factory allocates housing, but since 1982 it has required money for a flat – 2,000 yuan as a kind of 'registration fee'. The system is that you have to apply, then register, then they will investigate your situation, then decide if they can give you a flat. Good connections with the people in the housing committee of the factory are important. But only a small number of people has the money to get a housing allocation. The point system is: points for position, seniority, leading functions (5–20 depending on grade), labour model (5), the family having two jobs in the unit (10). Concerning seniority I know that one year in the factory gives one point, but the rest of the details I am not quite sure about. One child does not give points because now everybody has only one child.[11] Other units will reward one-child parents, but not his. I would have liked a housing allocation, but do not have the money. If I had the money I would

10. A brigade was the second administrative level in a people's commune, above the production team.
11. In some units one-child parents still get privilege in the housing queue.

buy a flat, but it costs 40,000 yuan for 70 square metres, even when it is subsidised by the work unit.

My household registration was moved to the city in 1983, three years after we returned from the countryside. It was a complicated process. The Public Security Bureau should give permission for a move. Then the original place should give permission, and then the new Street Office was consulted. The Neighbourhood Committee changes household registrations in groups. I did not use my good connections. That method was not so popular and important at that time. It took six years to change the registration of my husband and children from peasants to urban citizens. At that time the Neighbourhood Committee changed many registrations. Then they stopped for two years, so the registration of the second and third child was changed to a village nearby. Then their chances of an urban registration were greater, because the area soon would be given status as a district of the city. To change from one place to another with peasant registration (*nong zhuan nong*) is not as difficult as to change from peasant to urban registration (*nong zhuan fei*). When the children got registration in the new village, they could get land to farm and a chance to get a job when there were vacant positions in the village. In October their registration was changed to an urban one because the whole village changed at one time, as the town was enlarged.

F 35 XT

We live in a private house. My father-in-law bought it for 400 yuan back in time. I do not remember when. They sold a house in the countryside to be able to buy this and we live here with my husband's two brothers. There are three rooms, in all 40 square metres, each family has one room. We also built a small kitchen. We pay 12 yuan for electricity and 2 for water every month. My unit allocates housing in principle according to seniority but in reality flats are only given to cadres. We have applied many times because we have so little space but without result. It is cheaper to participate in pooling (*jizi jianfang*) than to buy flats in 'society'. When work units build houses they are not charged land tax, they do not have to buy land. Furthermore it is cheaper and easier to get electricity, water and gas in factory housing. An apartment costs 45,000 for three rooms for the family, the unit pays something. But our units do not build houses for lack of money so our only option now is to buy commercial housing. There are empty houses in the city because they are too expensive: top floor is 500 yuan per square metre, the most expensive is 1,000 yuan, average is 800 yuan. Last year we paid an advance of 1,000 yuan for a commercial flat, but they have not begun to build the building yet. It will amount to 40,000 in all for 60 square metres on the top floor, which is cheapest. We borrowed the money from friends and my parents gave some. We do not know where to get the last money from.

F 40 XT

We live six people in a private house, inherited from our grandparents, and we eat together every day. The house is 50 square metres in two storeys and we rebuilt it in 1990 for more than 10,000 yuan of our own money. When the area gets torn down we will only get compensation for the 20 square metres that was in the old house, so if a new house is built on the site we will have to pay market price for the 80 square metres that we have already paid to build once. Even if we do not have the money, we have to find it somewhere. We pay 20 to 30 yuan for water and electricity every month and last winter we used 400 yuan for coal.

The housing reform plan of Xingtai began in 1993 and every month 5 per cent from the workers' salary and 5 per cent from the work unit is transferred to a collective housing fund that is used to build houses sold under certain conditions, cheaper than commercial housing. My work unit participates, but we did not join because we would never reach a state where we had the qualifications for getting a flat, which includes 20 years seniority, no private housing and two jobs in the work unit.

J 17 GZ

We live in our own house, ownership rights belongs to my husband. It is 100 square metres, five rooms and one bathroom. We pay 95 yuan for water and electricity each month, no rent. It is built on the ground where our old house was. The area was renovated and we spent 20,000 yuan of our own savings to build a new house.

But the problem is that there is a plan to build a road, where our house is. I do not know how we can move the house. Things are not being run in a just manner in this part of the town. Some enterprise managers have several houses and some workers do not have a decent place to live. It is not fair. My husband's parents live by themselves in the village. They also get dividends of their own. My husband and his two brothers take turns looking after them.

J 1 GZ

My household registration is in Guangzhou and first we lived in a flat of less than 20 square metres. Our present flat belongs to the work unit. We have 74 square metres, four rooms, a kitchen and a bathroom. Water and electricity is 80 – 90 yuan a month, deducted from my salary. Three years after we moved to Guangzhou, we participated in the housing allocation process. On the basis of position, seniority and present housing conditions we were ranked after each other and then the housing allocation group of the leadership decided in the end. We invested 40,000 yuan of our own savings in building the blocks here; that is 30 per cent of the cost, the work unit paid 70 per cent. We paid the money in 1994 and in October 1995 we could move into our new address. I was lucky. Very few people can buy their own housing with the living standards and the price level of today. My mother still lives in Henan together with my elder brother. Every year we send some money to her.

F 21 XT

My work unit began to pool money to build houses in 1988 but we hesitated to participate. The criteria for participating were the same as for getting a housing allocation: seniority, need, etc. because the unit contributed two-thirds while the family should only pay one third. But we did not have the money and we also thought about our son getting married. If we used money just for one living place, what could he get? We would rather save money for our son. This year we have bought, though. The rent kept going up, it had gone up to 70 yuan per month, so we thought we had to buy. We paid 20,000 yuan for four rooms at 70 square metres in all. I studied the rules and found that there were deductions for seniority, position and something else. We have 60 years of seniority in all, my husband's position also counted something. Xingtai is the only town where position also counts. All together we got deducted 30,000 yuan, the market price was 50,000 yuan – more than 700 yuan for one square meter.

After we bought our hearts were easy, owning one's own house is a good feeling. You do not have to worry about the rent going up. We had to borrow money from family members and friends – a little from each – to pay for the place. When we bought we were not told that the houses have to be demolished within a five-year plan. We bought in October 1996 and in January 1997 we were told about the plan. We attended a meeting about it, chaired by the Construction Bureau that has set up a small group in charge of renovation of old districts. The houses will be ranked and exchanged on the basis of ranking and size (*gongjia tiaozheng fang*). We have heard from someone else that after having been compensated for the square metres one already has, there will be an offer of 10 square metres for 400 yuan each and if one wants more it will be at the market price, which is around 800 yuan a square metre. Now we hope to get a bigger place after the reconstruction so we can all live together, also with my parents-in-law who now live by themselves. They have bought a flat from the City Commercial Bureau. It is an old house from the 1970s, it is not earthquake-safe so they paid 10,000 yuan for 100 square metres, which is very cheap, only 100 yuan for one square metre. One of our neighbours – an old lady in the street – is very unhappy about it and is crying because they will demolish her ancestors' property.

In the old form of housing allocation seniority was the most important, then whether you were a cadre or a technician, and these restrictions also applied to pooling of funds for housing. But now the housing policy is to *sell* houses and so anyone can participate if they have money. Money was not so important before. At that time people were not like they are now. We did not think about a bonus, we worked 8 hours a day. Now, when workers have worked just a few hours they want a bonus. We miss the spirit of the old days and we also lack resources because of the low salary.

F 8 XT

We live in the house of my uncle,[12] who provided the job at the Public Baths for me. Neither the Bath House nor the Hair Dresser Office have their own housing. The house is built by the Housing Bureau of the City Government. Usable area is 28 square metres. We bought the house for 12,000 yuan in the first half of 1997, which means a little more than 400 yuan a square metre. We borrowed the money. Buying a new house would be 880 yuan a square metre. We now own the house with a formal deed and we can sell it again after two or three years. I read the documents carefully before deciding. The price is related to seniority and other things also gave a deduction. We discussed it very carefully in the family and then we agreed to do it. We already have an urban household registration. You heard I grew up in the countryside but when I took over the job at the Public Baths from my uncle we exchanged our registration status so he got my agricultural one and I got his urban one.

F 0 XT

We live in a house belonging to one of our relatives, 20 square metres in two rooms. We cannot get allocated housing from the work unit because my husband has been away for so long. We got a unit flat in 1981, but that was on the fourth floor and when he got sick it was not very convenient. It also was worn out, the roof was leaking so we gave it back to the unit and moved to where we live now. We tried to change the flat with one on the first floor, but the Housing Bureau was extremely strict those first years, when it had to go on market terms. We were not told when the unit would repair the roof and anyway we could not get another flat. We do not pay any rent here, and we do not pay much attention to housing. We pay 20 yuan for water and electricity every month. If they renovate the surroundings here, we must see what happens. I am not worried about that and I have neither contacted my own nor his work unit about new housing. We cannot possibly get another housing allo-

12. He means the house was originally provided by the uncle, as he later says that they bought the house.

cation because we returned the flat. We take one step at a time (*zou yibu, shuo yibu*).

F 4 XT

Our house is private. My husband's father bought it in the 1950s. We have replaced the roof and the western wall. It is 30 square metres. We pay 10 yuan for water and 10 yuan for electricity. My work unit allocates housing but owns very few buildings so I never got anything from them. They recently started to sell houses but the prices are rather high. Our first son has got an apartment of 15 square metres from his work unit, the second son has a small place of 20 square metres that he built himself in 1983 for 300 yuan, and the third son bought his own flat in 1996. He borrowed some money and paid 36,000 yuan for three rooms on the fourth floor. His work unit also paid a share, but I am not clear about the ownership rights.

F 2 XT

After they [the children of the interviewee] moved out there were many empty apartments here so the army demolished the house and build a new building but they did not give a flat to us. We had to buy it, but our economy is strained. When the second son got married we spent some money and the other children thought the division between them were not fair, so we discussed it again and again. At last we had to give up buying the flat and moved into this house. Here we live now, all the rest of us. It is the office building of the Army Hospital no. 63, built during the Korean War. It is a very good building. We have not discussed this with the army. The principle is that those who live in the house own it. The family who lived here before gave it to us. I do not care. I have tried so many times to apply for an apartment and talk to the leaders. They have no shame. They only wait for you to come with gifts and otherwise they do not care. They have houses and flats but they rotate them within their own ranks. One cadre moves out and makes room for the next one. They can even rent rooms outside if they think they need more space. They built new houses in 1995, as I told you. They sold them and the prices were reasonable, but I learned about it too late. Nobody informed us and we live too far away so we did not know what was happening. But I was in the unit and I had applied so they ought to have informed me. I went to the city party secretary and he twisted and turned saying, 'sorry for all this bureaucracy, we forgot you, I apologise so much'. But there was still one apartment left on the fifth floor, I could get it if I wanted. It was just to pick up the phone. But I went home and talked to my wife and we agreed to save our money and go on living almost for free in this old office building. I just worry because I have three sons, one already has a flat, the other can take this over when we are gone, but the last one will also have to find a place. I contacted my daughter-in-law. She has money but she thinks otherwise. She was not willing to help us. So now we must see what will happen. It is impossible to get housing allocations for free now.

SOCIAL SECURITY

F 8 XT

My wife is on labour health insurance and this gives her less money than sick leave would. Women have to be 45 years old and have a seniority of more than 30 years to get sick leave. Her expenses for medicine and hospitals are not covered. Her medicine cost 2,000 yuan over the last two or three years. I have gone to her work unit many times to get compensation for the medical bill. She has many pains in her back and needs an operation but the unit cannot pay. I also have to take care of my parents in the countryside if they fall ill. My father is 89 and my mother also over 80, but luckily they are strong and healthy. The biggest happiness for a family nowadays is not to be sick!

F 15 XT

My husband was laid off from the factory in 1996 and now they do not care about his health expenses. They say the health insurance is in the salary but we don't get any salary! When he was working, he got treatment at the factory clinic, and when he had to go to the hospital he was compensated 80 per cent for costs over 2,000 yuan.

He has to take medicine for his lungs and it costs at least 30 yuan a month, in all I think we pay 100 yuan a month for medicine. I have heard about the social security regulations on TV and read it in the papers, but I do not think we are part of it. A couple of days ago the Neighbourhood Committee sent out a form to families with difficulties. We were asked to report if our work units were paying salary and tell about our economy in general. We filled it in with the true information about our situation. I do not know what they will do with it. The city has a quota for poverty cards, they are for the families most badly off. They give it in groups, twice a year. So who is the most needy? We do not want to be part of the quota. The factory got one for us the previous years, but this year we do not want it. At least we have some 50 yuan a month. We can eat and we do not fit the especially poor level, we just have to save a little. They say this year prices will not be lower for people with the card. You will only be exempt from taxes, if you do trading. So if you have the card and you want to sell melons, you go to your factory and they can write an application for you to the Neighbourhood Committee and give it a stamp. The years after you will not have to pay tax. Last year the City Government passed a regulation saying that 120 yuan was the lowest living expense. If people do not have that they should be paid up to that. But too many people are in that category. The government does not have the money. Our family only have 50 yuan a month but too many families are in that situation, so we are not the worst off.

F 21 XT

For example concerning health insurance: For us old people there should be some kind of safety net. We have worked for one whole generation, so we cannot go without. Headache or fever, we have to get medicine. We get 15 yuan a month, it is not much, just for small ailments you can spend many tens of yuan. Seen from the nation as such, the system is not very good. But the state is not rich either. The enterprises are not doing well and they cannot all stretch their hands to the state. There has to be some kind of insurance. In society to establish health insurance companies where individuals can contribute their savings is a good method. It should be arranged by the work units, not by people themselves. But the units are collapsing and do not have money. Banks, tax bureaus and security organs are the best units to work in but one needs a good education and then both money and connections to get in there. These things were not so important before. Anyway, our life is better now, we are very well. The biggest change is that we eat well and dress well. But Xingtai city as a whole is not a very good place these days.

F 35 XT

The Textile Mill in principle covered health care, but in reality they stopped that service in 1992. In my new unit they have to cover expenses over 3,000 yuan (it is a rule), then no further compensation or reimbursement in the monthly salary. But I have not been compensated 1,000 yuan as I should, because I spent over 4,000 yuan last year.

F 40 XT

In our family, three people – my father, my wife and my sister – do not have effective health care insurance. Even though they all have kept a connection to a work unit, they will not get reimbursed for health expenses because their units do not have the money. At my wife's workplace they have a rule of reimbursing giving birth, but when we had our child, they could not compensate us. First they said they would pay half but later they stepped down on their promise and made us fill out a form, so if the unit gets money again some time in the future we could be compensated.

We have done nothing to secure my family members through other means. There are a lot of commercial insurances for sale, but we and the people around us do not care much about it, nobody insures themselves. We do not take the risk really seriously, I think it is a problem of mentality. We ought to do more about it and secure ourselves, I don't know why we just let it be.

J 17 GZ

On social security in my work unit I will get a pension of 90 per cent of my former salary after I reach 50 years of age.[13] This is more than I get now, being laid off. Health care expenses can be refunded up to 55 yuan a month but if it is a serious illness there are some other rules, I am not quite sure about them. To stay in the hospital the unit refunds 80 per cent. Health care security has gotten worse and worse. Before everything was paid, then it was lowered to 60 per cent and then to 50 per cent, and now it is down to the 55 yuan a month that one can get reimbursed. But I am lucky, I still have the connection to my work unit, so they will take care of me. They always pay in time. But my daughter is a problem, her health is not good, we have used more than 3,000 yuan on her this year. My unit only refunded half of my son's health expenses until he was 16 years old but they will not pay anything to my daughter. We got a child for whom we did not have a permit (*shengyu zhibiao*) and the units only pay social security for one child. My daughter's expenses we have to bear ourselves. And my husband is also self-supporting but he has not been ill.

J 1 GZ

Concerning welfare: 90 yuan is deducted every month to go into a pension fund, half from my salary and half is covered by the work unit. Before we were reimbursed all expenses on health care and the children had a card, so they would get 50 per cent reimbursed. Now a part of the personal income is put into a personal account. When that is spent there is progressive reimbursement: Under 5,000 yuan I pay 10 per cent, from 5,000 to 10,000 yuan I pay 8 per cent, over 10,000 I pay 2 per cent. We do not have unemployment insurance, and my wife does not have a pension guarantee. What is the use of that? She may be laid off, but then we must eat a little less. It is not important. What will we do if we get into trouble? I

13. This is the rule all right, but it seems unlikely she will get 90 per cent of her salary as 'really' retired, when she now only gets a basic living subsidy. Experiences from other interviews say that the pensioners keep getting the low subsidy after reaching formal retirement age.

have not thought about it. I know only a little about the possibilities of commercial insurance.

J 8 XT

My wife works in a machine tool factory, an SOE. She is now on labour health insurance (*chi laobao*) because of bad health. She gets 105 yuan a month. She has for the last 2–3 years helped a relative sell things now and then and gets 7–8 yuan a month. She began to work in the factory when she was 13 year old, because her family was in very tight circumstances. Her parents died early so she is almost illiterate. For 6 or 7 years she has been on labour insurance. She did very heavy work as a steel caster and it was bad for her health, especially because she started to work at so young an age. The leadership of her unit is no good. It might close. It cannot even pay salary, only the retired and the ones on labour health insurance will get their money, workers do not get paid.[14] My unit also has problems and pays a very low salary because we have become responsible for our own profit and loss. Salary is always low in the service industry. There is competition between the public hair dressers and the private sector. Xingtai is the only place in the country where there is a central Hair Dresser Office.

F 0 XT

My husband and I are both 47 years old. Neither of us are party members. We both graduated from lower middle school in 1968. He started to work immediately in a state-owned enterprise, making vehicles for mining. He was just an ordinary worker. Now he is on sick leave and gets 270 yuan a month. He has not been able to go to work since 1989. His sickness is not related to his work. His blood pressure is too high and until now he has had a cerebral haemorrhage three times. He suffers from hemiplegia and cannot take care of himself. So I cannot go to work, either, I have to stay at home and look after him, we have nobody else to do it. Our medical expenses are reimbursed, his unit has insurance. We pay our-

14. This situation is contrary to the policy of the unit of case F 33 XT in Appendix 1, where the interviewed person says that her unit tends only to pay the people who actually work.

selves and at the end of each quarter, we get the money back. Last year my husband spent more than one month in the hospital. It cost 4,000 yuan and we paid 400 ourselves, while the unit paid the rest. They reimbursed us 90 per cent so it is no problem but life is hard anyway. If he had not been ill it would be easier. But we do not even have 200 yuan a month per person, it is not up to the minimum living standard. Our income is around 500 yuan a month, it is only enough for eating. We cannot get a poverty card because we do not belong to a unit that does not pay salary.

I work as a salesperson at a market owned by the City Government. From end of school in 1968 until 1974 I was a sent-down youth in the vicinity of Xingtai. When I was allowed to go back to the city the market asked for people and I got in, but business is bad. The market is located in the wrong place and there are too few buyers. I have sick leave since last year to take care of my husband, but my own health is also not good, my heart is too big. I was never ill before, so I do not know about earlier health insurance systems. I have 260 yuan a month in illness allowance. My unit participates in an insurance scheme, each month 10 yuan is deducted. On top of that the unit paid 500 yuan, this arrangement just started. I do not quite understand what it is all about. I have heard that only if you go to the hospital your expenses will be refunded. For small illnesses you are not covered. All the retired persons in my unit have to participate in the scheme, but I do not really understand the rules.

J 16 GZ

None of us have health care or pension insurance. I have heard that the village can pay 80 per cent of hospital expenses but our health is good so I have not tried to get any expenses reimbursed. Basically we depend on ourselves, I do not know of any rules we can count on and we do not plan to buy any kind of insurance.

F 4 XT

Two weeks ago my husband was run over by a car from the City Procuratorate. His nose was bleeding badly and he got a concussion. The driver of the car took him to the hospital and paid for three days then he disappeared, leaving a telephone number. After my husband came back he feels dizzy all the time, his nose keeps bleeding and he is not well at all. He has been back to the hospital several times to get medicine and have the stitches taken out. Each time we have to pay ourselves, because we do not know the name of the person who hit him. It has already cost us more than 1,000 yuan. We have tried to phone the number the driver left, but no one answers. Then I have tried to phone the Procuratorate, but they send me from one place to another, and nobody will take responsibility. I have also consulted with the Trade Union, unsuccessfully. The driver was clever to just drive my old man to the hospital without asking for a policeman to record the accident. He was afraid of being involved with the police, therefore being so friendly at first, and then just walking away. Now we cannot find the guilty person and my husband's work unit will not pay the medical bills. They say the Procuratorate should pay. I have thought about sending my son to the City Government but I dare not, as he has a bad temper and I am afraid he will ruin the whole thing.

On health insurance I can get refunded 10 yuan a month and we share it with the whole family. No matter who is sick, if I go and buy the medicine my work unit will reimburse me up to these 120 yuan a year. My husband can get 6 yuan a month back for health care services. If you have had more expenses you can discuss with them, but these days they are not easy to deal with, because the economic situation is so bad. They do not care even if you have a serious disease, as the rules say they should. They stopped caring already from 1992.

When we do not get pensions and salary we go to the work unit and complain. We retired people have been going together, those of us who dare to go. Some are afraid of getting into trouble if they complain. But the leadership says they have spent all the money. They say that the more we complain, the less money we will get. We went to the head of the factory Trade Union, he said we should go to the manager, and the manager just says they have spent all the money. The obstructions are too many and we cannot really do anything. The state has its rules, but it is best to rely on oneself. We do not complain.

F 23 XT

In my job I do not have any health insurance and I cannot afford pension insurance, either. My husband has health care paid by his old unit. This system does not work any more. Now everyone is covered according to seniority. If you have worked a short time, you get less, and vice versa. The minimum living standard in Xingtai is 120 yuan per person per month. The Neighbourhood Committee registers the ones under that and they will get help from above i.e. the District Government. This does not go for the peasants that have started to come in from the outside to trade. Some are really trading, some just come here to bear children.

EDUCATION

F 15 XT

I would have liked to go to school longer, but conditions when I was a child did not allow it. Our own children at least got to junior middle school, except for our third son, who is a senior middle school graduate. But now we even have to pay for primary school. It is a big difference from before with all the fees that we have to pay for school. Before the teachers were obliged to help the children and give extra lessons, if somebody was behind. Now it all costs money; they tell you to buy some books, and sometimes do not even use them. The teachers' salary is paid by state money, but then there are training fees and other fees. I think something is wrong. But our grandchildren have to get a good schooling, otherwise it is difficult to find a job.

J 17 GZ

On schooling we pay 1,000 yuan for our daughter who attends a vocational school within the textile industry. Our son went to a vocational school for handicrafts for three years, 1993 to 1996. We paid 4,000 yuan in school fees in all. But it was all wasted, he cannot use it for anything. I myself only had one year in junior middle school, then came the Cultural Revolution. I would have liked to read more books, but there were no more books to read. I do not think my children are very good in school, but it is no use worrying about it or making a big fuss.

J 1 GZ

Regarding schools we pay 2,000 each school term (a half-year) for our daughter, and 500 for our son. On top of that for each of them we pay 3,500 yuan a term in different school fees (*shoufei*). My daughter went to middle school in Henan before, but because I was tranferred to Guangzhou she followed in 1992. We take our children's education very seriously. My hottest wish is that my son will pass the entrance test for senior middle school.

J 8 XT

Our son is in senior middle school. We got a poverty card from my work unit so we only pay half of the school fees, that is, 800–900 yuan each year. Our daughter is at home. She does not want to go to school or apply for a job so we let her stay here because of her young age. She is too young to go out in society.

F 0 XT

Just to keep our son in school costs 200 yuan a month for daily expenses. He is 21 years old and attends a vocational school in Shijiazhuang. When he entered last year we had to pay 6,000 yuan in school fees for two years. We did not have the money so our relatives paid. Our son will graduate next year. If times had been what they used to be it would have been fine, because he could have gotten a job in a factory, or he could have gotten into my husband's work unit. We will contact the leadership there directly to ask if there is any possibility that he can get a job there. But it is impossible to tell what will happen, it is a great pain to get a job today. Anything will do, either a work unit or being self-employed. Each year is different from the one before. I do not know what we will do in the future. We wait until he has graduated, then we must see what happens. I think the government should help young people get employment. My biggest worry in life is that the child cannot find a job. Of course I would like him to get into a state-owned unit, but it should be one that pays salary!

F 2 XT

I am retired now and still get my pension through the army. The situation of our family is different from others. The field army is extremely mobile. My children all grew up in the countryside and moved to Xingtai in 1976. So their schooling has been rather erratic. Only my daughter got to senior middle school. The life in the countryside for my wife alone with three children was difficult. The school was far away and the teachers often pressed the children to do them favours and give them gifts.

This is the same now. We recently had a problem with my grandson. He was about to finish fourth grade, but he did not get the books to do the preparations for the examination. I asked him how many did not have books and he said that five pupils apart from himself did not have the books they needed. I thought this could not be right, so I first tried several bookstores in the city but these books were sold out. Then I contacted some former teachers, relatives of some people in the army, and they had some good advice, so in the end I got the books from a small bookshop in a county outside Xingtai. I just described the book and the grade they were meant for to the bookseller and he fetched six copies from his store room in the back. It took many days to run around so it is good I am retired now, else the children would not have been able to prepare properly for their exam.

F 23 XT

In junior middle school we paid 300 yuan for a school transfer for our grandson. I have seen that there is a rule that schools must not charge fees for transfers, but they did it anyway. The schools only want money, but they do not even give a receipt. I think it is all swindel and humbug. Our country has very clear rules for charging school fees but they are not obeyed. The State Education Commission has several times expressed concern about the disorderly way of imposing fees (*luan shoufei*) and the State Council has done the same, but they stick to their own rotten ways. Many units act according to the saying, 'policies from above (create) countermeasures from below'.

The middle school where my grandson is now does not guarantee a job after graduation. They will recommend you, but for the job for which our grandson is trained there is only one factory in Xingtai and it demands an investment for hiring new people. They spent one year at that factory during the education. I have heard of the daughter-in-law of somebody, who paid 6,000 yuan as an investment when her unit merged with another one. On paper it is voluntary, but in fact people are forced to pay if they want to stay. For permanent workers it was 6,000 yuan and for temporary workers 3,000 yuan. When the social style is so bad, no wonder the schools' behaviour is also not good. There is a change in attitude. In the 1970s people's thinking was different. Nobody talked of pay, we built bridges and factories, I led people in voluntary labour (*yiwu laodong*). If you asked them to come, they came at once. No talk of pay. Not like now, they want pay, before they move anywhere.

REACTIONS

F 15 XT

We cannot count on our children. They do not even have enough for themselves. My greatest worry is that the children don't have jobs, so that they will not have enough to eat. 200 or 300 yuan will do for us. We old people are used to suffering, we can stand it. We have better food now than before. We just wish the young people should not suffer the same way as we did. The important thing is to keep going, looking for jobs, pulling people. Only if you have friends, will you succeed. The government should pay some attention to people who do not have a job, but there are too many. The problem is whether the government actually has the capacity now.

F 40 XT

The good changes in society since the reforms started are that it is more convenient to buy things and people are much more lively and dynamic. But the problem to worry about is how to find work. I just hope my work unit will come back on track like it was before 1994. In this situation we cannot count on the government, there are too many laid off people and too many enterprises are operating at a loss, how should the government be able to care for all those? I think now we have to depend on ourselves and then the most important thing is to depend on your own qualities and resources, more than on power or money or family. We are lucky that we still live with my parents. If we have to separate our economies at some point, I don't think we will be able to make ends meet.

J 17 GZ

I am somewhat confident about the future because my husband has the land and we have rooms for rent. I am not familiar with the reforms in welfare policy. And it does not matter whether we ordinary people understand it or not, it is of no use for us. The economy is much better now, if one has money one can buy a lot of things. We have more freedom than before, we do not have to cut off the tail of capitalism! But there are too many laid off people. In my factory we were 900 employees, now they have laid off 600 people in two rounds. Those more than 45 years old (like me) 'retire', those under 45 get one month's salary each year, calculated according to their seniority. Otherwise the unit does not care about them.

J 1 GZ

Generally speaking the changes in living standards are very big, for most people the change is for the better. A minority cannot uphold their former living standard, if for instance they are laid off. The personal greed of people is swelling, housing is difficult to pay and the quality of education is not satisfactory.

J 8 XT

I became a party member in 1996 because my boss encouraged me. In economic terms it does not matter if you are a party member. But if you do not have anything else to give your children at least they can say that their father is a party member. Besides, membership gives you something to look forward to. If not on the economic, then on the political side you have a goal, people believe in this and that. I believe in the CCP.

J 16 GZ

Relationships between people have suffered a lot because of the new times. Before, our contact with our neighbours was very good and close but this has disappeared. One reason is that people only think of making money, another is that there are so many outsiders here and we all have to live together. Public security is harmed. But in the future society will certainly develop into a better place.

F 23 XT

In my life I have been working so much for so little pay. I am proud of having been in the forefront of political mobilization, at least earlier. We did not have to promote our children, they got jobs because of their own good behaviour. We have not been knocking on doors but the situation in Xingtai is bad. There are more people selling than buying things. The people are just too pitiable, I know because I hear about it when I collect the sanitation fee. Some cannot even pay the 7 yuan a year for sanitation. They have not been paid for years. The difference between good and bad units is too big today. When we meet each other, we say: 'How are you? Are you getting your salary?' If the answer is 'yes', it is good![15]

15. Refer to the Chinese custom of greeting with a concrete question, like 'Have you had lunch?' or 'Are you back from work?' instead of just 'Hello'. The custom is often referred to in historical literature in connection with the greeting 'Have you eaten today?' alleged to have been common in Imperial China and taken as a proof of the existence of starvation.

Appendix 3 只能靠自己

Key to Cases

F 15 XT

The Liu household consists of five people: a couple in their late 50s, their second son and his wife, both 32 years old, and their third son at 24. Their first son and a daughter live in separate households and there are an unspecified number of grandchildren. We interviewed the mother.

F 35 XT

The Guo family consists of three persons: father, 36, mother and a boy, nine years old. Both parents participated in the interview.

F 40 XT

The Xing Family has a household of six persons: father and mother, 54 and 51 years old, the interviewed person (whose age was not given) and his wife; a sister at 23; and a child, two months old. The interviewed son works in a state-owned enterprise, the biggest factory in Xingtai with 8,000 employees.

J 17 GZ

The Kong family has four members: A couple of in their late 40s; a son at 22 and a daughter at 19. The interviewed person is the woman, 46 years old.

J 1 GZ

The Li family has four members: father, 45; mother, 43; son, 15; daughter, 17. (The son is mentioned first even though he is the youngest). The father was interviewed.

F 21 XT

The Liang household has six members: a couple of 52 and 50 years; their son, 28 years old, with a wife at 27 and a two-year-old child;

finally a daughter of the old couple/sister to the son at 21. The interviewed person is Bianshu, the older woman.

F 8 XT

The Mu family consists of four people: two parents, 43 and 40 years old, and two teen-age children, 16 and 17. The interviewed person is the father, who has been a party member since 1996.

J 16 GZ

The Che household in Guangzhou consists of three women: a mother (widow), 55 years old, and two daughters, 31 and 28 years old. The oldest daughter was interviewed.

F 0 XT

The Li family is a household of three persons: a married couple in their 40s and their child, 21 years old. The interviewed person is the wife/mother.

F 4 XT

The Zhao family household consists of 11 people: a retired couple of 61 and 62 years old, three sons at the age of 40, 38 and 35, three daughters-in-law and three grandchildren. We interviewed the oldest woman.

F 2 XT

The Zhu family consists of six persons: the couple, 58, three sons, 30, 28, 25, and a daughter of 19. The first son and his wife live by themselves with a son. The second son and his wife, third son and daughter live with their parents. The interviewed person is the father who has served in the army for 39 years.

F 23 XT

Peng Gongfen, 60, and her husband, 69, live with their grandson. They have two daughters and a son who all live in their own households. They are both party members and one of their daughters is, too.

只能靠自己

Bibliography

Ash, Robert A. and Y.Y. Kueh (eds) (1996) *The Chinese Economy under Deng Xiaoping*. Oxford: Clarendon Press.

Asian Development Bank (2001) 'Technical Assistance to the People's Republic of China for Policy and Institutional Support for the Social Security Reform Pilot Program'. TAR: PRC 34096.

Bakken, Børge (2000) *The Exemplary Society: Human Improvement, Social Control, and the Dangers of Modernity in China*. Oxford: Oxford University Press.

Bell, Daniel and Joanne R. Bauer (1996) *The East Asian Challenge for Human Rights*. Cambridge: Cambridge University Press.

Bian, Yanjie (1994) '*Guanxi* and the Allocation of Urban Jobs in China'. *The China Quarterly*, no. 140, pp. 971–999.

—— (1997) 'Bringing Strong Ties Back: Indirect Ties, Network Bridges, and Job Searches in China'. *American Sociological Review*, vol. 62, pp. 366–384.

—— and John R. Logan (1996) 'Market Transition and the Persistence of Power: The Changing Stratification System in Urban China'. *American Sociological Review*, vol. 61, pp. 739–758.

—— (et al.) (1997) 'Work Units and Housing Reform in Two Chinese Cities'. In Xiaobo Lü and Elizabeth Perry (eds), *Danwei. The Changing Chinese Workplace in Historical and Comparative Perspective*. Armonk: M.E. Sharpe, pp. 223–250.

Bloom, Gerry, Y. Lu and J. Chen (2001) 'Financing Health Care in China's Cities: Balancing Needs and Entitlements'. *Paper presented at China Social Policy Conference*, Oxford, October 19–20.

BR: *Beijing Review*. Before 1979 *Peking Review* (*PR*).

Brooks, Douglas H. and Myo Thant (1998) *Social Sector Issues in Transitional Economies of Asia*. Oxford: Oxford University Press.

Brudholm, Thomas (2001) 'Conviction and Critique: Addressing the Sceptic'. In Kirsten Hastrup (ed.), *Human Rights on Common Grounds. The Quest for Universality.* The Hague: Kluwer Law International, pp. 25–38.

Bruun, Ole (1995) 'Political Hierarchy and Private Entrepreneurship in a Chinese Neighborhood'. In Andrew Walder (ed.), *The Waning of the Communist State. Economic Origins of Political Decline in China and Hungary.* Berkeley: University of California Press, pp. 184–212.

—— and Michael Jacobsen (2000) *Human Rights and Asian Values. Contesting National Identities and Cultural Representations in Asia.* Nordic Institute of Asian Studies, Democracy in Asia Series, no. 6. Surrey: Curzon Press.

Buhmann, Karin (2001) *Implementing Human Rights through Administrative Law Reforms.* Copenhagen: Djøf Publishing.

Burell, Mattias (2001) *The Rule-Governed State. China's Labour Market Policy, 1978–1998.* Uppsala: Uppsala University.

—— (2002) 'Enforcing the Labor Law: Labor Dispute Resolution in the 1990s'. *Paper presented at Conference on Legal and Political Reform in the PRC. 3–4 June.* Lund University, Sweden.

Cao, Yang, Victor Nee and Xuguang Zhou (2000) 'Comment: Controversies and Evidence in the Market Transition Debate/ Reply: Beyond the Debate and toward Substantive Institutional Analysis'. *The American Journal of Sociology*, vol. 105, no. 4, pp. 1175–1195.

Cassese, Antonio (1990) *Human Rights in a Changing World.* Oxford: Polity Press.

CEL: Compulsory Education Law: *Zhonghua Renmin Gongheguo yiwu jiaoyu fa*, adopted 4 April 1986 at the 4th Session of the 6th NPC (*GWYGB*, no. 12, 1986: 400–402).

Chan, Anita (1997) 'Chinese *Danwei* Reforms: Convergence with the Japanese Model?' In Xiaobo Lü and Elizabeth Perry (eds), *Danwei. The Changing Chinese Workplace in Historical and Comparative Perspective.* Armonk: M. E. Sharpe, pp. 91–113.

—— (1998) 'Labor Standards and Human Rights: The Case of Chinese Workers Under Market Socialism'. *Human Rights Quarterly*, vol. 20, pp. 886–904.

Chan, Cecilia L.W. (1993) *The Myth of Neighbourhood Mutual Help. The Contemporary Chinese Community-Based Welfare System in Guangzhou.* Hong Kong: Hong Kong University Press.

Chan, Kam Wing and Li Zhang (1999) 'The *Hukou* System and Rural–Urban Migration in China: Processes and Changes'. *The China Quarterly*, no. 160, pp. 819–855.

Chen, Aimin (1998) 'China's Urban Housing Market Development: Problems and Prospects'. *Journal of Contemporary China*, vol. 7, no. 17, pp. 43–60.

Chen, Jianfu (2002) 'Implementation of Law as a Politico-Legal Battle in China'. *Paper presented at Conference on Legal and Political Reform in the PRC. 3–4 June.* Lund University, Sweden.

'Chengzhen zhufang zhidu gaige zongheng 1–4' [Casual talk about urban housing reform, 1–4] (1997). *Jingji cankao bao*, 19, 22, 24, 25 April.

'China Revises its Pharmaceutical Administration Law' (2001). *China Law*, April.

Cheung, Gordon C.K. (1997) 'An Analysis of 1993 Chinese Taxation Reform'. *Journal of Contemporary Asia*, vol. 27, no. 4, pp. 511 – 517.

Chiu, Catherine C.H. (et al.) (1998) 'A Comparison of Occupational Values between Capitalist Hong Kong and Socialist Guangzhou'. *Economic Development and Cultural Change*, vol. 46, no. 4, pp. 749–770.

Cook, Sarah and Naila Kabeer (eds) (2000) 'Social Policy in the South: Revisioning the Agenda'. *IDS Bulletin*, vol. 31. no. 4.

Craven, Matthew (1995) *The International Covenant on Economic, Social and Cultural Rights. A Perspective on its Development.* Oxford: Clarendon Press.

CTN: *Chengshi tongji nianjian* [Urban statistical yearbook]. Beijing: Zhongguo tongji chubanshe.

Dalberg-Larsen, Jørgen (1995) 'The Nordic Welfare Model – What Separates the Nordic Countries from the Rest of Europe?'. In *Reconceptualizing the Welfare State. Proceedings from Symposium in connection with Maastricht II.* Copenhagen: The Danish Centre for Human Rights, pp. 22–32.

Davis, Deborah (1989) 'Chinese Social Welfare: Policies and Outcomes'. *The China Quarterly*, no. 119, p. 576–597.

—— (1992) 'Job Mobility in post-Mao Cities: Increases on the Margins'. *The China Quarterly*, no. 132, pp.1062–1085.

—— (ed.) (1995) *Urban Spaces in Contemporary China.* Cambridge: Woodrow Wilson Center Press and Cambridge University Press.

Deacon, Bob (1983) *Social Policy and Socialism.* London: Pluto Press.

—— (1993) 'Developments in East European Social Policy'. In Catherine Jones (ed.), *New Perspectives on the Welfare State in Europe.* London and New York: Routledge, pp.177–197.

—— (2000) *Globalization and Social Policy: the Threat to Equitable Welfare.* Geneva: United Nations Research Institute for Social Development, Occasional Paper 5.

—— and Julia Szalai (eds) (1990) *Social Policy in the New Eastern Europe. What Future for Socialist Welfare?* Aldershot: Avebury.

Devereux, Stephen and Sarah Cook (2000) 'Does Social Policy Meet Social Needs?'. *IDS Bulletin*, vol. 31. no. 4.

Dixon, John (1981) *The Chinese Welfare System, 1949–1979.* New York: Praeger Publishers.

Drzewicki, Krzysztof (2001) 'The Right to Work and Rights in Work'. In Asbjørn Eide, Catarina Krause and Allan Rosas (eds), *Economic, Social and Cultural Rights. A Textbook.* Dordrecht: Martinus Nijhoff Publishers, pp. 223–243.

Duckett, Jane 2001 'Political Interests and the Implementation of China's Urban Health Insurance Reform'. *Social Policy and Administration*, vol. 35, no. 3, pp. 290–306.

Dutton, Michael (1998) *Streetlife China.* Cambridge: Cambridge University Press.

EL: Education Law: *Zhonghua Renmin Gongheguo jiaoyu fa*, adopted 18 March 1995 at the 3rd session of the 8th NPC (*GWYGB*, no. 10, 1995: 373–383).

Eckstein, Alexander (1977) *China's Economic Revolution.* Cambridge: Cambridge University Press.

Eide, Asbjørn, Catarina Krause and Allan Rosas (1995) *Economic, Social and Cultural Rights. A Textbook.* Dordrecht: Martinus Nijhoff Publishers.

—— (2001) *Economic, Social and Cultural Rights. A Textbook.* Second revised edition. Dordrecht: Martinus Nijhoff Publishers

Esping-Andersen, Gøsta (1990) *The Three Worlds of Welfare Capitalism.* Cambridge: Polity Press.

—— (1999) *Social Foundations of Postindustrial Economies.* Oxford: Oxford University Press.

—— (2000) 'Social Indicators and Welfare Monitoring'. *Social Policy and Development Programme Paper*, no. 2. Geneva: United Nations Research Institute for Social Development.

—— (ed.) (1996) *Welfare States in Transition. National Adaptations in Global Economies.* London: Sage Publications.

Fairbank, John King (1986) *The Great Chinese Revolution: 1800–1985.* New York: Harper & Row Publishers.

—— (1992) *China. A New History.* Cambridge, MA: The Belknap Press of Harvard University Press.

Fanggai wenjian xuanbian [Selected documents on housing reform] (1997). Xingtai: Zhufang weiyuanhui bangongshi.

Fischer, Georg and Guy Standing (eds) (1993) *Structural Change in Central and Eastern Europe: Labour Market and Social Policy Implications.* Paris: OECD.

Francis, Corinna-Barbara (1996) 'Reproduction of *Danwei* Institutional Features in the Context of China's Market Economy: The Case of Haidian District's High-Tech Sector'. *The China Quarterly*, no. 147, pp. 839–859.

FEER: *Far Eastern Economic Review*, Hong Kong.

Ferge, Zsuzsa (1997) 'The Changed Welfare Paradigm: The Individualization of the Social'. *Social Policy and Administration*, vol. 31, no. 2, pp. 20–44.

Funü bao: Women's Daily, Beijing.

Fultz, Elaine and Markus Ruck (2001) 'Pension Reform in Central and Eastern Europe: Emerging Issues and Patterns'. *International Labour Review*, vol. 140, no. 1, pp. 19–43.

Fung, Ho-lup (2001) 'The Making and Melting of the 'Iron Rice Bowl' in China 1949 to 1995'. *Social Policy and Administration*, vol. 35, no. 3, pp. 258–273.

Gaubatz, Piper Rae (1995) 'Urban transformation in post-Mao China: Impacts of the reform era on China's urban form'. In Deborah Davis (ed.), *Urban Spaces in Contemporary China*. Cambridge: Woodrow Wilson Center Press and Cambridge University Press, pp. 28–60.

Ge, Yanfeng (1997) 'Gaige yu fazhan guocheng zhong de shehui baozhang zhidu jianshe wenti' [Problems in building a social security system in the process of reform and development]. *Unpublished Report*, Beijing: State Council Research Development Centre.

—— (et al.) (2003) *Zhongguo jiguan shiye danwei yanglaojin zhidu gaige yanjiu. Yizhong ansheji. Research into the reform of the pension system in state institutions and public service units in China. One scheme design.* (In Chinese and English). Beijing: Foreign Languages Press.

Ghai, Yash (1995) 'Asian Perspectives on Human Rights'. In J.T.H. Tang, *Human Rights and International Relations in the Asia-Pacific Region*, London: Pinter, pp. 54–67.

—— (1998) 'Rights and Globalization: East Asian Experience'. *Peoples for Human Rights. IMADR YEARBOOK*, vol. 6.

Goodman, David S.G. (ed.) (1997) *China's Provinces in Reform*. London: Routledge.

Goodman, Roger and Ito Peng (1996) 'The East Asian Welfare States: Peripatetic Learning, Adaptive Change, and Nation-building'. In Gøsta Esping-Andersen (ed.), *Welfare States in*

Transition. National Adaptations in Global Economies. London: Sage Publications, pp. 192–224.

Goodman, Roger, Gordon White and Huck-ju Kwon (eds) (1998) *The East Asian Welfare Model. Welfare Orientalism and the State.* London: Routledge.

GTN: *Guangzhou tongji nianjian* [Guangzhou statistical yearbook]. Beijing: Zhongguo tongji chubanshe.

Gu, Edward X. (2001a) 'Beyond the Property Rights Approach: Welfare Policy and the Reform of State-Owned Enterprises in China'. *Development and Change*, vol. 32, pp. 129–150.

—— (ed.) (2001b) 'Labor Market Reform. Central Government Policy'. *Chinese Law & Government*, vol. 34, no. 1, pp. 5–99.

Guan, Xinping (2001) 'Globalization, Inequality and Social Policy: China on the Threshold of Entry into the World Trade Organization'. *Social Policy and Administration*, vol. 35, no. 3, pp. 242–257.

Guangzhou shi tigaiwei (1994) 'Guanzhou shi shehui baoxian, baozhang zhidu gaige de jiben huigu' [The present situation and future of Guangzhou's social security and insurance system). In *International Conference on the Establishment and Improvement of Social Security System in Guangzhou.* Guangzhou: kaifang shidai zazhi she, pp. 29–32.

Guangzhou Ribao: *Guangzhou Daily.*

Guangzhou shi zhi [Guangzhou local gazeteer] (1995) vol. III.

Guangzhou sishinian 1949–1988 (1997). Guangzhou: Tongji chubanshe.

Hastrup, Kirsten (ed.) (2001) *Human Rights on Common Grounds. The Quest for Universality.* The Hague: Kluwer Law International.

Havel, Vaclav (et al.) (1985) *The Power of the Powerless. Citizens Against the State in Central-Eastern Europe.* Edited by John Keane. London: Hutchinson.

He, Qinglian (1997) *Xiandaihua de Xianjing – Dangdai Zhongguo de jingji wenti* [The trap of modernization – economic and social problems in contemporary China]. Beijing: Jinri Zhongguo chubanshe.

HJN: *Hebei jingji nianjian* [Hebei statistical yearbook]. Beijing: Zhongguo tongji chubanshe.

Hong, Yang (1998) 'Hebei: Development through Economic Integration'. *Provincial China*, no. 5, pp. 18–31.

Hort, Sven E. O. and Stein Kuhnle (1999) 'The Coming of East and South East Asian Welfare States?' Paper presented at the International Conference on 'Family, Social Policy and Financial Strategy'. Sun Yat-sen Institute for Social Sciences and Philosophy, Academia Sinica, Taipei, 16–17 April 1999.

—— (2000) 'The Coming of East and South East Asian Welfare States?'. *Journal of European Social Policy*, vol. 10, no. 2, pp. 162–184.

Hsiung, Ping-chun, Maria Jaschok and Cecilia Milwertz (eds) (2001) *Chinese Women Organizing. Cadres, Feminists, Muslims, Queers*. Oxford: Berg.

Howe, Christopher, Y.Y. Kueh and Robert Ash (2001) *China's Economic Reform: A Study with Documents*. Richmond: Curzon.

Hu, Xiaoyi (1998) *Zouxiang 21 shiji de Zhongguo shehui baoxian* [Towards Chinese social insurance of the 21st century]. Beijing: Zhongguo laodong chubanshe.

—— (2001) 'Sannian quebao, sange sikao' [Three years of guarantees, three times food for thought]. *Zhongguo shehui baozhang*, no. 6, pp. 4–7.

Hunt, Paul (1996) *Reclaiming Social Rights. International and Comparative Perspectives*. Aldershot: Dartmouth.

Ikels, Charlotte (1990) 'The Resolution of Intergenerational Conflict. Perspectives of Elders and their Family Members'. *Modern China*, vol. 16, no. 4, pp. 379–406.

—— (1996) *The Return of the God of Wealth. The Transition to a Market Economy in Urban China*. Stanford: Stanford University Press.

International Conference on the Establishment and Improvement of Social Security System in Guangzhou (1994). Guangzhou: Kaifang shidai zazhi she.

Jacobs, Bruce J. (1997) 'Shanghai: an Alternative Centre?' In David Goodman (ed.), *China's Provinces in Reform*. London: Routledge, pp. 163–193.

Jiang Wanrong (1998) '1997–1998 nian: Zhongguo shangpin zhuzhai jianshe yu zhufang zhidu gaige' [Housing reform in 1997–1998]. In Ru Xin (et al.) (eds), *1998 nian: Zhongguo shehui xingshi fenxi yu yuce* [1998: Analysis and forecast of social situation]. Beijing: Shehui kexue wenxian chubanshe, pp. 296–309.

Jiaoyu fa jiqi peitao guiding [Laws on education and related regulations] (2001). Beijing: Zhongguo fazhi chubanshe.

Jiaoyu fa quanshu [Collection of laws on education] (1995). Beijing: Beijing guangbo xueyuan chubanshe.

Jones, Catherine (1993) 'The Pacific Challenge: Confucian Welfare States'. In Catherine Jones (ed.), *New Perspectives on the Welfare State in Europe*. London and New York: Routledge, pp. 198–217.

—— (ed.) (1993) *New Perspectives on the Welfare State in Europe*. London and New York: Routledge.

Kabeer, Naila and Sarah Cook (2000) 'Re-visioning Social Policy in the South. Challenges and Concepts'. *IDS Bulletin*, vol. 31, no. 4, pp. 1–10.

Kapstein, Ethan B. and Michael Mandelbaum (1997) *Sustaining the Transition: The Social Safety Net in Postcommunist Europe*. New York: Council of Foreign Relations.

Kent, Ann (1993) *Between Freedom and Subsistence. China and Human Rights*. Hong Kong: Oxford University Press.

—— (1999) *China, the United Nations, and Human Rights. The Limits of Compliance*. Philadelphia: University of Pennsylvania Press.

Kinglun, Ngok (ed.) (2000) 'The Development of the Labor Law of the People's Republic of China'. *Chinese Law & Government*, vol. 33, no. 1, pp. 3–95.

Koch, Ida Elisabeth (2001a) 'Sociale grundrettigheder som judiciable rettigheder' [Social rights as judiciable rights]'. *Eu-ret & Menneskeret*, no. 4, pp. 169–181.

—— (2001b) 'Legal Pluralism in the Human Rights Universe'. In Kirsten Hastrup (ed.), *Human Rights on Common Grounds. The Quest for Universality*. The Hague: Kluwer Law International, pp. 139–156.

Kornai, Janos (1997) *Struggle and Hope. Essays on Stabilization and Reform in a post-Socialist Economy*. Cheltenham, UK: Edward Elgar.

Kuhnle, Stein (1995) 'History of the Welfare State'. In *Reconceptualizing the Welfare State. Proceedings from Symposium in connection with Maastricht II*. Copenhagen: The Danish Centre for Human Rights, pp. 9–21.

Kwon, Huck-ju (1997) 'Beyond European Welfare Regimes: Comparative Perspectives on East Asian Welfare Systems'. *Journal of Social Policy*, vol. 26, no. 4, pp. 467–484.

Lai, On-kwok (2000) 'Housing Reforms at Fifty (1949–1999): The Political Economy of a Production-biased Housing Regime in Transition'. *China Review 2000*. Hong Kong: The Chinese University Press, pp. 481–508.

Lassen, Eva Maria (2001) 'World Religions, World Values: In Dialogue with the Bible'. In Kirsten Hastrup (ed.), *Human Rights on Common Grounds. The Quest for Universality*. The Hague: Kluwer Law International, pp. 177–194.

Leckie, Scott (1991) *From Housing Needs to Housing Rights*. London: The International Institute for Environment and Development.

Lee, Ming-kwan (2000) *Chinese Occupational Welfare in Market Transition*. London: MacMillan Pres, Ltd.

Lee, Peter Nan-shong (1995) 'Housing Privatization with Chinese Characteristics'. In Linda Wong and Stewart MacPherson (eds), *Social Change and Social Policy in Contemporary China*. Hong Kong: Avebury, pp. 113–139.

—— (1993) (ed.) 'Housing Reform under Deng Xiaoping. Editor's Introduction'. *Chinese Law and Government*, vol 26, no. 1, pp. 3–14.

Leung, Joe C.B. and Richard Nann (1995) *Authority and Benevolence. Social Welfare in China*. Hong Kong: The Chinese University Press.

Li, Buyun (1997) 'Chinese Citizens' Right to Work' In *Domestic Implementation of Obligations under the UNCESCR*. Oslo: Norwegian Institute of Human Rights, pp. 1–13.

Li, Hanlin and Wang Qi (1996) *Research on the Chinese Work Unit Society*. Frankfurt am Main: Peter Lang.

Li, Hanlin, Li Lulu and Wang Fenyu (1996) *Work Unit – the Basic Structure of Chinese Society–Data Material*. Beijing: Beijing Publishing House.

Li, Hua (1999) 'Zhuanxing shehui zhong de hunhe jiegou' [The mixed structure of social transformation]. *Boshi xuewei lunwen* [Ph.d. thesis], Renmin daxue. Copy with author.

Li, Jingwen (ed.) (2000) *Zhongguo shehui qianjing* [The future of China's society]. Beijing: tuanjie chubanshe.

Li, Lulu and Wang Fenyu (1991) *Dangdai Zhongguo xiandaihua jincheng zhong de shehui jiegou jiqi biange* [Changes in the social structure of China's present modernization process]. Zhejiang: Renmin chubanshe.

Li, Shuzhi (1996) 'Chenzhen zhuzhai shichang fenxi' [Analysis of the housing market]. *Zhongguo gaige bao*, 10 October.

Lin, Ka (1999) *Confucian Welfare Cluster. A Cultural Interpretation of Social Welfare*. Tampere: University of Tampere.

—— (2001) 'Chinese Perceptions of the Scandinavian Social Policy Model'. *Social Policy and Administration*, vol. 35, no. 3, pp. 321–340.

Lin, Lihong (et al.) (2001) 'Cong xianding quanli dao xianshi quanli' [From constitutional rights to real rights]. *Shehui baozhang zhidu*, no. 5, pp. 30–41.

Lindholm, Tore (1999) 'Article 1'. In Asbjørn Eide and Gudmundur Alfredsson (eds), *The Universal Declaration of Human Rights:*

A Common Standard of Achievement. The Hague: Kluwer, pp. 41–73.

Liu, Hainian, Li Lin and Morten Kjærum (eds.) (1999) *Human Rights and Administration of Justice.* Beijing: China Legal System Publishing House.

Liu, Jianjun (2000) *Danwei Zhongguo – shehui tiaokong tixi chonggou zhong de geren, zuzhi, yu guojia* [Work unit China – individual, organization, and state during the process of reconstruction of social regulation system]. Tianjin: Tianjin renmin chubanshe.

Liu, Zhiqiang (1998) 'Earnings, Education, and Economic Reforms in Urban China'. *Economic Development and Cultural Change*, vol. 46, no. 4, pp. 697–726.

Lo, Wing and Joseph Cheng (eds) (1996) *Social Welfare Development in China, Constraints and Challenges.* Chicago: Imprint Publications.

Lu, Aiguo (1996) 'Welfare Changes in China during the Economic Reforms'. *Research for Action* 26. Helsinki: United Nations University, World Institute for Development Economics Research.

Lu, Feng (1993) 'The Origins and Formation of the Unit System'. *Chinese Sociology and Anthropology*, vol. 25, no. 3, pp. 7–91.

Lu, Xueyi and Li Peilin (eds) (1997) *Zhongguo xin shiqi shehui fazhan baogao (1991–1995)* [Social development 1991–1995]. Shenyang: Liaoning renmin chubanshe.

Lu, Xueyi and Zheng Yefu (1997) 'Zhongguo jianli chengzhen zhufang xin tizhi de jiben silu' [Some ideas on housing system reform in China]. In Lu Xueyi and Li Peilin (eds) *Zhongguo xin shiqi shehui fazhan baogao (1991–1995)* [Social development 1991–1995]. Shenyang: Liaoning renmin chubanshe, p. 633–672.

Lü, Xiaobo and Elizabeth J. Perry (eds) (1997) *Danwei. The Changing Chinese Workplace in Historical and Comparative Perspective.* Armonk: M. E. Sharpe.

Lubman, Stanley B. (1999) *Bird in a Cage: Legal Reform in China after Mao.* Stanford, California: Stanford University Press.

Luo, Yanhua (1998) *Dongfang ren kan renquan* [An Eastern look at human rights]. Beijing: xinhua chubanshe.

MacFarquhar, Roderick (1974) *The Origins of the Cultural Revolution, 1: Contradictions among the People 1956 – 1957*. London: Oxford University Press.

MacPherson, Stewart (1995) 'Social Policy in China in Contemporary Perspective'. In Linda Wong and Stewart MacPherson (eds), *Social Change and Social Policy in Contemporary China*. Hong Kong: Avebury, pp. 216–250.

—— and J.S. Cheng (eds) (1996) *Economic and Social Development in South China*. Cheltenham, UK: Edward Elgar.

—— and James Midgley (1987) *Comparative Social Policy and the Third World*. New York: St. Martin's Press.

Maixiang xiandaihua yu guojihua – zhongwai xuezhe xinlun [Toward modernization and internationalization – a new talk between Chinese and foreign scholars] (1996). Guangzhou: Guangdong renmin chubanshe.

Mallee, Hein (ed.) (1996) 'Reform of the Hukou System'. *Chinese Sociology and Anthropology*, vol. 29, no. 1.

Meng, Xin (2000) *Labour Market Reform in China*. Cambridge: Cambridge University Press.

Michelson, Ethan (ed.) (1998) 'Tradition in the Shadow of Modern Legal Practice'. *Chinese Law and Government*, vol. 31, no. 5–6 (2 vols.).

Midgley, James (1981) *Professional Imperialism: Social Work in the Third World*. London: Heinemann.

Milwertz, Cecilia (1997) *Accepting Population Control: Urban Chinese Women and the One-Child Family Policy*. Richmond: Curzon.

MOFA: Ministry of Foreign Affairs (2002) 'White Paper on Labor and Social Security in China'. Beijing: Ministry of Foreign Affairs of the PRC.

Mok, Ka-ho (2001) 'Education Policy Reform'. In Linda Wong and Norman Flynn (eds), *The Market in Chinese Social Policy*. Basingstoke: Palgrave, pp. 88–111.

—— and David Chan (1996) 'The Emergence of Private Education in the Pearl River Delta: Implications for Social Development'. In Stewart MacPherson and J.S. Cheng (eds), *Economic and Social Development in South China.* Cheltenham, UK: Edward Elgar, pp. 242–265.

Moore, Mick (2000) 'States, Social Policies and Globalisations'. *IDS Bulletin*, vol. 31, no. 4, pp. 21–31.

Nathan, Andrew (1997) *China's Transition.* New York: Columbia University Press.

Nee, Victor (1989) 'A Theory of Market Transition: From Redistribution to Markets in State Socialism'. *American Sociological Review*, vol. 54, pp. 663–681.

Ness, Peter van (1999) *Debating Human Rights: Critical Essays from the United States and Asia.* London: Routledge.

Nowak, Manfred (2001) 'The Right to Education'. In Asbjørn Eide, Catarina Krause and Allan Rosas (eds) *Economic, Social and Cultural Rights. A Textbook.* Dordrecht: Martinus Nijhoff Publishers, pp. 245–271.

Odinkalu, Chidi Anselm (2001) 'Analysis of Paralysis or Paralysis by Analysis? Implementing Economic, Social, and Cultural Rights under the African Charter on Human and Peoples' Rights'. *Human Rights Quarterly*, vol. 23, pp. 327–369.

Oksenberg, Michel, Lawrence Sullivan and Marc Lambert (eds) (1990) *Beijing Spring, 1989. Confrontation and Conflict. The Basic Documents.* Armonk: M.E. Sharpe.

'Out of Business' (1999). *Far Eastern Economic Review*, 18 and 25 March.

Peerenboom, Randall (1993) 'What's Wrong with Chinese Rights?: Toward a Theory of Rights with Chinese Characteristics'. *Harvard Human Rights Journal*, vol 6, pp. 29–57.

—— (2001) 'Seek Truth From Facts: An Empirical Study of Enforcement of Arbitral Awards in the PRC'. *The American Journal of Comparative Law*, vol. 49, pp. 249–328.

Philion, Stephen (1998) 'Chinese Welfare State Regimes'. *Journal of Contemporary Asia*, vol. 28, no. 4, pp. 518–536.

Postiglione, Gerard A. (ed.) (1998) 'Popularizing Nine-Year Compulsory Education. Selection from China Education News'. *Chinese Education and Society*, vol. 31, no. 5.

—— (ed.) (2001) 'Educational Research Selections'. *Chinese Education and Society*, vol. 34, no. 5.

Potter, Pitman B. (2001) *The Chinese Legal System. Globalization and Local Legal Culture.* London: Routledge.

PR: *Peking Review*, Beijing. After 1979 *Beijing Review* (*BR*).

Pudney, Stephen and Wang Limin (1994) *Housing and Housing Reform in Urban China: Efficiency, Distribution and the Implications for Social Security.* Programme of Research into Economic Transformation and Public Finance, London School of Economics.

Qian, Yingyi (1999) 'The Institutional Foundations of China's Market Transition'. *Annual World Bank Conference on Development Economics.*

Reconceptualizing the Welfare State. Proceedings from Symposium in connection with Maastricht II. (1995). Copenhagen: The Danish Centre for Human Rights.

'Resolution on the Political Report of the CCP Central Committee to the 8th National Congress of the Party' (1971). In *Documents of Chinese Communist Party Central Committee, Sept. 1956–Apr. 1969.* Hong Kong: Union Research Institute, pp. 31–32.

Robertson, Robert E. (1994) 'Measuring State Compliance with the Obligation to Devote the "Maximum Available Resources" to Realizing Economic, Social and Cultural Rights'. *Human Rights Quarterly*, vol. 16, pp. 693–714.

Rosen, Stanley (ed.) (1997) 'Recent Developments in Chinese Education'. *Chinese Education and Society*, vol. 30, no. 3.

—— (ed.) (2000) 'Education and the Economy on the Eve of the Twenty-First Century'. *Chinese Education and Society*, vol. 33, no. 1.

Ru, Xin, Lu Xueyi and Dan Tianlun (1998) *1998 nian: Zhongguo shehui xingshi fenxi yu yuce* [1998: Analysis and forecast of social situation]. Shehui lanpishu [Social blue-book]. Beijing: Shehui kexue wenxian chubanshe.

—— (1999) *1999 nian: Zhongguo shehui xingshi fenxi yu yuce* [1999: Analysis and forecast of social situation]. Shehui lanpishu [Social blue-book]. Beijing: Shehui kexue wenxian chubanshe.

—— (2000) *2000 nian: Zhongguo shehui xingshi fenxi yu yuce* [2000: Analysis and forecast of social situation]. Shehui lanpishu [Social blue-book]. Beijing: Shehui kexue wenxian chubanshe.

—— (2001) *2001 nian: Zhongguo shehui xingshi fenxi yu yuce* [2001: Analysis and forecast of social situation]. Shehui lanpishu [Social blue-book]. Beijing: Shehui kexue wenxian chubanshe.

Sabin, Lora (1994) 'New Bosses in the Workers' State: The Growth of non-State Employment in China'. *The China Quarterly*, no. 140, pp. 944–970.

Said, Edward (1995) *Orientalism: Western Conceptions of the Orient.* London: 1995.

Sano, Hans Otto (2000) 'Development and Human Rights: The Necessary, but Partial Integration of Human Rights and Development'. *Human Rights Quarterly*, vol. 22, pp. 734–752.

Saunders, Peter and Xiaoyuan Shang (2001) 'Social Security Reform in China's Transition to a Market Economy'. *Social Policy and Administration*, vol. 35, no. 3, pp. 274–289.

SCMP: *South China Morning Post*, Hong Kong.

Scheinin, Martin (2001a) 'The Right to Social Security'. In Asbjørn Eide, Catarina Krause and Allan Rosas (eds), *Economic, Social and Cultural Rights. A Textbook.* Dordrecht: Martinus Nijhoff Publishers, pp. 211–221.

—— (2001b) 'Economic and Social Rights as Legal Rights'. In Asbjørn Eide, Catarina Krause and Allan Rosas (eds), *Economic, Social and Cultural Rights. A Textbook.* Dordrecht: Martinus Nijhoff Publishers, pp. 29–54.

Scott, Craig (1999) 'Reaching Beyond (Without Abandoning) the Category of "Economic, Social and Cultural Rights"'. *Human Rights Quarterly*, vol. 21, pp. 633–660.

Scott, Suzie (1994) *The Long March to a Market Economy: An Account of Housing Reform in China.* Glasgow University: Centre for Housing Research and Urban Studies.

Shi, Guang and Li Weiping (2000) 'Summary of Conference on China Rural Health Reform and Development, 7–9.11.2000'. China Health Economics Institute and Institute of Development Studies, UK.

Shehui Baozhang Zhidu [Social Security System]. Photocopy series from the People's University, Beijing.

Shirk, Susan (1993) *The Political Logic of Economic Reform in China.* Berkeley: University of California Press.

Smyth, Russell (2000) 'Asset Stripping in Chinese State-Owned Enterprises'. *Journal of Contemporary Asia*, vol. 30, no. 1, p. 3–16.

Solinger, Dorothy (1995) 'The Floating Population in the Cities: Chances for Assimilation'. In Deborah Davis (ed.), *Urban Spaces in Contemporary China.* Cambridge: Woodrow Wilson Center Press and Cambridge University Press, pp. 113–139.

—— (1997) 'The Impact of the Floating Population on the *Danwei*: Shifts in the Pattern of Labour Mobility Control and Entitlement Provision'. In Xiaobo Lü and Elizabeth Perry (eds), *Danwei. The Changing Chinese Workplace in Historical and Comparative Perspective.* Armonk: M.E. Sharpe, pp.195–222.

—— (2001) 'Why We Cannot Count the "Unemployed"'. *The China Quarterly*, no. 167, pp. 671–688.

Standing, Guy (1996) 'Social Protection in Central and Eastern Europe: A Tale of Slipping Anchors and Torn Safety Nets'. In Gøsta Esping-Andersen (ed.), *Welfare States in Transition. National Adaptations in Global Economies.* London: Sage Publications, pp. 225–255.

State Council Information Office (1999) 'Progress in China's Human Rights Conditions in 1998'. Beijing: State Council Information Office.

Sun, Liping (1996) 'Shehui, shehui guanxi yu shehui jiegou' [Society, social relations and social structure]. *Shehuixue yanjiu*, no. 5.

Svensson, Marina (1996) *The Chinese Conception of Human Rights. The Debate on Human Rights in China, 1898–1949*. Lund: Department of East Asian Languages, Lund University.

—— (2000) 'The Chinese Debate on Asian Values and Human Rights: Some Reflections on Relativism, Nationalism, and Orientalism'. In Ole Bruun and Michael Jacobsen (2000), *Human Rights and Asian Values. Contesting National Identities and Cultural Representations in Asia*. Surrey: Curzon Press, pp. 199–226.

Szalai, Julia (1990) 'Outline for the Radical Reforms of Social Policy in Hungary'. In Bob Deacon and Julia Szalai (eds), *Social Policy in the New Eastern Europe. What Future for Socialist Welfare?* Aldershot: Avebury, pp. 91–102.

Szelenyi, Ivan and Eric Kostello (1996) 'The Market Transition Debate: Towards a Synthesis?' *American Journal of Sociology*, vol. 101, no. 4, pp. 1082–1096.

Tang, J.T.H. (1995) *Human Rights and International Relations in the Asia-Pacific Region*, London: Pinter.

Tang, Kwong-leung (2000) *Social Welfare Development in East Asia*. Hampshire: Palgrave.

Tang, Wenfang (2001) 'Political and Social Trends in the post-Deng Urban China: Crisis or Stability?' *The China Quarterly*, no. 168, pp. 890–908.

—— and William L. Parish (2000) *Chinese Urban Life under Reform. The Changing Social Contract*. Cambridge: Cambridge University Press.

Tang, Ying (1997) 'Shilun geren zhufang danbao diya daikuan jiqi fengxian kongzhi' [On individual housing mortgage and how to control the risk]. *Chengshi yanjiu*, no. 4, pp. 17–20.

Tanner, Murray Scott (1999) *The Politics of Lawmaking in China. Institutions, Processes, and Democratic Prospects*. Oxford: Clarendon Press.

Thelle, Hatla (ed.) (1998) *Political Development and Human Rights in China*. Copenhagen: The Danish Centre for Human Rights.

Tian, Donghai (1997) 'Shehui zhufang chixuxing shengcun de tansuo: Xinxing suoyou xingshi' [Explorations into the sustainability of social housing: New patterns of ownership]. *Chengshi wenti*, no. 5, pp. 58–61.

Titmuss, Richard (1958) *Essays on 'The Welfare State'*. London: George Allen & Unwin Ltd.

—— (1974) *Social Policy – an Introduction*. London: George Allen & Unwin, Ltd.

Toebes, Brigit (2001) 'The Right to Health'. In Asbjørn Eide, Catarina Krause and Allan Rosas (eds), *Economic, Social and Cultural Rights. A Textbook*. Dordrecht: Martinus Nijhoff Publishers, pp. 169–190.

Tomasevski, Katarina (1995) 'International Prospects for the Future of the Welfare State'. *Re-conceptualizing the Welfare State*, pp.100–117.

—— (2001) 'Indicators'. In Asbjørn Eide, Catarina Krause and Allan Rosas (eds), *Economic, Social and Cultural Rights. A Textbook*. Dordrecht: Martinus Nijhoff Publishers, pp. 531–543.

Tong, James (1987) 'Urban Economic Reforms in Sichuan under Zhao Ziyang, 1978–1980'. *Chinese Law & Government*, vol. 20, no. 3, pp. 3–18.

Tu, Weiming and Theodore de Bary (eds) (1997) *Confucianism and Human Rights*. New York: Columbia University Press.

UNDP (1990) *Human Development Report 1990*. Oxford and New York: Oxford University Press.

—— (2000) *Human Development Report 2000. Human Rights and Human Development*. Oxford and New York: Oxford University Press.

UNRISD (2000) 'Social Policy in a Development Context'. *Report of the UNRISD International Conference 23–24 September 2000*. Tammsvik, Sweden.

Walder, Andrew (1986) *Communist neo-Traditionalism. Work and Authority in Chinese Industry*. Berkeley: University of California Press.

—— (ed.) (1995) *The Waning of the Communist State. Economic Origins of Political Decline in China and Hungary*. Berkeley: University of California Press.

Waldron, Jeremy (1993) *Liberal Rights. Collected Papers 1981–1991.* Cambridge: Cambridge University Press.

Wang, Feiling (1998) *From Family to Market. Labor Allocation in Contemporary China.* Oxford: Rowman & Littlefield Publishers.

Wang, Fenyu and Li Lulu (2001) *Zhongguo chengshi laodongli liudong* [Labour mobility in Chinese cities]. Beijing: Beijing chubanshe.

Wang, Mengkui (2001) *Zhongguo shehui baozhang tizhi gaige* [Reform of the social security system in China]. Beijing: Zhongguo fazhan chubanshe.

Wang, Shaoguang and Hu Angang (1995) *Wang Shaoguang Proposal I, II.* 2 vols. *Chinese Economic Studies*, vol. 28, no. 3 and 4.

—— (2001) *The Chinese Economy in Crisis: State Capacity and Tax Reform.* Armonk: M. E. Sharpe.

Wang, Zhen (2000) 'Gender, Employment and Women's Resistance'. In Elizabeth Perry and Mark Selden (eds), *Chinese Society. Change, Conflict and Resistance.* London: Routledge, pp. 62–82.

Wang, Ya Ping and Alan Murie (1999) *Housing Policy and Practice in China.* London: Macmillan Press Ltd.

Wank, David (1999) *Commodifying Communism. Business, Trust, and Politics in a Chinese City.* Cambridge: Cambridge University Press.

White, Gordon (1993) *Riding the Tiger: The Politics of Economic Reform in post-Mao China.* Basingstoke: Macmillan.

Whyte, Martin K. (1996) 'The Chinese Family and Economic Development: Obstacle or Engine?' *Economic Development and Cultural Change*, vol. 45, no. 1, pp. 1–30.

—— (1997) 'The Fate of Filial Obligations in Urban China'. *The China Journal*, no. 38, pp. 1–31.

—— and William L. Parish (1984) *Urban Life in Contemporary China.* Chicago: University of Chicago Press.

Wong, Linda (1998) *Marginalization and Social Welfare in China.* London: Routledge.

—— and Grace Lee (1996) 'Welfare in a Stratified Immigrant Society–Shenzhen's Social Policy Challenge'. In Stewart

MacPherson and J.S. Cheng (eds), *Economic and Social Development in South China*. Cheltenham, UK: Edward Elgar, pp.208–228.

—— and Norman Flynn (2001) *The Market in Chinese Social Policy*. Basingstoke: Palgrave.

—— and Stewart MacPherson (eds) (1995) *Social Change and Social Policy in Contemporary China*. Hong Kong: Avebury.

Woo, Wing Thye (1999) 'The Real Reasons for China's Growth'. *The China Journal*, no. 41, pp. 115–137.

World Bank (1991) *Urban Housing Reform in China. An Economic Analysis*. World Bank Discussion Papers 123. Washington D.C.: World Bank.

—— (1992) *China. Implementation Options for Urban Housing Reform*. Washington D.C.: World Bank Country Study.

—— (1993) *The East Asian Miracle: Economic Growth and Public Policy*. Washington D.C.: World Bank.

—— (1997a) *Financing Health Care*. China 2020 Series, Washington D.C.: World Bank

—— (1997b) *Old Age Security. Pension Reform in China*. China 2020 Series, Washington D.C.: World Bank

—— (2000) *Entering the 21st Century. World Development Report 1999/2000*. IBRD. Washington, D.C.: Oxford University Press.

Wu, Jinglian (et al.) (1998) *Guoyou jingji de zhanlüexing gaizu* [The strategic reorganization of state economy]. Beijing: Zhongguo fazhan chubanshe.

Xie, Yuchu (1997) 'Urban Unemployment in China'. *The China Strategic Review*, vol. II, no. 5, pp. 31–38.

Xin, Meng (2000) *Labour Market Reform in China*. Cambridge: Cambridge University Press.

Xin Zhongguo wushinian tongji ziliao huibian [Comprehensive statistical data and materials on fifty years of new China] (2002). Beijing: Zhongguo tongji chubanshe.

Xingtai shi (1996) *Guomin jingji he shehui fazhan tongji ziliao* [Statistical material on national economic and social development]. Hebei: Xingtai shi tongjiju.

Xu, Xianming (1992) 'Shengchunquan' [The right to subsistence]. *Zhongguo shehui kexue*, no. 5, pp. 39–56.

Xu, Yuebin (2001) 'Family Support for Old People in Rural China'. *Social Policy & Administration*, vol. 35, no. 3, pp. 307–320.

Yang, Jun and Liu Heng (2001) 'Woguo shehui baozhang lifa quexian ji lifa jianyi' [Suggestions concerning the defects of social security legislation in our country]. *Shehui baozhang zhidu*, no. 9, pp. 25–27.

Yang, Mayfair (1995) *Gifts, Favors and Banquets: The Art of Social Relationships in China*. Ithaca, New York: Cornell University Press.

Yang, Tuan, Yang Benren and Tang Jun (1996) *Zhongguo shehui baozhang zhidu de zai xuanze* [The re-selection of a Chinese social security system]. Beijing: Zhongyang guangbo dianshi daxue chubanshe.

Yang, Yiyong (1997) *Shiye chongjibo – Zhongguo jiuye fazhan baogao* [The wave of unemployment – report on employment development in China] (1998). Beijing: Jinri Zhongguo chubanshe.

Yao, Shujie and Zongyi Zhang (2001) 'Regional Growth in China Under Economic Reforms'. *The Journal of Development Studies*, vol. 38, no. 2, pp. 167–186.

Yin, Z. Jason, Shuanglin Lin and David F. Gates (2000) *Social Security Reform. Options for China*. Singapore: World Scientific.

Young, Nick (2001/2002) 'Inventing New Traditions'. *China Development Brief*, pp. 7–12.

—— with Anthony Woo (2000) *An Introduction to the non-Profit Sector in China*. Kent: CAF.

Yuen-Tsang, Angelina W.K. (1997) *Towards a Chinese Conception of Social Support. A Study on the Social Support Networks of Chinese Working Mothers in Beijing*. Aldershot: Avebury.

Zhang, Zhongjun (1993) 'An Overview of Housing Reform'. *Chinese Law and Government*, vol. 26, no. 1, pp. 31–53.

Zhongguo jiawu ji chengzhen jumin jiating shouzhi diaocha tongji nianjian [Statistical yearbook on survey of prices and income and expenses of urban families in China] (1997). Beijing: Zhongguo tongji chubanshe.

Zhonghua Renmin Gongheguo jiaoyu falü ji [The laws on education of the People's Republic of China] (1999). Beijing: Foreign Languages Press.

Zhou, Jianjun (1997) 'Kunjing zhong de fanggai' [Housing reform in trouble]. *Chengshi wenti*, no. 2, pp. 27–29.

Zhu, Ling (2000) 'An Analysis of Social Security under the Planned Economy'. *Social Sciences in China*, Vol. XXI, no. 1, pp. 79–90.

ZJJTN: *Zhongguo jiaoyu jingfei tongji nianjian* [China educational finance statistical yearbook]. Beijing: Zhongguo tongji chubanshe.

ZLTN: *Zhongguo laodong tongji nianjian* [China labour statistical yearbook]. Beijing: Zhongguo tongji chubanshe.

ZMTN: *Zhongguo minzheng tongji nianjian* [China civil affairs' statistical yearbook]. Beijing: Zhongguo tongji chubanshe.

ZRGLSBFQ : *Zhonghua Renmin Gongheguo laodong he shehui baozhang fagui quanshu* [Laws and regulations on labour and social security of the PRC] (1999) 2 vols. Beijing: Zhongguo laodong shehui baozhang chubanshe.

ZTN: *Zhongguo tongji nianjian* [Statistical yearbook of China]. Beijing: Zhongguo tongji chubanshe.

Zuo, Xuejin and Hu Suyun (2001) 'Chengzhen yiliao baoxian zhidu gaige: Zhengfu yu shichang de zuoyong' [Reform of the urban health care insurance system: The role of the state and the market]. *Zhongguo shehui kexue*, no. 5, pp. 102–111.

ZZZG: *Zhongguo zhufang zhidu gaige* [Reform of the housing system in China] (1996). Beijing: Gaige chubanshe.

只能靠自己

Index

The Nordic Institute of Asian Studies (NIAS) is funded by the governments of Denmark, Finland, Iceland, Norway and Sweden via the Nordic Council of Ministers, and works to encourage and support Asian studies in the Nordic countries. In so doing, NIAS has been publishing books since 1969, with more than one hundred titles produced in the last ten years.

Nordic Council of Ministers